Frommer's®

S0-CFR-437

PORTABLE

Savannah

4th Edition

by Darwin Porter & Danforth Prince

Here's what critics say about Frommer's:

"Amazingly easy to use. Very portable, very complete."

—*Booklist*

"Detailed, accurate, and easy-to-read information for all price ranges."

—*Glamour Magazine*

WILEY

Wiley Publishing, Inc.

Published by:

WILEY PUBLISHING, INC.

111 River St.
Hoboken, NJ 07030-5774

ISBN: 978-0-470-39902-6

Editor: Billy Fox
Production Editor: Eric T. Schroeder
Cartographer: Andrew Dolan
Photo Editor: Richard H. Fox
Production by Wiley Indianapolis Composition Services

For information on our other products and services or to obtain technical
support, please contact our Customer Care Department within the U.S. at
800/762-2974, outside the U.S. at 317/572-3993 or fax 317/572-4002.

Wiley also publishes its books in a variety of electronic formats. Some con-
tent that appears in print may not be available in electronic formats.

Manufactured in the United States of America

5   4   3   2   1

Contents

List of Maps

ABOUT THE AUTHORS

As a team of veteran travel writers, **Darwin Porter** and **Danforth Prince** have produced dozens of previous titles for Frommer's, including many of their guides to Europe, the Caribbean, Bermuda, The Bahamas, and parts of America's Deep South. A film critic, columnist, and radio broadcaster, Porter is also a noted biographer of Hollywood celebrities, garnering critical acclaim for overviews of the life and times of, among others, Marlon Brando, Katharine Hepburn, Humphrey Bogart, Howard Hughes, and Michael Jackson. Prince was formerly employed by the Paris bureau of the *New York Times,* and is today the president of *www.Blood MoonProductions.com* and other media-related firms. In 2008, Porter and Prince collaborated on the release of their newest book about Hollywood, sexuality, and sin as filtered through 85 years of celebrity excess, *Hollywood Babylon— It's Back!*

AN INVITATION TO THE READER

In researching this book, we discovered many wonderful places—hotels, restaurants, shops, and more. We're sure you'll find others. Please tell us about them, so we can share the information with your fellow travelers in upcoming editions. If you were disappointed with a recommendation, we'd love to know that, too. Please write to:

Frommer's Portable Savannah, 4th Edition
Wiley Publishing, Inc. • 111 River St. • Hoboken, NJ 07030-5774

AN ADDITIONAL NOTE

Please be advised that travel information is subject to change at any time—and this is especially true of prices. We therefore suggest that you write or call ahead for confirmation when making your travel plans. The authors, editors, and publisher cannot be held responsible for the experiences of readers while traveling. Your safety is important to us, however, so we encourage you to stay alert and be aware of your surroundings. Keep a close eye on cameras, purses, and wallets, all favorite targets of thieves and pickpockets.

FROMMER'S STAR RATINGS, ICONS & ABBREVIATIONS

Every hotel, restaurant, and attraction listing in this guide has been ranked for quality, value, service, amenities, and special features using a **star-rating system.** In country, state, and regional guides, we also rate towns and regions to help you narrow down your choices and budget your time accordingly. Hotels and restaurants are rated on a scale of zero (recommended) to three stars (exceptional). Attractions, shopping, nightlife, towns, and regions are rated according to the following scale: zero stars (recommended), one star (highly recommended), two stars (very highly recommended), and three stars (must-see).

In addition to the star-rating system, we also use **seven feature icons** that point you to the great deals, in-the-know advice, and unique experiences that separate travelers from tourists. Throughout the book, look for:

Finds	Special finds—those places only insiders know about
Fun Fact	Fun facts—details that make travelers more informed and their trips more fun
Kids	Best bets for kids and advice for the whole family
Moments	Special moments—those experiences that memories are made of
Overrated	Places or experiences not worth your time or money
Tips	Insider tips—great ways to save time and money
Value	Great values—where to get the best deals

The following **abbreviations** are used for credit cards:

AE	American Express	DISC	Discover	V	Visa
DC	Diners Club	MC	MasterCard		

FROMMERS.COM

Now that you have this guidebook to help you plan a great trip, visit our website at **www.frommers.com** for additional travel information on more than 4,000 destinations. We update features regularly to give you instant access to the most current trip-planning information available. At Frommers.com, you'll find scoops on the best airfares, lodging rates, and car rental bargains. You can even book your travel online through our reliable travel booking partners. Other popular features include:

- Online updates of our most popular guidebooks
- Vacation sweepstakes and contest giveaways
- Newsletters highlighting the hottest travel trends
- Podcasts, interactive maps, and up-to-the-minute events listings
- Opinionated blog entries by Arthur Frommer himself
- Online travel message boards with featured travel discussions

The Best of Savannah

If you have time to visit only one city in the Southeast, make it Savannah. It's that special.

The movie *Forrest Gump* may have put the city squarely on the tourist map, but nothing changed the face of Savannah more than the 1994 publication of John Berendt's *Midnight in the Garden of Good and Evil*. The impact has been unprecedented, bringing in millions in revenue as thousands flock to see the sights from the bestseller and the 1997 movie directed by Clint Eastwood. In fact, Savannah tourism has nearly doubled since the publication of what's known locally as The Book. Even after all this time, some locals still earn their living off The Book's fallout, hawking postcards, walking tours, T-shirts, and in some cases their own careers, as in the case of the Lady Chablis, the drag queen in The Book who plays herself in the film.

"What's special about Savannah?" we asked an old-timer. "Why, here we even have water fountains for dogs," he said.

The free spirit, the passion, and even the decadence of Savannah resemble those of Key West or New Orleans rather than the Bible Belt down-home "Red State" interior of Georgia. In that sense, it's as different from the rest of the state as New York City is from upstate New York.

Savannah—pronounce it with a drawl—conjures up all the clichéd images of the Deep South: live oaks dripping with Spanish moss, stately antebellum mansions, mint juleps sipped on the veranda, magnolia trees, peaceful marshes, horse-drawn carriages, ships sailing up the river (though no longer laden with cotton), and even General Sherman, no one's favorite military hero here.

Today, the economy and much of the city's day-to-day life still revolve around port activity. For the visitor, however, the big draw is Old Savannah, a beautifully restored and maintained historic area. For this we can thank seven Savannah women who, after watching mansion after mansion demolished in the name of progress, managed in 1954 to raise funds to buy the dilapidated Isaiah Davenport

House—hours before it was slated for demolition. The women banded together as the Historic Savannah Foundation, and then went to work buying up architecturally valuable buildings and reselling them to private owners who promised to restore them. As a result, more than 800 of Old Savannah's 1,100 historic buildings have been restored and painted in their original colors—pinks and reds and blues and greens. This "living museum" is now the largest urban National Historic Landmark District in the country—some 2½ square miles, including 21 1-acre squares that survive from Gen. James Oglethorpe's dream of a gracious city.

1 Frommer's Favorite Savannah Experiences

- **Experiencing 19th-Century Ambience**   Savannah is one of the top two cities in the Deep South (the other being Charleston) where you can experience what elegant life was like in the 19th century by checking into a B&B in a restored historic building. If you're a man sitting in one of these Victorian parlors, surrounded by wall paintings of bygone belles, you'll feel a little bit like Rhett Butler come to call on Scarlett O'Hara. Typical of these is the Eliza Thompson House, built around 1847 in Savannah's antebellum heyday.

- **Wandering the Isle of Hope**   Spanish conquistador Hernando de Soto came here 4 centuries ago looking for gold. The island later became a place of refuge for Royalists escaping the guillotine of the French Revolution. Today, the Isle of Hope, 10 miles south of Savannah, is an evocative and nostalgic reminder of Savannah's yesteryears. You can go for a stroll in a setting of oaks lining the bluff, plenty of Spanish moss, and Georgia pine, dogwood, magnolia, azalea, and ferns.

- **Having a Picnic Among Plantation Ruins**   There is no more evocative site in the Savannah area for a picnic than Wormsloe State Historic Site at 7601 Skidaway Rd., 10 miles southeast of town. A picnic here can be combined with an exploration of the Isle of Hope. Now ruins, these grounds were once part of a 900-acre estate that belonged to Noble Jones, an 18th-century Colonial who came to Savannah with James Oglethorpe in 1733. Nature trails are cut through the property, and there are picnic tables. The property is reached along a beautiful oak-lined drive that makes you think you're on the road to Tara.

Impressions

*Savannah is America's Mona Lisa. Gaze your fill, look all
you will. (For once it's quite polite to stare.) You may never
fathom the secret of her smile, but like those who love
and live with her, you will know the endless rich rewards
of trying.*

—Writer Anita Raskin

- **Pursuing Grits, Game & Gumbo**   In the state of Georgia, only the much larger city of Atlanta equals Savannah in the number of fine restaurants. Since the mid–18th century, Savannah and the Low Country have been known for their abundance and variety of food, and lavish eating and drinking have long been loyal customs. The surrounding area was (and is) rich in game and fish, including marsh hen, quail, crab, and even deer. To these hunters' trophies were added the bounty of local gardens, including those old favorites—collard greens, beets, turnips, peas, okra, and corn. That corn was ground into grits as well, and the okra was used to thicken gumbos, for which every Savannahian seems to have a favorite recipe.

- **Finding Your Own *Forrest Gump* Bench**   Arm yourself with a box of chocolates and set out to find your own historic Savannah square like Tom Hanks did in the film *Forrest Gump*, where he began to spin out his adventures. Find the square of your choice, perhaps Chippewa Square (where Forrest actually sat), sit down, enjoy those chocolates, and watch the world go by. Savannah revolves around its historic squares, and it's said that if you sit on a bench long enough, everybody in Savannah will eventually pass by.

- **Enjoying a Martini in Bonaventure Cemetery**   In The Book, Mary Harty invites John Berendt, the author of *Midnight in the Garden of Good and Evil*, for martinis in this moss-draped cemetery. It has since become a tradition to partake of this quaint custom. On the former grounds of an oak-shaded plantation, you can enjoy your libation in the midst of the long departed. Of course, the proper way to drink a martini, as in The Book, is from a silver goblet. Your seat? None other than the bench-gravestone of poet Conrad Aiken.

- **Taking a Pub-Crawl Along the Riverfront**   Savannah has the best, friendliest, and most atmospheric pubs in Georgia,

none more alluring than those along its historic waterfront. On
St. Patrick's Day, people drive down from South Carolina or up
from Florida to go pubbing. But on any night you can stroll
along the cobblestones searching for your favorite hangout.
Often you get staged entertainment. If not, count on the locals
to supply amusement. It's all in good fun. People having a hot
time in an atmospheric setting of old warehouses represents one
of the Deep South's best recycling programs.

- **Spending a Day at the Beach on Tybee Island**   East of the
  city, Tybee Island, with its golden sands, is a place to have fun.
  Sun worshipers, joggers, surf-casters, kite flyers, swimmers, and
  mere sightseers come to escape the oppressive heat of Savannah's summers. Join the pelicans, gulls, and shorebirds in the
  dunes for beach dynamics. You'll be following the footsteps of
  Blackbeard, who often took refuge here. It is believed that
  many of the pirate's treasures are still buried at Tybee. To cap off
  a perfect day, head for Fort Screven, a Civil War fort. Then
  climb to the top of the lighthouse for a panoramic view of
  coastal Georgia.

- **Camping It Up at Club One**   From Clint Eastwood to Demi
  Moore, from Meg Ryan to Bruce Willis, every visiting movie
  star or celebrity heads to this rollicking joint. 'Tis true that
  some Savannahians refer to it as a gay club, and there are those
  who would never darken its door. But the club attracts a wide
  spectrum of humanity because it's known for having the best
  entertainment in Savannah. Sometimes even the fabled Lady
  Chablis, empress of Savannah, appears here. This drag queen
  gained prominence in John Berendt's book, *Midnight in the
  Garden of Good and Evil,* and plays herself in the film (Diana
  Ross wanted to). The dancing here is the hottest in Savannah.

2 Best Hotel Bets

- **Best Boutique Hotel**   Built in 1888, the **Mansion on Forsyth
  Park** (© **888/711-5114** or 912/238-5158; www.mansionon
  forsythpark.com), is the most spectacular in Savannah. This
  hotel has both luxury and taste and is also the site of one of
  Savannah's leading restaurants.

- **Best River Street Rejuvenation**   The cotton warehouses along
  the Savannah River have been turned into hotels, shops, and
  restaurants, none restored better than the **River Street Inn**
  (© **800/253-4229** or 912/234-6400; www.riverstreetinn.com).

A flourishing storage warehouse for cotton until the boll weevil came, it dates from 1817, when it was constructed of ballast stones brought over from England. Today, it is the epitome of comfort and charm with memorable views of the Savannah River.

- **Best B&B in the Historic District**   Savannah's classic inn of charm and grace, **Ballastone Inn** (© **800/822-4553** or 912/236-1484; www.ballastone.com), an 1838 building, has been given the glamour treatment. You're housed in a 19th-century-style interior, but with far greater comforts than the antebellum wealthy of Savannah used to experience. Polished hardwoods, elaborate draperies, and well-polished antiques set the stage for a grand B&B experience.

- **Best Deals on Suites**   The **Ramada Hotel & Suites Midtown** (© **800/272-6232** or 912/352-2828; www.ramada.com) offers roomy and attractively furnished suites that begin at $103, each ideal for a family. With its upgraded decor and furnishings, you get first-class comfort. Many of the suites open onto private balconies. Rates include a generous buffet breakfast.

- **Best Rescue of a Decaying Building**   Dating from 1873, the **Hamilton-Turner Inn** (© **888/448-8849** or 912/233-1833; www.hamilton-turnerinn.com) has been much restored after falling into decay. Today, the four-story French Empire house is one of the most upscale B&Bs in Savannah. The building earned notoriety in John Berendt's *Midnight in the Garden of Good and Evil*, but those high-rolling party days are over. It's now a serene oasis.

- **Best & Most Opulent B&B**   Built in 1892, **Kehoe House** (© **800/820-1020** or 912/232-1020; www.kehoehouse.com) is no longer a funeral parlor but an inn of such grace that it ranks among the finest in Georgia. Its fabrics, furniture, and comfort make it an adult retreat of flawless taste. Tom Hanks stayed here during the filming of *Forrest Gump.*

- **Best for Grand Hotel–Style Living**   Built in 1890 as the city's grandest hotel, today's **Hilton Savannah DeSoto** (© **800/426-8483** or 912/232-9000; www.desotohilton.com) is a monument to the grand life. Completely renovated, it is once again an address of lavish comfort with a certain charm, especially for such a commercial hotel. The public rooms, such as the 18th-century drawing room, reflect a Colonial theme.

- **Best Moderately Priced Hotel**   The most appealing of the city's middle-bracket but large-scale hotels, the **Hampton Inn Historic District** (© 800/426-7866 or 912/721-1600; www.hampton-inn.com) opened in 1997, rising seven redbrick stories. Although modern, it pays homage to Savannah's past, including its big-windowed lobby designed to evoke an 18th-century city salon.
- **Best Value**   Adjacent to Chatham Square, **Bed & Breakfast Inn** (© 888/238-0518 or 912/238-0518; www.savannahbnb.com) lies in one of the oldest and most historic parts of Savannah. Its guest rooms are exceedingly comfortable and some of the most affordable for those wishing to stay in the historic core. Furnishings are a combination of antiques and tasteful reproductions.

3 Best Restaurant Bets

- **Best Restaurant**   In the Victorian District, **Elizabeth on 37th** (© 912/236-5547; www.elizabethon37th.net), with its modern Southern cuisine, is not only the most glamorous and upscale restaurant in Savannah, but it also serves the most refined cuisine. In a palatial neoclassical villa from the turn of the 20th century, you can carve some indelible culinary memories here. The menu is reinforced by an impressive wine list.
- **Best Southern Cuisine**   The **Lady & Sons** (© 912/233-2600; www.ladyandsons.com) is the domain of Paula Deen who, along with her sons and $200, launched this temple of gastronomy. She's Savannah's most well-known cookbook writer, sharing the secrets of her kitchen. We always drop in for her chicken potpie topped with puff pastry. It doesn't get much better than this.
- **Best International Cuisine**   In the Mansion on Forsyth Park, **700 Drayton** (© 912/238-5158; www.700drayton.com), is one of the culinary showcases of Savannah. Enticing every visiting celebrity to Savannah, it dazzles with a seductive, market-fresh cuisine.
- **Best Low Country Cuisine**   Stylish and casual, **Sapphire Grill** (© 912/443-9962; www.sapphiregrill.com) is an upscale bistro. The "coastal cuisine" of Christopher Nason wins raves among food critics. It's based on seafood harvested from nearby waters. Wait until you sample the James Island littleneck clams

tossed in foie gras butter. The able service and impressive wine list contribute to the allure.

- **Best Seafood**   Many restaurants in Savannah serve good seafood, or else they're soon out of business. But the **Olde Pink House Restaurant** (℗ **912/232-4286**) seems to put more flavor into its offerings than its competitors do. You don't get just fried fish here, but the likes of black grouper stuffed with blue crab and drenched in a Vidalia onion sauce, or else crispy scored flounder with a tangy apricot sauce. That the setting is both elegant and romantic makes the Pink House even more appealing.

- **Best Prime Rib**   Chain restaurants rarely make Frommer's "best of" lists. There is one exception in Savannah: the **Chart House** (℗ **912/234-6686;** www.chart-house.com). Its prime rib is slow roasted and served au jus. The specially supplied beef is corn fed, aged, and hand cut. Beefeaters are in heaven here. The chefs prepare a mean lobster as well.

- **Best Cajun/Creole Cuisine**   Overlooking the Savannah River, **Huey's** (℗ **912/234-7385**) has a kitchen that would hold its own in New Orleans. If you like all those good things like jambalaya, andouille sausage, crayfish étouffée, and oyster po'boys, welcome home. Even homesick Louisiana visitors show up here "for a feasting."

- **Best Barbecue**   The good people of Savannah don't survive on oyster po'boys or catfish suppers all week. At least once a week they like barbecue. For that tasty treat, many of them show up at **Wall's** (℗ **912/232-9754**). This is an affordable, casual, family-style restaurant, where the barbecue is something to write home about. The sauce and the slow cooking are part of the secret—that and the hickory wood used. Of course, no Southern chef reveals all his secrets for barbecue!

- **Best Breakfast**   Everybody, or so it seems, shows up at **Clary's Café** (℗ **912/233-0402**) for breakfast. A Savannah tradition since 1903, the cafe today has an aura of the 1950s. You expect James Dean to show up on a motorcycle wearing bluejeans and a leather jacket. The cafe is featured in the film *Midnight in the Garden of Good and Evil.* Among the dozens of breakfast offerings, we go for the chef's special: Hoppel Poppel (scrambled eggs with chunks of kosher salami, potatoes, onions, and green peppers).

- **Best Down-Home Favorite** For "belly-busting food," **Mrs. Wilkes' Dining Room** (© **912/232-5997**; www.mrswilkes. com) is a Savannah tradition. Visitors and locals have been standing in line here since the 1940s for real down-home Southern fare. Mrs. Wilkes' time-tested recipes get a workout every day, feeding generations of the local citizenry on barbecued chicken, red rice and sausage, corn on the cob, squash and yams, and any dish with okra. And what would a meal be without Mrs. Wilkes' cornbread and collards?

- **Best Fusion Cuisine** The most eclectic bistro in town, **Bistro Savannah** (© **912/233-6266**) serves a mixture of Southern with fusion cuisine, inspired by a culinary geography that ranges from the bayou country of Louisiana to Thailand. Not only does it make the best seafood bouillabaisse in town, but it also serves such temptations as crisp pecan chicken with a blackberry bourbon sauce.

2

Savannah's History & Culture

In this chapter, we'll take you from the city's founding in Colonial days, through its many stages of growth, decline, and rebirth, with special attention paid to the art and architecture that make this Southern city unique. We'll also learn about the city and its people through a tour of Low Country cuisine.

Savannah's history is the subject of countless novels, most of them centered on its rich antebellum heyday. When General Sherman made it the final goal of his infamous March to the Sea, Savannah earned a dubious distinction in the annals of American history.

From battles with American Indians, British troops, Yankees, Spaniards, and, ultimately, civil rights advocates, the role of Savannah has been unique in the South, although it closely parallels the history of its neighbor, Charleston.

Before Savannah became General Sherman's Christmas gift to Abraham Lincoln, how did it all begin?

1 Savannah Today

Attracting millions of visitors every year, Savannah is now mentioned in the same breath as Charleston, as one of the most historic cities in the Southeast. In 1966, the U.S. government designated Savannah's downtown area as the Savannah Historic District, which is one of the largest such zones in America.

Like New Orleans, Savannah is prone to floods because of its flat topography, but it is the largest port along the Savannah River, lying along the U.S. Intracoastal Waterway.

Unlike most cities in the U.S., Savannah may have actually lost population since the official U.S. Census of 2000 that determined it had 131,510 residents. Today its population is estimated at fewer than 128,000.

The majority of the population, some 57%, is African American. Most of the other residents are white. Unlike many cities of the Southeast, the Hispanic or Latin population is small—some 2.23%.

Savannah is not a rich city, with some 21% of the population below the poverty line.

The port, along with tourism, is the mainstay of the economy. One of the world's largest paper mills, now owned by International Paper, is one of the biggest employers. The Gulfstream Aerospace Company, maker of private jets, also has its home base in Savannah.

Savannah is hardly the safest city in Georgia, with some 25 homicides every year and about 1,200 violent crimes. Home burglaries are a particular problem.

As a former mayor of Savannah told us, "we're not as big or as important as Atlanta, but we've forgotten more about true Southern hospitality than those good folks will ever know."

2 Looking Back at Savannah

COLONIAL DAYS

It was in 1733 that British general James Edward Oglethorpe (1696–1785) landed on the historic bluff above the Savannah River to found what was to become the 13th colony in America. The land was wilderness, but the British wanted to build a buffer zone between their colony in South Carolina and the "Spanish menace" to the south in Florida.

Still in his 30s when he sailed into the port of Savannah, Oglethorpe had already served in the military for 21 years, been a member of Parliament for 11 years, and served on a committee that uncovered widespread abuse of prisoners in England's jails. He had also spent 5 months in jail for killing a man in a brawl. After one of Oglethorpe's friends died in debtor's prison, Oglethorpe vowed to prevent similar deaths by establishing a debtor's colony (his own stay in the slammer must have motivated him as well). On June 9, 1732, King George II granted a charter to Oglethorpe and 20 others (the "Trustees") for the creation of a new colony to be called Georgia, after the king.

Hundreds of people in London applied to sail west, but only 114 men and women were chosen, as well as a doctor and a pastor. There would be freedom of worship in this new land on America's southeast coast, providing a settler wasn't a slave, a Roman Catholic, or a lawyer.

Seven months after being granted the charter, the colonists sailed from the port at Gravesend, England, aboard an overcrowded vessel called the *Anne*. They were heading west on a rough, wave-tossed voyage into an uncertain future. The crew and passengers were close to starvation when they landed at Savannah. It was good for them that the Native Americans were friendly, because the Indians could easily have overpowered the weakened colonists.

Like Columbus in the Bahamas, Oglethorpe and his colonists did not discover an unoccupied Savannah, but encountered an already inhabited land of Native Americans. The Low Country area of Georgia, or so it is believed, had actually been inhabited by nomadic Indian tribes since the end of the Ice Age, when vegetation returned to the land and animals roamed its plains.

The Yamacraws, a small tribe, had fled the Spanish conquistadors in Florida and had moved north to settle in Georgia. It was this group of Indians that was on hand to greet Oglethorpe. Instead of attacking, the Yamacraws were hospitable to these invaders who would change their continent forever. The Indians not only lived in peace with Oglethorpe's colonists, but they would also later help them fight off invasions by the Spaniards and other hostile tribes.

While in London, Oglethorpe had fantasized about the new city he wanted to found in the Americas. For this dream city, he wanted rectilinear streets that would cross at right angles. The core of town would be filled with squares that would be earmarked as "green lungs," or public parks, so settlers could "breathe the fresh air." Savannah would be laid out in "wards" around these central squares.

Once in Savannah, Oglethorpe also set aside space for markets and public areas. He established a 10-acre Trustees' Garden, modeled after the Chelsea Botanical Garden in London. The garden was doomed to failure because many of the plants were not hardy enough for the hard clay soil of coastal Georgia. The mulberry trees died, denying a home to silkworms, and the vines planted in the vineyards didn't bear grapes.

Oglethorpe viewed himself as the spiritual leader of the colony, and indeed he was called "Father Oglethorpe" by the colonists. His new city was founded only 6 months before a new set of colonists arrived from Europe, many escaping religious persecution. The ban on Catholics was rescinded. Not just Catholics, but Jews and Protestants also arrived, many coming from Iberia, especially Portugal.

By the mid–18th century, colonists in Georgia began to import slaves. They'd seen how their wealthy neighbors to the north in South Carolina were prospering in an economy fueled by slave labor. In a few short years, one out of every three persons in the colony was a slave, working the rich plantations that enveloped Savannah to its west.

Politically, the colonists in Georgia turned back further expansion by the Spanish coming north from Florida. Originally, the Spanish had wanted to make Georgia a colony. Oglethorpe, helped at the time by his Native American friends, thwarted their plans.

The founding father stayed in Savannah until 1743, finally giving up his dream and sailing back to London. The throne felt that Oglethorpe had failed as an administrator, and he was replaced by William Stephens, who was sent to govern in his place. The Trustees originally named by the king held onto their charter until 1752 before finally abandoning it. A political movement at the time wanted to turn their Low Country area into another royal colony like that enjoyed by South Carolina, centered at prosperous Charleston.

By 1754, a royal colony was established. Savannah became one of the leading ports of the Southeast, although it never overtook its major rival, Charleston. That prosperity of Low Country plantations became especially marked when the French and Indian War of 1763 came to an end. Britain won Florida, which ended Spain's attempts to forge colonies along the east coast of America.

The slaves began to build plantations for the growing of cotton, and these Colonial buildings soon came to dominate the landscape in the Low Country enveloping Savannah.

THE AMERICAN REVOLUTION

At least a decade before the American Revolution, the residents of Savannah were beginning to defy their English rulers. British property was being destroyed, and so-called Liberty Boys often fought openly with Loyalists. The much-hated Stamp Act of 1765 didn't go over with the colonists, who objected to the tax on every printed item. Savannah even staged its own version of the Boston Tea Party.

The raucous Peter Tondee's Tavern at Whitaker and Broughton streets became the center of a growing rebellion in Georgia led by the Liberty Boys. The name came from their compatriots in Charleston, who had adopted it from Boston's Sons of Liberty. In defiance of royal authority, they flew a flag, featuring a rattlesnake with 13 rattles. Each of these rattles symbolized a different American colony.

These grog-swilling colonists defiantly wore homemade Liberty stocking caps and went so far as to erect a so-called Liberty Pole in front of Tondee's Tavern. The Declaration of Independence was read in Georgia for the first time in front of this tavern, and it was also at Tondee's Tavern that the Liberty Boys first heard the news of the battles of Lexington and Concord. The die was cast: America's war of freedom had begun, even though there were many Loyalists still residing in Georgia.

By June 28, 1776, the battles had come to South Carolina and Georgia as well. The first major victory for the American freedom fighters came on that day, when Gen. William Moultrie defeated an invading fleet of 50 British warships. Although outnumbered and lacking adequate ammunition, the revolutionaries battled the British from a fort hastily assembled on Sullivan's Island.

This early victory was followed by disaster. Before Christmas of 1778, the city of Savannah fell to British troops, with Charleston falling in the spring 2 years later. In their victory, British troops sought vengeance. They executed many patriots and robbed and pillaged from the richest homes in the area.

In October 1781, word reached Savannah that the British "sword of surrender" had been presented to the American forces at Yorktown. "Mad" Anthony Wayne and his troops arrived to reclaim the city in 1782. The British were defeated, and many die-hard Loyalists in Georgia returned to Mother England, never to be seen again.

After the war, Savannah was made the capital city of Georgia, a position it would lose in 1786 to Augusta, which in time would lose out to Atlanta.

ANTEBELLUM TRIUMPH & TRAGEDY

In the years following the American Revolution, commerce in Savannah boomed. The demand grew for Sea Island cotton. On the Low Country plantations, cotton was king, and Savannah was the port from which to ship it north or abroad.

In 1793, Eli Whitney invented the cotton gin on a plantation near Savannah. A former schoolteacher from the North, Whitney invented the gin with the aid of a widow, Catherine ("Caty") Greene, who ran the plantation and had been married to Nathanael Greene of Revolutionary War fame. The cotton gin allowed seeds to be removed with far greater speed and efficiency than by existing methods. Low Country cotton plantations would flourish for at least the next 6 decades.

Both Europe and America focused on Savannah in 1819 when the SS *Savannah* became the first steam-powered vessel to cross the Atlantic. The vessel departed Savannah on May 22 of that year, arriving at the port of Liverpool a record 29 days later. Triumphantly, the ship went on to Glasgow, Stockholm, and even to St. Petersburg in Russia. But in 1821, the vessel was caught in gale winds and capsized off the shores of Long Island.

Disaster struck Savannah in 1796 and 1820, when two major fires left half the city in ruins. The famous Savannah City Market was burned in both instances. As if the fire of 1820 didn't devastate Savannah enough, a yellow fever epidemic broke out. It is estimated that about one-tenth of the city's population died. Yellow fever was to strike again and again for the rest of the 19th century.

Antebellum Savannah was at the peak of its prosperity, fueled by cotton and slavery. But ominous clouds were on the horizon as tensions between the North and South grew steadily worse.

THE CIVIL WAR ERA

There was rejoicing on the streets of Savannah as its neighbor South Carolina seceded from the Union on December 20, 1860. The election of President Abraham Lincoln, who was despised in Savannah, had demoralized the city. In 1861, Georgia followed South Carolina in separating itself from the Union, and when Confederate troops fired on Fort Sumter that same year, war was declared. Calling it "the War of Northern Aggression," Savannahians hoped for an easy, quick victory.

Within a few months, federal troops occupied much of the coastal lowlands of the Carolinas and Georgia, leaving only the port cities of Wilmington, Charleston, and Savannah in Confederate hands, albeit blockaded by the Union navy.

On April 11, 1862, Union cannons fired on Fort Pulaski, 15 miles east of Savannah. They overcame the masonry fortification, but Savannah was months from occupation. In just 30 hours, Union forces had captured Pulaski, signaling the end of masonry fortifications.

With its port blockaded by the Union, Savannah suffered greatly during the war. Goods were hard to come by, as Savannah had always looked to the sea for its livelihood. The city endured bravely, both men and women aiding the war effort.

Except for a few skirmishes and the bombardment of Charleston in 1863, the Carolinas and Georgia escaped heavy fighting until May 1864, when Union general Ulysses S. Grant told Gen. William Tecumseh Sherman to "get into the interior of the enemy's country as far as you can, inflicting all the damage you can against their war resources." Thus began Sherman's famous March to the Sea, the world's first modern example of total war waged against a civilian population. Savannah was the final target.

Sherman fought his way south from Chattanooga, Tennessee, to Atlanta, a key railroad junction, which the Confederates evacuated on September 1, 1864. Leaving Atlanta burning, he departed for the sea on October 17, cutting a 60-mile path of destruction across central and eastern Georgia. "We have devoured the land, and our animals eat up the wheat and corn fields close," Sherman reported. "All the people retire before us, and desolation is behind. To realize what war is, one should follow our tracks."

Despite his orders, looting and pillaging were rampant, but there were few attacks on civilians and none against women.

Sherman arrived at Savannah on December 10, in time to make the port city a Christmas present to Lincoln. (Fortunately, he did not burn the city.) In January 1865, he turned northward into South Carolina. He torched 80 square blocks of Columbia in February. Confederate general Joseph E. Johnston made several attempts to slow Sherman's advance. One such attempt was the Battle of Rivers Bridge, between Allendale and Erhardt, South Carolina, in February; the last was the Battle of Bentonville, near Durham in central North Carolina, in March. On April 26, 2 weeks after Gen. Robert E. Lee surrendered to Grant at Appomattox Courthouse in Virginia, Johnston met Sherman at Durham and handed over his sword. The war in the Carolinas and Georgia was over.

SCALAWAGS, CARPETBAGGERS & JIM CROW

The Confederate survivors straggled home to face Reconstruction. At first, Confederate war veterans dominated the state legislatures in Georgia. They enacted so-called black code laws, which gave some rights to the newly freed slaves but denied them the vote. This and other actions infuriated the Republicans who controlled the U.S. Congress and wanted to see the South punished for its rebellion. In 1867, Congress passed the Reconstruction Act, which gave blacks the right to vote and divided the South into five districts, each under a military governor who had near-dictatorial powers. Approximately 20,000 federal troops were sent to the South to enforce the act.

Recalcitrant white officials were removed from state office, and with their new vote, the ex-slaves helped elect Republican legislatures in all three states, and many blacks won seats. Despite doing some good work, these legislatures were corrupt. They enacted high taxes to pay for rebuilding and social programs, further alienating the struggling white population.

White Georgians also complained bitterly about "scalawags" (local whites who joined the Republican Party) and "carpetbaggers" (Northerners who came South carrying all their possessions in bags made of carpet). The animosity led to the formation of two secret white organizations—the Knights of the White Camelia and the Knights of the Ku Klux Klan—that engaged in terrorism to keep blacks from voting or exercising their other new rights. The former slaves were also disappointed with the Republicans when it became obvious that they wouldn't receive the promised "40 acres and a mule." Those who did vote began to cast them for their former masters. Factions also developed among the local scalawags and the Northern carpetbaggers.

During Reconstruction, blacks from plantations from throughout Georgia flooded into Savannah, living in poverty. For the planters, though, cotton returned as king and would reign supreme until the arrival of the boll weevil.

All this set the stage for whites to regain control of Georgia in 1871. By 1877, President Rutherford B. Hayes, a Republican, withdrew federal troops from the South. Reconstruction was over.

During the next 20 years, white governments enacted Jim Crow laws, which imposed poll taxes, literacy tests, and other requirements intended to prevent blacks from voting. Whites flocked to the Democratic Party, which restricted its primaries—tantamount to elections throughout the South—to white voters. Blacks who did try to vote faced having the Ku Klux Klan burn crosses on their lawns, or even being lynched. Indeed, "strange fruit" hung from many Southern trees during this period.

Racial segregation became a legal fact of life, from the public drinking fountains to the public schools. The U.S. Supreme Court ratified the scheme in its 1896 *Plessy vs. Ferguson* decision, declaring "separate but equal" public schools to be constitutional. Black schools in the South were hardly equal, but they surely were separate.

Throughout the 19th century, Savannah remained rigidly segregated. In 1878, the first public school for blacks was opened. That was followed in 1891 by the first public college for blacks. Educational segregation remained in place until well into the 20th century.

Savannah was sucked up in the Spanish-American War of 1898, when it was a port of embarkation for troops headed for Havana.

SAVANNAH IN THE 20TH CENTURY

As Savannah entered a new century, it was economically powerful, its ships fanning out to take Georgia exports such as lumber around the world. Savannah's men marched off to World War I.

Upon their return, economic devastation set in. The boll weevil attacked the cotton fields in the Low Country plantations around Savannah. King Cotton was dethroned. If that weren't enough, America entered a grave Depression during the Hoover era.

The Democrats remained supreme in Savannah, and racial segregation was a way of life. The city's economy was helped when the Eighth Air Force was founded outside Savannah, restoring some vigor to a sagging economy.

But Savannah was literally falling apart. Its historic buildings were being torn down or left to rot. In 1955, a group of determined ladies saved the historic Davenport House from the wrecking ball, and Savannah began to take preservation seriously.

Savannah took a back seat in the civil rights movement of the 1950s. The shots and the drama, for the most part, where being fired in Atlanta, under the leadership of Martin Luther King, Jr.

As late as 1959 and 1960, segregation in Savannah was firmly entrenched and backed by official state law. Unlike much of the more rural South, however, Savannah had a more progressive attitude regarding race relations. Even before the surge of the civil rights movement, there was relative tolerance between the races here, as African Americans slowly integrated themselves into the city's social fabric.

Local leader after local leader urged the city to face its problems of race relations with decency and dignity—and without hate. By 1961, Savannah was desegregating its public schools.

In May 1981, antiques dealer Jim Williams shot his lover-assistant, a hustler named Danny Hansford, 21. As a result, through a complicated legal process, Williams became the first person in Georgia to be tried four times for murder before he was finally acquitted.

The case could have slipped into history as another gay murder. However, writer John Berendt drifted into town one day, became intrigued by the story, and eventually wrote his megabestseller, *Midnight in the Garden of Good and Evil.*

His original agent turned down the story as too bizarre and "too regional." Buyers of books felt otherwise, and, in time, Clint Eastwood even directed it as a movie.

To the amazement of Savannah, the Berendt book put the city on the tourist map, as millions began to visit. Through the interest created by what is locally called "The Book," Savannah became a tourist attraction to compete with Charleston to the north.

3 Savannah's Architecture & Art

For art and architecture, Savannah is outclassed by Charleston to the north. But Savannah is not without its own accomplishments.

The greatest collection of evocative architecture lies in the Historic District, around which you can walk at your leisure, discovering the area's old buildings, churches, and squares. Some structures are from the Colonial era, others perhaps inspired by the Adam brothers or built in the Regency style. There are tons of ironwork and antique buildings in brick or clapboard. Even modest town houses from the 18th century are restored and have become coveted addresses and homes of charm.

Because many of its residents lacked money in the final decades of the 19th century and the beginning of the 20th, antique structures were allowed to stand, whereas many American cities destroyed their heritage and replaced them with modern buildings. By the time Savannahians got around to tearing down their old structures, a forceful preservation movement was launched—and just in time.

What you won't see, as you travel through the Low Country around Savannah, are a lot of plantations where cotton was king. Many of these have "gone with the wind."

THE FIRST CITY

In 1733, at the founding of Savannah, James Oglethorpe faced a daunting challenge. He not only had to secure homes for Trustees and colonists, but he also had to construct forts around the new town of Savannah to fend off possible Indian raids, even though the local Native Americans were friendly.

Since they weren't well built and were later torn down to make way for grander structures, none of the founding fathers' little wooden homes remain today. But that town plan as envisioned by Oglethorpe back in London still remains. He wanted an orderly grid composed of 24 squares. In case of rebellion he also wanted "mustering points" where troops could gather to squelch the problem.

Nine years after the colonists arrived in port, they had enough money and building materials to construct their first church, which quickly became the most elaborate structure in town. Called "The Orphan House," the church took its name from the Bethesda Orphanage founded by the evangelist George Whitefield in 1738. Along with Oglethorpe, Whitefield believed that rum drinking caused a yellow fever–like disease but that beer drinking was acceptable. This philosophy was expounded to the congregation of Georgia's first church. Unfortunately, this landmark building no longer stands.

After the Revolutionary War, the port of Savannah began to grow rich on profits it made shipping sago powder, beef, pork, animal skins, tar, turpentine, and other exports. Money generated from this thriving trade with Europe, especially London, was poured into architecture. Grander homes began to sprout on the squares of Savannah. Still, none of these early structures equaled the glory of the rival city of Charleston. While visiting the family of Gen. Nathanael Greene, Eli Whitney invented the cotton gin in 1793, bringing even greater prosperity to the area, which led to even grander building.

Only one structure remains from this post–Revolutionary era. Built by James Habersham, Jr., in a Georgian style, it is covered in pink stucco. Underneath the stucco is a solid brick foundation. Today it is a well-recommended restaurant and bar, known as the Olde Pink House Restaurant (p. 61), open to the general public at 23 Abercorn St.

The reason so little architecture from the post–Revolutionary era survived is that a disastrous fire struck in 1796, burning block after block of the city. In 1820, another devastating fire swept over Savannah, destroying architectural gems that had been erected by builders from both Charleston and the North. The fire erupted just at the time an epidemic of yellow fever broke out. Thousands of slaves died from the fever, temporarily slowing down building efforts because they provided the hard labor on the construction projects. Work on rebuilding Savannah was further slowed when cholera broke out in 1834.

But through it all, Savannahians survived and prospered and continued to pour money into elaborate structures, many of which remain today, especially those constructed of brick. The Federal style was very prevalent, as it was along the east coast of America. Some builders, perhaps those with Loyalist hearts, preferred the Georgian style. Locals continued to spend money on churches, notably the Independent Presbyterian Church of Savannah, whose architectural beauty competes with that of some of the finest churches of Charleston.

THE REGENCY STYLE SWEEPS SAVANNAH

The cotton planters with their newfound money invited William Jay of London to come to Savannah in 1817. He introduced the Regency style, which became all the rage in Savannah.

Some of his structures still stand today. His greatest achievement is the Owens-Thomas House, the best example of English Regency architecture in the United States. Inspired by classical buildings, the flourishing style was named for King George IV, who ruled as prince regent from 1811 to 1820. The house overlooks Oglethorpe Square and was standing in 1825 to welcome the Marquis de Lafayette when he was a guest of honor in Savannah. The French war hero addressed a crowd of Savannahians from the cast-iron veranda on the south facade of the building. This landmark building was constructed in the main from tabby, a concrete mixture of oyster shells, sand, and lime. The Grecian-inspired veranda on the southern facade was the first major use of cast iron in Savannah. As an architectural device, cast iron later swept the city.

Jay also designed the Telfair Mansion in a neoclassical Regency style. It was constructed in 1818 for Alexander Telfair, the scion of Edward Telfair, a former Georgia governor and Revolutionary War hero. The mansion was bequeathed to the city for use as a museum, and formally opened in 1886. Many notables attended; most of the crowd's interest focused on Jefferson Davis, the former president of the Confederacy.

The Irish-born architect Charles B. Cluskey (1808–71) arrived in Savannah in 1838 and stayed for almost a decade, becoming known for his antebellum architecture influenced by the Greek Revival style. The elite of Savannah, prospering from neighboring plantations, hired him to design their town houses, including the Champion-McAlpin-Fowlkes house in 1844. He served as city surveyor of Savannah from 1845 to 1847, when he went to Washington with plans to renovate the White House and Capitol (few of his ideas were carried out, however).

Another antebellum architect, John Norris (1804–76), flourished in Savannah between 1846 and 1860. His most famous landmark is the Savannah Customs House, which was constructed between 1848 and 1852 in the Greek Revival style, with its mammoth portico. In the same general style, he also designed many more notable structures throughout the city, including the Andrew Low House in 1849.

A competitor of his was John B. Hogg, who hailed from South Carolina. Hogg's most notable structure is the Trinity United Methodist Church at 225 W. President St. The church was built of stucco over gray brick, the famous "Savannah grays" form of architecture. The building became known in Georgia as the "Mother Church of Methodism."

As Georgia, along with South Carolina, moved closer to the horror of the Civil War, Savannah architecture stood at the peak of its beauty and charm. A visitor from London claimed, "Savannah puts on a hell of a good show. It's not London but not bad for a colony."

WAR, RECONSTRUCTION & PRESERVATION

Unlike Atlanta, Savannah was not burned to the ground, with no Scarlett O'Hara fleeing into the night to escape the flames. Even in 1864, after all the wartime deprivation suffered by the long blockade of its port, Savannah was still a worthy gift when Sherman presented it as a Christmas present to Lincoln.

The Civil War brought poverty to most Savannahians, and the decades of Reconstruction meant the end of opulence. Oglethorpe's original town plan had stretched from 6 to 24 city squares. Architects of renown avoided building in Savannah, going to richer cities.

The famous "Savannah grays" (bricks) ceased production in the 1880s. Many buildings fell into ruin or decay. Modern structures outside the Historic District were haphazardly constructed, although the Victorian era produced some notable structures to grace the cityscape.

Just when it appeared that Savannah was going to rot away in the hot Georgia sun, the preservation movement of the 1950s came at the 11th hour. Historic Savannah was saved and restored during the latter part of the 20th century and awaits your discovery in the 21st century.

THE ART OF SAVANNAH

In antebellum days, portraiture was the most common form of art in the Colonial era. Any moderately well-off family commissioned rather idealized portraits of its family members, at least the gentleman and lady of the house. Most of the portraits were either in oil on canvas or in watercolor. In some rare instances, the portraits were done on ivory.

The subjects of the portraits are attired in their "Sunday go-to-meeting" garb. If a setting was used as a backdrop, it was romanticized—an elegant drapery, a Grecian column, a distant view of the ocean.

With the coming of the deprivations caused by the Civil War and the lean poverty years of the Reconstruction era, Savannah was more in survivalist mode than in the mood for painting.

Slowly, Savannahians began to find time for art again, although the decades produced no known national painters.

As time went on, a number of self-taught artists emerged in Savannah and the Low Country. Many of them were black, working in a folk art medium. Sometimes they painted on unpainted clapboard from some abandoned barn or other structure. The Telfair Museum is the exhibition center for these self-taught artists, exhibiting Low Country art in various temporary exhibitions.

Among the other artists who have distinguished themselves in modern times is Leonora Quarterman (1911–79), who became one of the best-known watercolorists in the South. Her silk-screen prints of Savannah and Georgia coastal scenes are highly prized by collectors today.

Christopher P. H. Murphy (1902–69) was a native of the city who became known for drawings that captured both the cityscape of Savannah and the coastal landscape of the Low Country coastline. His originals and reproductions still come on the market from time to time and are as sought after as those of Ms. Quarterman.

4 Savannah in Popular Culture: Books, Films & Music

BOOKS

- **Berendt, John.** *Midnight in the Garden of Good and Evil* (1994). This is the book that put Savannah on the tourist map—with a little help from Forrest Gump. Characters such as Lady Chablis (a wickedly funny black drag queen) and Danny Hansford (a hustler) are introduced in this brilliantly conceived and seductive story of murder (or was it self-defense?) in the steamy Old South. It has been called both a travel book and a murder mystery. Berendt's book—called "The Book" in Savannah—was a bestseller, but the sappy movie of the same title, directed by Clint Eastwood, didn't fare as well with viewers.
- **Jones, Jacqueline.** *Saving Savannah* (2008). This is a meticulous re-creation of the Civil War in Georgia's rice kingdom. It documents how locals surrendered to Sherman's invading forces rather than face destruction like Atlanta. The book is the best yet to document the struggles and conflicts between blacks and whites during the tumultuous Reconstruction years.
- **Kennett, Lee.** *Marching Through Georgia* (1995). Gen. William Tecumseh Sherman pledged "to make a trail that would be visible for 50 years"—250 miles long and 60 miles wide, from Atlanta to Savannah. This carefully researched book, the story of both soldiers and civilians, tells how he did it.

FILMS

Set in Savannah, *Forrest Gump* (1994) was a huge worldwide commercial success, winning six Oscars, including a Best Actor Award for Tom Hanks. The movie tells the story of a man with an IQ of 75 and his epic journey through life. The film received rave reviews, except for a dissent here and there—*Entertainment Weekly* called it "a baby boomer version of Disney's America."

Director Clint Eastwood's *Midnight in the Garden of Good and Evil* (1997) is based on John Berendt's spectacular bestseller. Southern

Gothic in tone, it depicts the fabulously eccentric personalities of Savannah, including drag queen Lady Chablis. The book is based on the actual killing of Danny Hansford, a local hustler, by art dealer Jim Williams, an event that resulted in four murder trials before a final acquittal.

With Savannah as a setting, *The Legend of Bagger Vance* (2000) is directed by Robert Redford. It stars Will Smith as Bagger Vance and Matt Damon as Rannulph Junuh, the best golfer in the city. Bagger teaches Rannulph the secret of an authentic golf stroke, which turns out also to be the secret to mastering any challenge and finding meaning in life.

Bestselling novelist John Grisham wrote the story, *The Ginger-bread Man*, that director Robert Altman turned into a 1998 film. Kenneth Branagh stars as lawyer Rick Magtruder, who has a one-night stand with caterer Mallory Doss (played by Embeth Davidtz) and becomes hooked on her. For those who like strong suspense, heavy plotting, and a dark atmosphere, this one evokes the more famous *Midnight in the Garden of Good and Evil.*

MUSIC

Johnny Mercer, born in Savannah in 1909, is the most famous composer to hail from the city. This noted lyricist and songwriter wrote more than 1,000 songs, many of them hits, including "Blues in the Night" and "One for My Baby."

Jazz legend **Joe Steele** is a seminal figure from the golden age of jazz in the '20s to the Big Band era. Born in 1899, Steele reached the peak of his jazz career from 1932 to 1936 when he played piano in Chick Webb's band. Some of his playing can be heard in the Smith-sonian record collection titled "Big Band Jazz."

The career of **Connie Haines** (1921–2008) spanned decades of American music and 200 recordings. She was the first white artist to record for Motown Records, and she appeared before five U.S. presidents and in many films.

Called "The Lady from Savannah," **Irene Reid** (1930–2008) is in the grand tradition of such performers as Ella Fitzgerald and Sarah Vaughn. She won fame at Harlem's Apollo Theater in 1947, and was a fixture in New York nightclubs such as the Village Gate for years. In 1961 she joined Count Basie. After touring the world with the Basie band, she formed her own group, Ms. Irene Reid & Co. Throughout her life, she appeared on the stage with some of the biggest names in show business, including Flip Wilson, Carmen McRae, Aretha Franklin, and B. B. King.

5 Eating in Savannah

Savannah is the capital of the Georgia Low Country and the coastal Sea Islands, the site of many former rice and cotton plantations.

In recent years, Savannah chefs have moved far beyond the "grits-and-greens" type of cookery, creating fresh combinations from traditional ingredients. For example, instead of black-eyed peas cooked in bacon fat, you might get black-eyed-pea salsa. Instead of fried shrimp, you might get smoked shrimp and melon gazpacho. Instead of Southern fried chicken, you might get stuffed breast of chicken with a crabmeat-and-artichoke dressing.

COLONIAL CUISINE

Oglethorpe's Colonials found a Low Country made up of marshes and saltwater creeks. They turned to these for a harvest of shrimp and oysters. For meat, the forests were full of game such as rabbits. The Low Country also yielded marsh hens, doves, pigeons, and quail. Deer were hunted at night by torchlight. By 1800, visitors reported seeing the old City Market (since burned down) overflowing with corn, peas, okra, field greens, beets, squash, turnips, sweet potatoes, beans, and even eggplant. The bean of choice was the black-eyed pea, which was African in origin. Combined with rice, it became hoppin' John. Many Savannahians still eat hoppin' John on New Year's Day. Tradition has it that it will bring them luck in the coming year.

The Colonials roasted their meat over fires on spits. Rare meat was considered not only the best tasting but the healthiest. In time, however, beginning in the 1800s, the iron kitchen range was introduced. Cooks started cooking their meats well-done, and even today many Savannahians will only eat their meat well-done.

From the Native Americans Oglethorpe encountered when he landed, the Colonials learned how to make cornbread, which they called hoecake, pone, or dodgers. The seasoning in this first early American version of cornbread? Bear grease. For many Savannahians

Impressions

The land belongs to the women, and the corn that grows upon it; but meat must be got by the men, because it is they only that hunt. This makes marriage necessary, that the women may furnish corn and the men meat.

—James Oglethorpe on Savannah's Native Americans (1733)

Impressions

Oh, lady, if yo' want to tas'e somethin' sweet,
Jes' take a li'l onion an' a li'l piece o' met
An' mix 'em wid yo' tender, pure, raw s'rimp.

—Traditional vendor call

during the blockade of the Civil War, cornbread and some milk were all they had to sustain life.

In the Savannah tradition, meat was preferred if it had "streak of lean and a streak of fat." Some early settlers liked boiled fat—no lean.

When slavery became a factor in the colony, many Africans introduced recipes remembered from their distant homelands. Dishes became hotter and spicier, especially with the use of red pepper.

Sometimes vendors came around from door to door (back door, that is) hawking fresh produce or seafood. The shrimp man, for example, sold fresh shrimp carried in a basket on his head.

FAVORITE SAVANNAH FOODS

The Southern love for pork was and is economical. Hogs are easier to raise than cattle, because they more or less take care of themselves by foraging for their food, and cows take longer to raise. A succulent hog can add to its body weight 150 times in just 1 year of life. Savannahians found that all parts of the hog, even the head, could be consumed.

From the hog they smoked hams, made sausages, dried cracklings for cornbread, and saved the fat for lard, which they used in virtually every dish, most often to season greens and other vegetables. Salt pork preserved the meat during long cold winters and came in most handily during the long siege caused by the Civil War.

BBQ'd pork remains the favorite meat dish of Savannah, followed by fried chicken, of which every Southern chef has a special recipe. Beef lags a distant third. Even today, many Savannahians do not eat lamb.

Quail is the favorite game bird of Savannah and the Low Country. In fact, it is a staple on most tables and is served grilled, stuffed, or sautéed at breakfast, lunch, or dinner.

The tomato, which is now integral to most Southern meals, from fried green tomatoes to soups, was thought to be poisonous before the Civil War. Some Savannahians believed that it had the power to act as a love potion—hence they called it the "love apple." After the

Civil War, the tomato came into favor and started to appear in okra-laced gumbos, in soups, in catsup and, miracle of miracles, to be eaten raw by the most daring of diners.

Although the tomato is botanically a fruit, the Supreme Court in 1893 declared it a vegetable. At the same time, eggplants, peppers, avocados, peas, beans, cucumbers, and squash, though botanical fruits, were also ruled vegetables. All of these found favor with the diners of Savannah. A true Savannahian will eat a fresh tomato only between late May and early August.

Lima beans, sometimes cooked with okra, became the best-known beans for consumption in Savannah. Named for their place of origin, Lima, Peru, the beans became known as "butter beans" in Savannah.

Savannahians also love sweet potatoes, and they are fashioned in countless dishes, with sweet potato pancakes a favorite, especially at Sunday brunches.

Southerners also take to greens, especially collards, which are served almost invariably cooked in pork stock, with cornbread used to mop up the "pot liquor."

Grits appear frequently, most often at breakfast. Savannahians like to spice them up in several versions, including cheese grits.

3

Planning Your Trip
to Savannah

Savannah is to Georgia what Charleston is to South Carolina—
Georgia's grandest, most historic, and most intriguing city to visit. In
fact, it's one of the 10 most historic cities in America.

Because much of the interest focuses on the easily walkable historic core, getting the hang of navigating Savannah comes relatively
quickly for most visitors from more congested urban areas.

Even more than Charlestonians, the people of Savannah are noted
for their old-fashioned Southern hospitality. You'll frequently hear
them say, "Y'all come back, you hear?"

In the pages that follow, we've compiled everything you need to
know to handle the practical details of planning your trip: a calendar
of events, visitor information, and more.

1 Visitor Information

You can contact the **Division of Tourism,** Georgia Department of
Industry, Trade & Tourism, PO Box 1776, Atlanta, GA 30301-1776
(© **800/VISIT-GA** [847-4842] or 404/962-4000; www.georgia.
org/travel). Ask for information on your specific interests, as well as
a calendar of events (Jan–June or July–Dec).

VISITOR INFORMATION

The **Savannah Information Visitor Center,** 301 Martin Luther
King Jr. Blvd., Savannah, GA 31401 (© **912/944-0455**), is open
Monday to Friday 8:30am to 5pm and Saturday and Sunday 9am to
5pm. The staff is friendly and efficient. The center offers an audio-
visual presentation ($4 adults, $1 children), organized tours, and
self-guided walking, driving, or bike tours with excellent maps, cas-
sette tapes, and brochures.

Tourist information is also available from the **Savannah
Area Convention & Visitors Bureau,** 101 E. Bay St., Savannah,
GA 31402 (© **877/728-2662** or 912/644-6401; www.savannah
visit.com).

2 When to Go

CLIMATE

The average high and low temperatures in Savannah show Low Country coastal areas to be warmer year-round than farther inland. Winter temperatures seldom drop below freezing. Spring and fall are the longest seasons, and the wettest months are December to April.

Spring is a spectacular time to visit Savannah. Many areas become a riot of color as azaleas, dogwoods, and camellias burst into bloom.

Savannah Average Temperatures & Rainfall

	Jan	Feb	Mar	Apr	May	June	July	Aug	Sept	Oct	Nov	Dec
High (°F)	60	62	70	78	84	89	91	90	85	78	70	62
High (°C)	16	17	21	26	29	32	33	32	29	26	21	17
Low (°F)	38	41	48	55	63	69	72	72	68	57	57	41
Low (°C)	3	5	9	13	17	21	22	22	20	14	14	5
Rain (in.)	3.6	3.2	3.8	3.0	4.1	5.7	6.4	7.5	4.5	2.4	2.2	3.0

SAVANNAH CALENDAR OF EVENTS

February

Georgia Days Colonial Faire and Muster. Georgians turn out to celebrate the founding of their colony in Savannah on February 12, 1733, by James Oglethorpe. Various events are staged, including costumed demonstrators depicting skills used by the early settlers. Tickets cost $2 for adults and $1 for children. Call ⓒ 912/651-2125 or go to www.georgiahistory.com for more information. First Saturday and Sunday in February.

Savannah Irish Festival. This Irish heritage celebration promises fun for the entire family, with music, dancing, and food. There's a children's stage and a main stage. Contact the Irish Committee of Savannah at ⓒ 912/232-3448 or go to www.savannahirish.org for more information. Mid-February.

March

St. Patrick's Day Celebration on the River. The river flows green and so does the beer in one of the largest celebrations held on River Street each year. Enjoy live entertainment, lots of food, and tons of fun. Contact the Savannah Waterfront Association at ⓒ 912/234-0295 or visit www.riverstreetsavannah.com for more information. St. Patrick's Day weekend.

Savannah Music Festival. Featuring everything from indigenous music from the South to world premieres, this annual music festival attracts fans from all over America. Chamber music and even ballet troupes perform before appreciative audiences. For more information, call ⓒ **912/234-3378** or visit www.savannahmusic festival.org. Begins mid-March.

The Savannah Tour of Homes & Gardens. During this annual festival, now more than 70 years old, each day a different district of historic Savannah is featured on a tour, including private homes and gardens not available to visitors the rest of the year. For more information, call ⓒ **912/234-8054** or visit www.savannahtourof homes.org. Mid-March.

May

Memorial Day at Old Fort Jackson. The commemoration includes a flag-raising ceremony and a memorial service featuring "Taps." Contact the Coastal Heritage Society at ⓒ **912/651-6840** or visit www.chsgeorgia.org for more information. Late May.

June

Juneteenth. This event highlights the contributions of more than 200,000 African Americans who fought for their freedom and the freedom of future generations. This event is a celebration of the Emancipation Proclamation. Although this promise of freedom was announced in January, it was not until the middle of June (actual date unknown) that the news reached Savannah, thus prompting the remembrance of "Juneteenth." For more information, contact the Savannah Convention & Visitors Bureau at ⓒ **877/728-2662** or visit www.savannahvisit.com. Mid-June.

September

Savannah Jazz Festival. This festival features national and local jazz and blues legends. A jazz brunch and music at different venues throughout the city are among the highlights. For details, call ⓒ **912/525-5050** or visit www.savannahjazzfestival.org. Late September.

November

Cane Grinding and Harvest Festival. More than 75 craftspeople from four states sell and demonstrate their art at this annual festival. Music is provided by the Savannah Folk Music Society. Contact Oatland Island at ⓒ **912/898-3980** or go to www.oatland island.org for more information. Mid-November.

December

Christmas 1864. Fort Jackson hosts the dramatic re-creation of its evacuation on December 20, 1864. More than 60 Civil War reenactors play the part of Fort Jackson's Confederate defenders, who were preparing to evacuate ahead of Union general William

Tecumseh Sherman. Contact Old Fort Jackson at ℂ **912/232-3945** or go to www.chsgeorgia.org/jackson/home.htm for more information. Early December.

Holiday Tour of Homes. The doors of Savannah's historic homes are opened to the public during the holiday season. Each home is decorated, and a different group of homes is shown every day. Contact the Savannah Downtown Neighborhood Association at ℂ **912/236-8362** or visit www.dnaholidaytour.net for more information. Early December.

3 Money & Costs

You won't have any problem finding ATMs that are connected to the major national networks. For specific locations of **Cirrus** machines, call ℂ **800/424-7787** or go to www.mastercard.com; for the **PLUS** network, call ℂ **800/843-7587** or go to www.visa.com.

What Things Cost in Savannah	US$
Taxi from Savannah airport to downtown	22.00
One-way bus fare	1.00
Double room at The Westin Savannah Harbor (expensive)	265.00
Double room at The River Street Inn (moderate)	139.00
Double room at Bed & Breakfast Inn (inexpensive)	129.00
Lunch for one at Huey's (moderate)	20.00
Lunch for one at Clary's Café (inexpensive)	12.00
Dinner for one, without wine, at 700 Drayton (very expensive)	50.00
Dinner for one, without wine, at Il Pasticcio (moderate)	38.00
Dinner for one, without wine, at Wall's (inexpensive)	15.00
Bottle of beer	4.00
Coca-Cola	2.00
Cup of coffee in a cafe	2.50
Admission to Telfair Mansion and Art Museum	10.00
Movie ticket	9.00
Theater ticket to Savannah Theater	33.00

If you run out of funds on the road, you can have a friend or relative send you some money through **MONEYGRAM,** www.money gram.com, which allows you to transfer funds from one person to another in less than 10 minutes from thousands of locations. An American Express phone representative will give you the names of four or five offices nearby.

4 Specialized Travel Resources

FOR TRAVELERS WITH DISABILITIES   Many hotels and restaurants in Georgia provide easy access for persons with disabilities, and some display the international wheelchair symbol in their brochures. However, it's always a good idea to call ahead.

The **Governor's Developmental Disabilities Council** (✆ 888/275-4233 or 404/657-2126; www.gcdd.org) may also be of help. The Georgia Department of Industry, Trade & Tourism publishes a guide, *Georgia on My Mind,* that lists attractions and accommodations with access for persons with disabilities. To receive a copy, contact **Tour Georgia,** 75 5th St., Technology Sq., Atlanta, GA 30308 (✆ 800/VISIT-GA [847-4842], ext. 1903; www.georgia.org/travel).

For transportation within Georgia, individuals with disabilities can contact **Handicapped Driver Services** (✆ 877/437-8267 or 457-9851; www.hdsvans.com) or **Wheelchair Getaways, Inc.** (✆800/642-2042; www.wheelchairgetaways.com).

Amtrak (✆ 800/USA-RAIL [872-7245]; www.amtrak.com), with 24 hours' notice, provides porter service, special seating, and a substantial discount.

Many travel agencies offer customized tours and itineraries for travelers with disabilities. **Flying Wheels Travel** (✆ 507/451-5005; www.flyingwheelstravel.com) offers escorted tours and cruises that emphasize sports and private tours in minivans with lifts. **Access-Able Travel Source** (✆ 303/232-2979; www.access-able.com) offers extensive access information and advice for those with disabilities traveling around the world. **Accessible Journeys** (✆ 800/846-4537 or 610/521-0339; www.disabilitytravel.com) caters specifically to slow walkers and wheelchair travelers and their families and friends.

Organizations that offer travel assistance to people with disabilities include **MossRehab** (✆ 800/225-5667; www.mossresource net.org), which provides a library of accessible-travel resources online; and **SATH** (Society for Accessible Travel & Hospitality; ✆ 212/447-7284; www.sath.org; annual membership $45 adults, $30 seniors and students), which offers a wealth of travel resources for people with all types of disabilities and informed recommendations on destinations, access guides, travel agents, tour operators, vehicle rentals, and companion services. **AirAmbulanceCard.com** is now partnered with SATH and allows you to preselect top-notch hospitals in case of an emergency. The **American Foundation for the Blind (AFB; ✆ 800/232-5463;** www.afb.org), is a referral resource for the blind or visually impaired that includes information on traveling with Seeing Eye dogs.

For more on organizations that offer travel resources to people with disabilities, go to **www.frommers.com**.

FOR GAY & LESBIAN TRAVELERS   Homophobia is rampant in "Red State" Georgia, which does not approve, according to voter turnout, of same-sex marriage. Nor does it approve, in the words of one gay bartender, "of homosexuals in general." That said, Savannah and Atlanta are the most gay-friendly places to travel in Georgia. Even so, open displays of affection between same-sex couples may be met with glares of hostility.

The **International Gay and Lesbian Travel Association (IGLTA; ✆ 800/448-8550** or 954/776-2626; www.iglta.org) is the trade association for the gay and lesbian travel industry and offers an online directory of gay- and lesbian-friendly travel businesses; go to their website and click on "Travel."

FOR SENIORS   Nearly all major U.S. hotel and motel chains now offer a senior discount, so ask for the reduction *when you make the reservation;* there may be restrictions during peak days. Then be sure to have proof of your age (driver's license, passport, and so on) when you check in. Among the chains that offer the best discounts are **Marriott Hotels (✆ 800/228-9290;** www.marriott.com) for those 62 and older and **La Quinta Inns & Suites (✆ 800/531-5900;** www.lq.com) for ages 55 and older.

AARP, 601 E. St. NW, Washington, DC 20049 (✆ **888/687-2277;** www.aarp.org), is one organization for seniors that offers a wide variety of travel benefits.

FAMILY TRAVEL   The Savannah Convention & Visitors' Bureau offers, without charge, their 115-page *Savannah Travel Planner* that's loaded with ideas about how to effectively choreograph a trip to Savannah. A subsection of this travel planner, "Savannah for Kids," places special emphasis on the museums and Tybee Island beach-oriented destinations that kids love. Look for insights into family-friendly approaches to local forts, historic sites, wetland and wildlife refuges, and museums in and around the city. The brochure also includes maps scaled for both pedestrians and motorists and information about tours, events, and attractions. You can pick up a copy of this planning guide at the Savannah Convention & Visitors' Bureau, 301 Martin Luther King Jr. Blvd., Savannah, GA 31401; by calling **877/728-2662,** or by visiting www.savannahvisit.com.

5 Getting There & Getting Around

GETTING THERE

BY PLANE   Depending on where you are coming from, many visitors fly first to Atlanta's **Hartsfield International Airport (ATL),** 13 miles south of downtown Atlanta off I-85 and I-285. From Atlanta, there are many connecting flights into Savannah. There are also direct flights into **Savannah/Hilton Head International Airport (SAV)** on many airlines.

Savannah/Hilton Head International Airport is about 8 miles west of downtown just off I-16. **American** (© 800/433-7300; www.aa.com), **Delta** (© 800/221-1212; www.delta.com), **United** (© 800/241-6522; www.united.com), and **US Airways** (© 800/428-4322; www.usairways.com) have flights from Atlanta and Charlotte, with connections from other points.

BY TRAIN   Amtrak (© 800/USA-RAIL [872-7245]; www.amtrak.com) has stops in Atlanta and Savannah. Be sure to ask about Amtrak's money-saving "All Aboard America" regional fares or any other current fare specials. Amtrak also offers attractively priced rail-drive packages in the Carolinas and Georgia. The **train station** in Savannah is at 2611 Seaboard Coastline Dr. (© **912/234-2611**), some 4 miles southwest of downtown; cab fare into the city is around $5.

BY CAR   Georgia is crisscrossed by major interstate highways: I-75 bisects the state from Dalton in the north to Valdosta in the south; I-95 runs north-south along the Eastern Seaboard. The major east-west routes are I-16, running between Macon and Savannah, and I-20, running from Augusta through Atlanta and into Alabama. I-85 runs northeast-southwest in the northern half of the state.

In addition to the interstates, U.S. 84 cuts across the southern part of the state from the Alabama state line through Valdosta and Waycross, and eventually connects to I-95 south of Savannah.

The state-run welcome centers at all major points of entry are staffed with knowledgeable, helpful Georgians who can often advise you as to timesaving routes. The speed limit varies from 55 to 70 mph and the seat-belt law is strictly enforced.

Here is a list of approximate mileages to Savannah from other major cities in the East: Atlanta, GA, 248 miles; Charleston, SC, 107 miles; Charlotte, NC, 252 miles; Jackson, FL, 138 miles; Richmond, VA, 467 miles; Orlando, FL, 278 miles; New York, NY, 815 miles; and Washington, D.C., 579 miles.

For 24-hour road conditions, call © **404/656-5267. AAA** services are available in Savannah. The Savannah branch office of AAA is located at 712 Mall Blvd. (© **912/352-8222;** www.aaa south.com; open Mon, Wed, and Fri 8:30am–5:30pm and Tues and Thurs 10am–7pm).

BY BUS   Greyhound (© **800/231-2222;** www.greyhound.com) has good direct service to major cities in Georgia from out of state, including Savannah, with connections to almost any destination.

GETTING AROUND

The grid-shaped Historic District is best seen on foot—the real point of your visit is to take leisurely strolls with frequent stops in the many squares.

BY CAR   Though you can reach many points of interest outside the Historic District by bus, your own wheels will be much more convenient, and they're absolutely essential for sightseeing outside the city proper.

All major car-rental firms have branches in Savannah and at the airport, including **Hertz** (© **800/654-3131** or 912/964-9595 at the airport; www.hertz.com); **Avis** (© **800/831-2847;** www.avis.com), with locations at 422 Airways Ave. (© 912/964-1781) and at 2215 Travis Field Rd. (© 912/964-0234); and **Budget** (© **800/527-0700;** www.budget.com), with offices at 7070 Abercorn St. (© 912/966-1771).

BY BUS   You'll need exact change for the $1 fare, plus $1 for a transfer. For route and schedule information, call **Chatham Area Transit (CAT)** at © **912/233-5767.**

BY TAXI   The base rate for taxis is 60¢, with a $1.80 additional charge for each mile. For 24-hour taxi service, call **Adam Cab Co.** at © **912/927-7466.**

6 Neighborhoods in Brief

CITY LAYOUT

Every other street—north, south, west, and east—is punctuated by greenery. The grid of **21 scenic squares** was laid out in 1733 by Gen. James Oglethorpe, the founder of Georgia. The design—still in use—has been called "one of the world's most revered city plans." It's said that if Savannah didn't have its history and architecture, it would be worth a visit just to see the city layout.

Bull Street is the dividing line between east and west. On the south side are odd-numbered buildings, and on the north side are even-numbered buildings.

Historic District   The Historic District—the real reason to visit Savannah—takes in both the Riverfront District and the City Market, described below. It's bordered by the Savannah River and Forsyth Park at Gaston Street and Montgomery and Price streets. Within its borders are more than 2,350 architecturally and historically significant buildings in a 2½-square-mile area. About 75% of these buildings have been restored.

Riverfront District   In this popular tourist district, River Street borders the Savannah River. Once lined with warehouses holding King Cotton, it has been the subject of massive urban renewal, turning this strip into a row of restaurants, art galleries, shops, and bars. The source of the area's growth was the river, which offered a prime shipping avenue for New World goods bound for European ports. In 1818, about half of Savannah fell under quarantine during a yellow-fever epidemic. River Street never fully recovered and fell into disrepair until its rediscovery in the mid-1970s. The urban-renewal project stabilized the downtown and revitalized the Historic District. Stroll the bluffs along the river on the old passageway of alleys, cobblestone walkways, and bridges known as **Factors Walk.**

City Market   Two blocks from River Street and bordering the Savannah River, the City Market was the former social and business mecca of Savannah. Since the late 18th century, it has known fires and various devastations, including the threat of demolition. But in a major move, the city of Savannah decided to save the district. Today former decaying warehouses are filled with restaurants and shops offering everything from antiques to collectibles, including

Greater Savannah

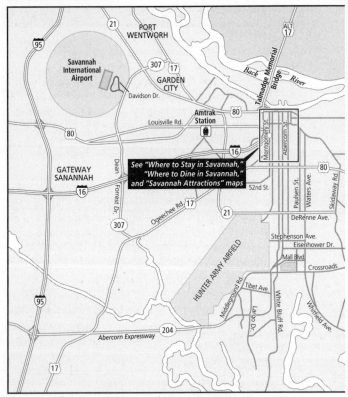

many Savannah-made products. And everything from seafood and pizza to French and Italian cuisine is served here. Live music often fills the nighttime air. Some of the best jazz in the city is presented here in various clubs. The market lies at Jefferson and West Julian streets, bounded by Franklin Square on its western flank and Ellis Square on its eastern.

Victorian District   The Victorian District, south of the Historic District, holds some of the finest examples of post–Civil War architecture in the Deep South. The district is bounded by Martin Luther King Jr. Boulevard and by East Broad, Gwinnett, and Anderson streets. Houses in the district are characterized by gingerbread trim, stained-glass windows, and imaginative architectural details. In all,

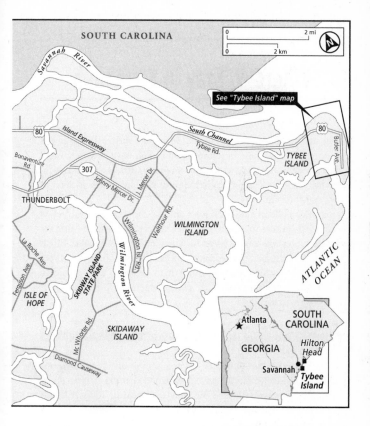

the district encompasses an area of nearly 50 blocks, spread across some 165 acres. The entire district was added to the National Register of Historic Places in 1974. Most of the two-story homes are wood frame and were constructed in the late 1800s on brick foundations. The district, overflowing from the historic inner core, became the first suburb of Savannah.

4

Where to Stay in Savannah

The undisputed stars of Savannah lodging are the small inns in the Historic District, most in restored homes that have been renovated with modern conveniences while retaining their original charm. Staying in one of these converted historic properties is sure to enhance your visit.

Savannah's hotel and B&B rates are like the weather—subject to change. **High season** is from April to October. You will find that the cheapest rates will usually be on weekdays during **low season,** which is January, February, and sometimes late August. The price ranges listed below include both low and high seasons. Very expensive hotels often have some smaller, more moderately priced units. It always pays to ask.

1 Along the Riverfront

EXPENSIVE

Hyatt Regency Savannah 🐾 There was an outcry from Savannah's historic preservation movement when this place went up in 1981. Boxy, massively bulky, and fully renovated in 2006, it stands in unpleasant contrast to the restored warehouses flanking it along the legendary banks of the Savannah River. Today it is grudgingly accepted as one of the biggest and flashiest hotels in town. It has a soaring atrium as well as glass-sided elevators. The comfortable rooms, often with paper-thin walls, are international and modern in their feel, all with good-size bathrooms and some with balconies overlooking the atrium. Room prices vary according to their views—units without a view are quite a bargain. Chances are, you'll find better food by dining outside the hotel at one of the independent restaurants recommended.

2 W. Bay St., Savannah, GA 31401. © **800/223-1234** or 912/238-1234. Fax 912/944-3678. www.hyatt.com. 351 units. $169–$409 double; $400–$600 suite. AE, DC, DISC, MC, V. Parking $17. **Amenities:** Restaurant; bar; indoor pool; fitness center; room service; laundry service; dry cleaning; nonsmoking rooms; rooms for those w/limited mobility. *In room:* A/C, TV, Wi-Fi, coffeemaker, hair dryer, iron, safe.

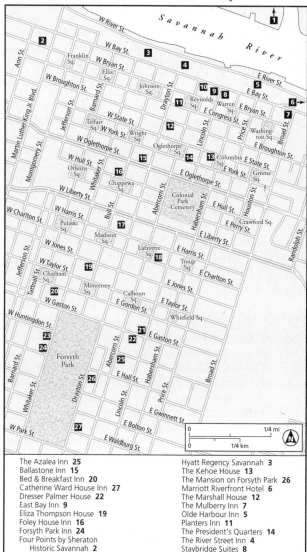

The Azalea Inn **25**
Ballastone Inn **15**
Bed & Breakfast Inn **20**
Catherine Ward House Inn **27**
Dresser Palmer House **22**
East Bay Inn **9**
Eliza Thompson House **19**
Foley House Inn **16**
Forsyth Park Inn **24**
Four Points by Sheraton
    Historic Savannah **2**
The Gastonian **21**
Hamilton-Turner Inn **18**
Hampton Inn Historic District **10**
Hilton Savannah DeSoto **17**

Hyatt Regency Savannah **3**
The Kehoe House **13**
The Mansion on Forsyth Park **26**
Marriott Riverfront Hotel **6**
The Marshall House **12**
The Mulberry Inn **7**
Olde Harbour Inn **5**
Planters Inn **11**
The President's Quarters **14**
The River Street Inn **4**
Staybridge Suites **8**
The Westin Savannah Harbor
    Golf Resort & Spa **1**
Whitaker Huntingon Inn **23**

The Mansion on Forsyth Park ★★★   This is the most opulent and spectacular boutique hotel in Savannah. Its core, known as the Kayton Family Mansion, was built in 1888 of terra-cotta bricks in a high-ceilinged, neo-Romanesque style. This place is international and more of a (tasteful) version of a Las Vegas blockbuster hotel than anything else in southeastern Georgia. The place is tasteful, highly entertaining, and stimulating.

Part of its allure derives from the rotating series of more than 400 paintings (depending on what artist is being showcased at the time) that sheath the walls of both the public areas and the upper hallways. Expect a plush environment with gilded cove moldings; Beaux Arts marble statues of, among others, turn-of-the-20th-century rococo goddesses at their baths; lavish antique chandeliers; and Versace copies of 19th-century French armchairs upholstered in faux zebra or leopard skin. The hotel's focal point is a courtyard and a small but artfully postmodern swimming pool. Bedrooms are avant-garde and plush, and among the most spacious in Savannah. Urban and very comfortable, they were inspired by posh boudoirs in New York and Milan.

700 Drayton St., Savannah, GA 31401. ℭ **888/711-5114** or 912/238-5158. Fax 912/721-1123. www.mansiononforsythpark.com. 126 units. $199–$350 double; from $400 suite. AE, DC, DISC, MC, V. Parking $19. **Amenities:** Restaurant; 2 bars; outdoor pool; fitness center; spa; business center; room service; cooking school. *In room:* A/C, TV, Wi-Fi, minibar, safe.

Marriott Riverfront Hotel ★   At least the massive modern bulk of this place is far enough from the 19th-century restored warehouses of River Street not to clash with them aesthetically. Towering eight stories, with an angular facade sheathed in orange-and-yellow brick, it doesn't quite succeed at being a top-rated luxury palace, but nonetheless it attracts lots of corporate business and conventions to its comfortable, modern units. The rooms aren't style setters but are generous in space, with bathrooms containing tub/shower combinations that are large enough to store your stuff and a generous supply of towels. In 2005, the Magnolia Spa opened on-site.

100 General McIntosh Blvd., Savannah, GA 31401. ℭ **800/228-9290** or 912/233-7722. Fax 912/233-3765. www.marriott.com. 387 units. $179–$259 double; from $270 suite. Children 12 and under stay free in parent's room. AE, DC, DISC, MC, V. Parking $12. **Amenities:** 2 restaurants; 2 bars; lounge; 2 pools (1 indoor); fitness center; spa; Jacuzzi; business center; room service; laundry service; dry cleaning; nonsmoking rooms; rooms for those w/limited mobility. *In room:* A/C, TV, Wi-Fi, coffeemaker, hair dryer, iron.

The Westin Savannah Harbor Golf Resort & Spa ★   Savannah's largest hotel opened in late 1999 in a 16-story blockbuster format that dwarfs the city's existing B&Bs. It rises somewhat jar-ringly from what were until the late 1990s sandy, scrub-covered flat-lands on the swampy, rarely visited far side of the river from Savannah's historic core. Conceived as part of a massive resort devel-opment project, and very concerned with managing the way it fits into the ecosystems around it, it derives the bulk of its business from corporate groups who arrive for large conventions throughout the year. It's the largest of the four large-scale hotels that dominate the city's convention business, yet despite a worthy collection (more than 200 pieces) of contemporary art that accents the labyrinth of high-ceilinged public rooms here, there's something just a bit sterile, even lifeless, about this relatively anonymous blockbuster hotel. Compounding the problem is its isolated position, both geographi-cally and emotionally, from the bustle, grace, and charm of central Savannah—this in spite of cross-river shuttle ferries that deposit clients into the center of the River Street bar and restaurant frenzy. The most elaborate guest rooms are on the two top floors and con-tain extras and comforts designated as Club Level. Otherwise, rooms are comfortable but bland, outfitted in pale colors and conservative furnishings.

1 Resort Dr. (PO Box 427), Savannah, GA 31421. ℂ **800/937-8461** or 912/201-2000. Fax 912/201-2001. www.westinsavannah.com. 403 units. $265–$419 double; from $450 suite. AE, DC, DISC, MC, V. Water taxis shuttle you across the river to Rousakis Plaza on River St. at 20-min. intervals. From I-95 and Savannah/Hilton Head International Airport, take exit 17A to I-16 toward Savannah. Follow the sign for Rte. 17–Talmadge Bridge. Take the Hutchinson Island exit onto Resort Dr. **Ameni-ties:** 3 restaurants; 3 bars; outdoor pool; 18-hole golf course; 4 tennis courts; fitness center; Jacuzzi; sauna; beauty treatments; room service; babysitting; laundry service; dry cleaning; all nonsmoking rooms; rooms for those w/limited mobility. *In room:* A/C, TV, Wi-Fi, minibar, coffeemaker, hair dryer, iron, safe.

MODERATE

Olde Harbour Inn 🕵   The neighborhood has been gentrified and the interior of this place is well furnished, but you still get a whiff of riverfront seediness as you approach from Factors Walk. It was built in 1892 as a warehouse for oil, and its masonry bulk is camouflaged with shutters, awnings, and touches of wrought iron. Inside, a labyrinth of passages leads to small but comfortable suites, many of which reveal the building's massive timbers and structural iron brackets and offer views of the river. Some decors feature the origi-nal brick, painted white. Each unit contains a well-maintained bath-room along with its own kitchen—useful for an extended stay. Despite the overlay of chintz, you'll have a constant sense of the building's thick-walled bulk. Breakfast is the only meal served.

Family-Friendly Hotels

Hampton Inn Historic District (p. 50)   One of the most appealing of the city's middle-bracket hotels, this family favorite rises on historic Bay Street. Rooms are spacious, and there's a pool and sun deck on the roof.

The Mulberry Inn (p. 47)   In the heart of the Historic District is this family hotel that lets kids 17 and under stay free if they share a room with their parents. Children enjoy the pool, and cribs are provided free.

River Street Inn (see below)   The best bet along the riverfront for families with children is this converted cotton warehouse from 1817. Large rooms make family life easier, and children 12 and under stay free. The inn also has a game room, and there are many fast-food joints just outside the front door.

508 E. Factors Walk, Savannah, GA 31401. © **800/553-6533** or 912/234-4100. Fax 912/233-5979. www.oldeharbourinn.com. 24 units. $159–$450 suite. Rates include continental breakfast. AE, DC, DISC, MC, V. **Amenities:** Breakfast room; nonsmoking rooms. *In room:* A/C, TV, Wi-Fi, kitchenette (in some), coffeemaker, hair dryer, iron, safe.

River Street Inn ★★ *Kids*   When Liverpool-based ships were moored on the nearby river, this building stored massive amounts of cotton produced by upriver plantations. After the boll weevil decimated the cotton industry, it functioned as an icehouse, a storage area for fresh vegetables, and (at its lowest point) the headquarters of an insurance company. Its two lowest floors, built in 1817, are made of ballast stones, which were carried in the holds of ships from faraway England.

In 1986, a group of investors poured millions into its development as one of the linchpins of Savannah's Riverfront District, adding a well-upholstered colonial pizazz to the public areas and converting the building's warren of brick-lined storerooms into some of the most comfortable and well-managed rooms in town. In 2007, the owners poured nearly $2.5 million into renovations of its guest rooms and corridors, as part of an ongoing effort to keep this charming, well-located inn a viable competitor. If night-crawls among the bars and restaurants of River Street are a priority, there is no other hotel better positioned than this one.

124 E. Bay St., Savannah, GA 31401. ℰ **800/253-4229** or 912/234-6400. Fax 912/
234-1478. www.riverstreetinn.com. 86 units. $139–$245 double; $275 suite. Chil-
dren 13 and under stay free in parent's room. AE, DC, DISC, MC, V. Parking $8.
Amenities: 2 restaurants; lounge; gym; all nonsmoking rooms. *In room:* A/C, TV,
Wi-Fi, hair dryer, safe.

2 In the Historic District

VERY EXPENSIVE

Ballastone Inn ⭐⭐ This glamorous inner-city B&B occupies a
dignified 1838 building separated from the Juliette Gordon Low
House (original home of the founder of the Girl Scouts of America)
by a well-tended formal garden; it's richly decorated with all the
hardwoods, elaborate draperies, and antique furniture you'd expect.
For a brief period (only long enough to add a hint of spiciness), the
place functioned as a bordello *and* a branch office for the Girl Scouts
(now next door). It has an elevator, unusual for Savannah B&Bs, but
no closets (they were taxed as extra rooms in the old days and so
never added). It also has many truly unusual furnishings—cachepots
filled with scented potpourri, and art objects that would thrill the
heart of any decorator. A full-service bar is tucked into a corner of
what was originally a double parlor. Each suite has a Jacuzzi tub as
well as a private dressing area.

14 E. Oglethorpe Ave., Savannah, GA 31401. ℰ **800/822-4553** or 912/236-1484.
Fax 912/236-4626. www.ballastone.com. 16 units. $235–$375 double; $395 suite.
Rates include full breakfast, afternoon tea, and evening hors d'oeuvres. AE, MC, V.
Free parking. No children 15 and under. **Amenities:** Breakfast room; lounge; spa
treatments; nonsmoking rooms. *In room:* A/C, TV, hair dryer, fireplace (in some).

Four Points by Sheraton Historic Savannah ⭐ This tasteful
and well-managed newcomer lies in Savannah's historic zone, close
to the emerging shopping district known as Ellis Square. This five-
story brick-fronted inn is a winner, thanks to a location only 3 blocks
from Broughton Street. Accommodations are comfortable, contemporary, monochromatic, and unfussy, appropriate nests for explo-
rations of the historic zone without the lack of privacy you'll
sometimes experience in a smaller inn or B&B.

520 W. Bryan St., Savannah, GA 31401. ℰ **912/790-1000**. Fax 912/721-1270. www.
fourpoints.com/historicsavannah. 127 units. $95–$210 double; $175–$285 suite. AE,
DC, DISC, MC, V. **Amenities:** Restaurant; piano bar; rooftop pool; health club; laundry service; coin-op laundry. *In room:* A/C, TV, fridge (in some).

The Gastonian ⭐⭐ One of the two or three posh B&Bs in
Savannah, the Gastonian incorporates a pair of Italianate Regency
buildings constructed in 1868 by the same unknown architect. Hard

times began with the 1929 stock market crash—the buildings were divided into apartments for the payment of back taxes. In 1984, the Lineberger family, who were visiting from California, saw the place and fell in love with it. They poured $2 million into restoring it. Today everything is a testimonial to Victorian charm, except for a skillfully crafted serpentine bridge connecting the two buildings curving above a semitropical garden. The guest rooms are appropriately plush, comfortable, cozy, and beautifully furnished. The Gastonian has received the AAA Four Diamond Award for excellence.

220 E. Gaston St., Savannah, GA 31401. ℭ 800/322-6603 or 912/232-2869. Fax 912/232-0710. www.gastonian.com. 17 units. $189–$365 double; $385–$425 suite. Rates include full breakfast. AE, DISC, MC, V. No children 11 and under. **Amenities:** Breakfast room; lounge; nonsmoking rooms. *In room:* A/C, TV, Wi-Fi, hair dryer.

Hamilton-Turner Inn ✦✦   This is one of the most noteworthy B&Bs in Savannah, boasting a unique (and sometimes bizarre) pedigree that's unlike any other in town. It was built for the then-astronomical price of $100,000 by a local power broker, Samuel Hamilton, in 1873. Mayor of Savannah, president of the Shriners, a reputed blockade runner during the Civil War, and owner of the local electrical company, the waterworks, the icehouse, and the town's biggest "fancy goods store," Hamilton was one of the inspirations for Margaret Mitchell's character of Rhett Butler in *Gone With the Wind.* His four-story French Empire house was almost obscenely ostentatious at the time. Today, with more than 10,000 square feet, it's the largest upscale B&B (in terms of sheer square footage) in Savannah.

Most of the modern-day notoriety associated with this place comes from its portrayal, in John Berendt's *Midnight in the Garden of Good and Evil,* as the party house of Savannah's favorite rakish twosome, Joe and Mandy Odom. Long after all that died down, in 1997, the building was acquired by native Savannahians Charles and Sue Strickland, who poured money and a strong dose of respectability back into the place, restoring it to a grandiose testimonial to a robber baron's Gilded Age fortune in the South. Guest rooms—most with 14-foot ceilings and fireplaces—are outfitted with Empire, Eastlake, and/or Renaissance Revival antiques and a kind of dignified, slightly chilly looking grandeur.

330 Abercorn St., Savannah, GA 31401. ℭ 888/448-8849 or 912/233-1833. Fax 912/233-0291. www.hamilton-turnerinn.com. 17 units. $189–$369 double. Rates include full breakfast and afternoon wine and cheese. AE, DC, DISC, MC, V. Free parking. **Amenities:** Breakfast room; all nonsmoking rooms; 1 room for those w/limited mobility. *In room:* A/C, TV, Wi-Fi.

The Kehoe House 𝘾𝘾𝘾   The Kehoe was built in 1892. In the 1950s, after the place had been converted into a funeral parlor, its owners tried to tear down the nearby Davenport House (see chapter 6, "Exploring Savannah") to build a parking lot. The resulting outrage led to the founding of the Historic Savannah Association and the salvation of most of the neighborhood's remaining historic buildings.

Today the place functions as a spectacularly opulent B&B, with a collection of fabrics and furniture that's almost forbiddingly valuable. However, it lacks the warmth and welcome of the Ballastone. Breakfast and afternoon tea are part of the ritual that has seduced such former clients as Tom Hanks, who stayed in room no. 301 during the filming of parts of *Forrest Gump.* The rooms are spacious, with the typical 12-foot ceilings, and each is tastefully furnished with English period antiques.

123 Habersham St., Savannah, GA 31401. ℂ **800/820-1020** or 912/232-1020. Fax 912/231-0208. www.kehoehouse.com. 13 units. $239–$389 double. Rates include full breakfast, evening tea, and hors d'oeuvres. AE, DC, DISC, MC, V. **Amenities:** Breakfast room; all nonsmoking rooms; rooms for those w/limited mobility. *In room:* A/C, TV, Wi-Fi, hair dryer.

EXPENSIVE

The Azalea Inn 𝘾 *(Finds)*   The furnishings of this B&B are a little richer, its colors a bit more evocative, and its decor more appealingly cluttered than those of many of its nearby competitors. The setting is an Italianate house (ca. 1889) set less than 2 blocks east of Forsyth Park, within a "historically correct" garden laid out as a garden might have been in Victorian times, contrary to the modernity of its swimming pool. It was originally built for Capt. Walter Coney, an army officer whose fortune derived from a then-flourishing maritime supply company. Rooms are furnished with period antiques, and each has its own distinctive Victorian-era decor. Especially appealing is the Gentleman's Parlor, a ground-floor room once dominated by men discussing manly things, which still carries a hint of the bourbon and cigars consumed liberally within its confines. More frilly and feminine is the Magnolia Room, where cream-colored walls offset a four-poster bed with upholsteries depicting—you guessed it—magnolia blossoms. The Cotton Exchange Room features a massive four-poster bed and a deck overlooking the swimming pool.

217 E. Huntingdon St., Savannah, GA 31401. ℂ **800/582-3823** or 912/236-2707. Fax 912/236-0127. www.azaleainn.com. 10 units. $219–$290 double; $275–$300 2-bedroom suite. Rates include full breakfast. AE, DISC, MC, V. **Amenities:** Outdoor pool; all nonsmoking rooms. *In room:* A/C, TV, Wi-Fi, hair dryer, iron.

Catherine Ward House Inn ✹ *Finds*   It isn't as spectacular or desirable as it was when it was newer, but the 2005 restoration of this house has won several civic awards, and it's so evocative of Savannah's "carpenter Gothic" Victorian revival that Clint Eastwood inserted a long, graceful shot of its exterior in *Midnight in the Garden of Good and Evil*. Built by a sea captain for his wife in 1886 in a location a short walk from Forsyth Park, it offers one of the most lavishly decorated interiors of any B&B in Savannah, but at prices that are significantly less than those offered at better-known B&Bs a few blocks away. A garden in back encourages languid sun-dappled dialogues. Each midsize guest room is richly decorated.

118 E. Waldburg St., Savannah, GA 31401. ℂ **800/327-4270** or 912/234-8564. Fax 912/231-8007. www.catherinewardhouseinn.com. 9 units. $159–$329 double. Rates include full breakfast. AE, DISC, MC, V. Children 13 and under discouraged. **Amenities:** Breakfast room; tennis courts (nearby); all nonsmoking rooms. *In room:* A/C, TV, Wi-Fi, hair dryer.

Foley House Inn ✹   Decorated with all the care of a private home, this small B&B occupies a brick-sided house built in 1896. Its owners doubled its size in the early 1990s by acquiring the simpler white-fronted house next door, whose pedigree predates its neighbors by half a century. All rooms are neatly furnished. The staff will regale you with tales of the original residents of both houses. Breakfast and afternoon hors d'oeuvres, tea, and cordials are served in a large, verdant space formed by the two houses' connected gardens.

The inn is the recipient of the AAA Four Diamond Award and has been featured on HGTV's *Great Homes Across America* and some of the TV features of Turner South. Enjoy home-baked sweets every afternoon in the parlor wing and homemade appetizers from 6 to 7pm.

14 W. Hull St., Savannah, GA 31401. ℂ **800/647-3708** or 912/232-6622. Fax 912/231-1218. www.foleyinn.com. 18 units. $230–$392 double. Rates include full breakfast, afternoon hors d'oeuvres, wine, and cordials. AE, MC, V. No children 11 and under. **Amenities:** Breakfast room; laundry service; all nonsmoking rooms. *In room:* A/C, TV, Wi-Fi, hair dryer, safe, Jacuzzi (in some).

Hilton Savannah DeSoto ✹   The name still evokes a bit of glamour—built in 1890, this hotel was for many generations the city's grandest. In 1967, thousands of wedding receptions, Kiwanis meetings, and debutante parties later, the building was demolished and rebuilt in a bland, angular, modern format. The guest rooms are conservatively modern, and reached after you register in a stone-floored lobby whose decor was partly inspired by an 18th-century colonial drawing room. Despite the absence of antique charm, many guests like this place for its polite efficiency and modernism. Guest rooms were renovated in 2007.

15 E. Liberty St. (PO Box 8207), Savannah, GA 31401. © 800/426-8483 or 912/232-9000. Fax 912/232-6018. www.desotohilton.com. 246 units. $169–$289 double; $280–$399 suite. AE, DC, DISC, MC, V. Valet parking $15; self-parking $11. **Amenities:** 2 restaurants; bar; outdoor pool; fitness center; business center; limited room service; massage; babysitting; laundry service; dry cleaning; nonsmoking rooms; rooms for those w/limited mobility. *In room:* A/C, TV, Wi-Fi, hair dryer, iron.

The Mulberry Inn ⟨ *(Kids* Locals point with pride to the Mulberry as a sophisticated adaptation of what might've been a derelict building into a surprisingly elegant hotel. Built in 1868 as a stable and cotton warehouse, it was converted in 1982 into a simple hotel, and in the 1990s it received a radical upgrade and a dash of decorator-inspired Chippendale glamour. Today its lobby looks like that of a grand hotel in London, and the rooms, though small, have a formal decor (think English country house with a Southern accent). The hotel's brick-covered patio, with fountains, trailing ivy, and wrought-iron furniture, evokes the best aspects of New Orleans.

601 E. Bay St., Savannah, GA 31401. © 877/468-1200 or 912/238-1200. Fax 912/236-2184. www.savannahhotel.com. 145 units. $179–$294 double. Children 17 and under stay free in parent's room. AE, DC, DISC, MC, V. Parking $10. **Amenities:** Restaurant; lounge; outdoor pool; fitness center; Jacuzzi; limited room service; nonsmoking rooms; rooms for those w/limited mobility. *In room:* A/C, TV, Wi-Fi, microwave, fridge, hair dryer, iron.

The President's Quarters ⟨ President's Quarters combines the coziness of a B&B with the advantages of a small and elegant inn. Its design of labyrinthine hallways is quirky enough to be within a much-renovated private home. It's composed of two interconnected 1850s-era brick-built town houses whose modern-day gazebo and walled garden jut out into Oglethorpe Square. This is the only B&B in Savannah with enough on-site parking for all of its guests and a working fireplace in every room. Furnishings include a mixture of French and English Victorian antiques interspersed with reproductions. Each guest room is named after a U.S. president: JFK, FDR, Dwight Eisenhower, Jimmy Carter, Calvin Coolidge, and so on. Breakfast is a big deal here, served in a somewhat cramped dining room with old-fashioned accessories. Complimentary wine and hors d'oeuvres are served every evening between 5:30 and 6:30pm.

225 E. President St., Savannah, GA 31401. © 800/233-1776 or 912/233-1600. Fax 912/238-0849. www.presidentsquarters.com. 16 units. $229–$300 double; $325 suite. Rates include evening wine and hors d'oeuvres. AE, DC, MC, V. Free parking. **Amenities:** Business facilities. *In room:* A/C, TV, Wi-Fi, minibar (in suite), hair dryer, iron, fireplace.

Whitaker-Huntingdon Inn ⭐ Dignified and permeated with a sense of decency and Southern honor, this house was built in 1883 for a member of the eight-man Confederate delegation that surrendered the City of Savannah to General Sherman in December 1864. Later, a local cotton merchant who served a 4-year term as the city's mayor owned it. In 1923, the doctor who was using the house as the base for his medical practice added an all-brick addition onto the house's backside. Today the much-restored interior boasts 12-foot ceilings, period antiques, Oriental carpets, and pine floors—all of it gracefully arranged for a look that's faithful to the original decorative theme but a lot more comfortable than it was in the building's original days. Each of the two guest rooms is a two-bedroom suite, one with one bathroom and the other with two, and both have kitchenettes. There's also a resident ghost.

601 Whitaker St., Savannah, GA 31401. ✆ 877/232-8911 or 912/210-3422. Fax 912/772-6292. www.whinn.com. 2 units. $150–$175 double. Rates include continental breakfast. AE, DISC, MC, V. **Amenities:** Breakfast room; laundry service; all nonsmoking rooms. *In room:* TV, Wi-Fi, kitchenette, coffeemaker, iron.

MODERATE

Dresser Palmer House   This major investment in period restoration was built as two separate houses sharing an Italianate facade. In 1997, a lavish unification of the two houses was undertaken. Today the unified building bears the distinction of having the city's longest and most stately front porch (called a gallery in Savannah) and ceilings that are almost dizzyingly high. Each guest room, redecorated in 2005, is beautifully furnished, and most are equipped with a well-maintained bathroom containing a tub/shower combination. The breakfasts are social events, each featuring a different dish, like curried eggs or Southern grits casserole.

211 E. Gaston St., Savannah, GA 31401. ✆ 800/671-0716 or 912/238-3294. Fax 912/238-4064. www.dresserpalmerhouse.com. 15 units. $129–$249 double. Rates include evening wine and cheese. AE, DISC, MC, V. **Amenities:** Breakfast room; lounge; all nonsmoking rooms; 1 room for those w/limited mobility. *In room:* A/C, TV, Wi-Fi, ceiling fan, fireplace (in some).

East Bay Inn   Though the views from its windows might be uninspired, the East Bay is conveniently located near the bars and attractions of the riverfront. It was built in 1853 as a cotton warehouse; green awnings and potted geraniums disguise the building's once-utilitarian design. A cozy lobby contains Chippendale furnishings and elaborate moldings. The rooms have queen-size four-poster beds and reproductions of antiques. The hotel frequently houses tour groups from Europe and South America. In the cellar is **Skyler's**

(© 912/232-3955), an independently managed restaurant specializing in European and Asian cuisine. Midafternoon tea, wine, and cheese are a highly visible social ritual in this inn's daily schedule. The entire building is strictly nonsmoking.

225 E. Bay St., Savannah, GA 31401. © 800/500-1225 or 912/238-1225. Fax 912/232-2709. www.eastbayinn.com. 28 units. $159–$259 double. Rates include continental breakfast. AE, DC, DISC, MC, V. **Amenities:** Breakfast room; all nonsmoking rooms. *In room:* A/C, TV, Wi-Fi, coffeemaker, hair dryer, iron, safe, bathrobes.

Eliza Thompson House 𝒜𝒜 Many newer and less well-funded B&Bs attempt to re-create this inn's patina of historicity (ca. 1847), often with less success. It's set on a distinguished tree-lined street whose weather-beaten cobblestones demonstrate their long-ago craftsmanship. The wrought-iron accents and meticulously maintained details of its shutter-accented facade imply enormous care on the part of its owners. And inside, high ceilings, elaborate cove moldings, and well-chosen antiques imply a mixture of genteel propriety and discreetly romantic potential. Historical references abound within rich but understated interiors, and decorator wannabes often salivate at the ideas they garner for historical projects of their own. About half the rooms in the stately looking inn are within the main house; the other half lie within a much-restored and very tasteful building in back that was originally conceived as a stable and carriage house. Linking the two buildings is one of the largest and most lavishly landscaped courtyards in the city's historic core. In the words of a writer from *Georgia Magazine,* "Like its namesake, the Eliza Thompson House is a hospitable hostess."

5 W. Jones St., Savannah, GA 31401. © 800/348-9378 or 912/236-3620. Fax 912/238-1920. www.elizathompsonhouse.com. 25 units. $199–$239 double. Rates include continental breakfast. AE, DC, DISC, MC, V. **Amenities:** Breakfast room; lounge; nonsmoking rooms. *In room:* A/C, TV, Wi-Fi, hair dryer, iron.

Forsyth Park Inn 𝒜 One of the grandest houses on the western flank of Forsyth Park is this frame place built in the 1890s by a sea captain (Aaron Flynt, also known as Rudder Churchill). A richly detailed staircase winds upstairs from a paneled vestibule, and the Queen Anne decor of the formal salon extends through the rest of the house. Guest rooms have oak paneling and oversize doors that are testimonials to turn-of-the-20th-century craftsmanship. The more expensive guest rooms, including one in what used to be the dining room, are among the largest in town. Home-baked breads and pastries are a staple of the breakfasts.

102 W. Hall St., Savannah, GA 31401. © 866/670-6800 or 912/233-6800. Fax 912/233-6804. www.forsythparkinn.com. 11 units, including 1 cottage with kitchenette.

$185–$295 double; $225 cottage. Rates include full breakfast. AE, DISC, MC, V.
Amenities: Breakfast room; lounge; all nonsmoking rooms. *In room:* A/C, TV, Wi-Fi.

Hampton Inn Historic District *(Kids)*   This is one of the most
appealing of the city's middle-bracket large-scale hotels, and one of
the most charming and consistently praised Hampton Inns anywhere in the U.S. Opened in 1997, it rises seven redbrick stories
above the busy traffic of historic Bay Street, across from Savannah's
Riverwalk and some of the city's most animated nightclubs. Its big-
windowed lobby was designed to mimic an 18th-century Savannah
salon, thanks to the recycling of heart pine flooring from an old
sawmill in central Georgia and the use of antique Savannah bricks.
Comfortably formal seating arrangements, a blazing fireplace, and
an antique bar add cozy touches. The guest rooms are simple and
comfortable, with wall-to-wall carpeting, midsize tiled bathrooms,
and flowered upholstery. On the roof are a small pool and a sun deck
supplemented by an exercise room on the seventh floor. There's no
restaurant, but many eateries are a short walk away.

201 E. Bay St., Savannah, GA 31401. (✆) **800/426-7866** or 912/721-1600. Fax 912/
721-1610. www.hampton-inn.com. 144 units. $140–$180 double. AE, DC, DISC, MC,
V. Parking $10. **Amenities:** Breakfast room; lounge; rooftop pool; laundry service;
dry cleaning; nonsmoking rooms; rooms for those w/limited mobility. *In room:* A/C,
TV, coffeemaker, hair dryer, iron.

The Marshall House   Some aspects of this hotel—especially the
second-story cast-iron veranda that juts above the sidewalk—might
remind you of a 19th-century hotel in the French Quarter of New
Orleans. It originally opened in 1851 as the then-finest hotel in
Savannah. In 1864 and 1865, it functioned as a Union army hospital before housing such luminaries as novelist Conrad Aiken and Joel
Chandler Harris, author of *Stories of Uncle Remus*. After a ratty looking decline, it closed—some people thought permanently—in 1957.
In 1999, it reopened as a "boutique-style" inn. Despite the fact that
this place has some of the trappings of an upscale B&B, don't think
that it will provide the intimacy or exclusivity of, say, the Foley
House Inn. Some aspects of this place evoke a busy commercial
motel, albeit with a very elegant and spacious lobby filled with
upscale Colonial-inspired reproductions. Guest rooms succeed at
being mass-production-style cozy without being particularly opulent. Each is sheathed in one of three possibilities: yellow with
pinewood furniture, green with wrought-iron furniture, and blue
with white-painted furniture. Seven of the largest and most historically evocative rooms in the hotel are on the second floor, overlooking noisy Broughton Street, and are prefaced with wrought-iron

verandas with wrought-iron furniture. All rooms contain neatly kept bathrooms with showers. The bar has exposed brick, a very Southern clientele, and green leather upholstery. The **45 Bistro,** set beneath the glassed-in roof of what used to be the hotel's rear stable yard, is a restaurant serving Southern and international cuisine.

123 E. Broughton St., Savannah, GA 31401. © **800/589-6304** or 912/644-7896. Fax 912/234-3334. www.marshallhouse.com. 68 units. $185–$279 double; $249–$279 suite. Rates include continental breakfast. AE, DC, DISC, MC, V. **Amenities:** Restaurant; bar; nonsmoking rooms. *In room:* A/C, TV, Wi-Fi, hair dryer, safe.

Planters Inn   This small European-style inn is more businesslike than the average Savannah B&B. Built adjacent to Reynolds Square in 1912 as a seven-story brown-brick tower, it boasts a lobby with elaborate millwork and a scattering of Chippendale reproductions. The guest rooms are comfortably outfitted with four-poster beds and flowery fabrics; they're rather dignified and formal. Each room contains a neatly kept bathroom with a tub/shower combination. The Planters Inn isn't associated with the well-recommended Planters Tavern (which stands next door).

29 Abercorn St., Savannah, GA 31401. © **800/554-1187** or 912/232-5678. Fax 912/232-8893. www.plantersinnsavannah.com. 59 units. $159–$300 double. Rates include continental breakfast and evening wine reception. AE, DC, MC, V. Parking $12. **Amenities:** Breakfast room; lounge; nonsmoking rooms. *In room:* A/C, TV, Wi-Fi, coffeemaker, hair dryer, safe.

Staybridge Suites ★★   The five-story antique brick walls of this hotel originally housed a pickle factory and cannery in the 19th century; later it was an auto repair shop. Today it boasts one of the city's most striking fireplaces, deep sofas, and lots of exposed wood, evoking the lobby of a ski lodge in Vermont. Rooms are medium-size but well furnished, well upholstered, and surprisingly appealing, outfitted with formal, Queen Anne–inspired reproductions and thick carpeting. Each room has a writing table built into one corner and a full kitchen with stovetop, microwave, and refrigerator. It's the kind of setup where a traveling salesman could establish a headquarters during an extended business trip. Frankly, if you have even a hint of claustrophobia, you'll be happiest in a room with a bona fide window, rather than one that overlooks a narrow interior atrium (about a third of the rooms here are set up this way). But then again, if you appreciate calm and quiet, artificial lighting, and a sense of hermetically sealed, climate-controlled regularity, you might like one of the interior units just fine.

301 E. Bay St., Savannah, GA 31401. © **877/238-8889** or 912/721-9000. Fax 912/721-9019. www.ichotelsgroup.com. 104 units. $162–$249 double. Rates include

continental breakfast. AE, DC, MC, V. **Amenities:** TV lounge/lobby. *In room:* A/C, TV, Wi-Fi, kitchen.

INEXPENSIVE

Bed & Breakfast Inn *R̃ Value*   Adjacent to Chatham Square, in the oldest part of historic Savannah, this is a dignified stone-fronted town house built in 1853. You climb a gracefully curved front stoop to reach the cool, high-ceilinged interior, outfitted with a combination of antique and reproduction furniture. The guest rooms are good-size, comfortable, and tastefully furnished.

117 W. Gordon St. (at Chatham Sq.), Savannah, GA 31401. © 888/238-0518 or 912/238-0518. Fax 912/233-2537. www.savannahbnb.com. 18 units. $129–$219 double. Rates include full breakfast. AE, DISC, MC, V. **Amenities:** Breakfast room; lounge; nonsmoking rooms. *In room:* A/C, TV, Wi-Fi, hair dryer, iron, fireplace (in some).

3 Nearby Hotels & Inns

MODERATE

Baymont Inn & Suites   This motor lodge, one of the best in the Savannah area, appeals to motorists drawn to its location on Main Street. The location is also convenient for day trips to Hilton Head, lying only 18 miles to the north. The inn offers attractively furnished and good-size guest rooms. Each room features such extras as ergonomic chairs, free bottled water, and free cable TV, with pay-for-view movies and Nintendo. Many families visiting relatives at Hunter Army Airfield lodge here. Several affordable restaurants are nearby, but the hotel staff fills you up with complimentary morning treats such as waffles and French toast before you head out for the day. The hotel has such features as a senior discount program, interior-corridor room entrances, free local calls, and a 24-hour staffed front desk and switchboard.

357 Main St., Savannah, GA 31418. © 877/229-6668 or 912/964-8669. Fax 912/ 964-7770. www.baymontinn.com. 57 units. $79–$109 double. Rates include continental breakfast. Children 17 and under stay free in parent's room. AE, DC, DISC, MC, V. **Amenities:** Outdoor pool; nonsmoking rooms; rooms for those w/limited mobility. *In room:* A/C, TV, Wi-Fi, coffeemaker, hair dryer, iron.

Homewood Suites by Hilton   Built in 1990 about a 6-mile drive south of Savannah's historic core, this is a blandly modern member of a nationwide chain, wherein each room is a suite with either one or two bedrooms. Favored by business travelers who sometimes opt to stay in larger-than-usual quarters on extended business trips, it occupies a commercial neighborhood with suburban-style traffic and plenty of nearby restaurants and shopping malls. An evening cocktail party, hosted by the manager, takes the edge off the sense of anonymity that sometimes prevails here, but if you're looking for space to move around within a modern, uncontroversial setting, this place might be fine for you. Each room has a fully equipped kitchen with a microwave, full-size refrigerator, and cooking utensils.

5820 White Bluff Rd., Savannah, GA 31405. © **800/225-5466** or 912/353-8500. Fax 912/354-3821. http://homewoodsuites.hilton.com. 106 units. $159–$249 double. AE, DC, DISC, MC, V. **Amenities:** Restaurant; pool; gym; Jacuzzi; all nonsmoking rooms. *In room:* A/C, TV, Wi-Fi, kitchen, microwave, hair dryer, iron.

Ramada Hotel & Suites Midtown 𝑅 𝑉𝑎𝑙𝑢𝑒   One of the better deals in Savannah, this renovated property, with its upgraded decor and furnishings, offers first-class comfort but charges moderate prices. Guest rooms are large and well furnished. The suites don't cost a lot more, so these upgraded and oversize units may be the way to go. To make the suites even more attractive, a small kitchenette is included in each, with such extras as a microwave, dishware, and utensils for cooking light meals. Many of the guest rooms open onto balconies. A generous buffet breakfast, complete with such Southern favorites as biscuits and gravy, along with plenty of pancakes, bacon, and sausage, greets guests every morning. **Club Lounge** overlooks an outdoor courtyard and pool area.

6800 Abercorn St., Savannah, GA 31405. © **800/272-6232** or 912/352-2828. Fax 912/352-2828. www.ramada.com. 138 units. $92–$103 double; $149–$179 suite. Rates include buffet breakfast. Children 17 and under stay free in parent's room. AE, DC, DISC, MC, V. **Amenities:** Outdoor pool; health club privileges; business services; 24-hr. free coffee and tea; coin laundry. *In room:* A/C, TV, Wi-Fi, kitchenette (in suite), microwave (in suite), hair dryer, iron.

Savannah Midtown   If it's raining hard, and if every inn in the city's historic core is fully booked, and if you have no other option, you might stay in this modern hotel, built in 1983, where you can sustain life in between the visits you'll make, 7 miles north, to historic Savannah. Each room is divided by a lattice into a sleeping area and, on its other side, a sitting area where there's a small refrigerator, a coffeemaker, and a microwave—a somewhat uninspired setup that isn't by anyone's evaluation a genuine "suite," despite the large signs on the building's exterior advertising accommodations as such. Guest rooms have either two double beds or a king-size bed. Bathrooms are modern, tiled, and motel style in their design. At the center of the hotel is a glass-roofed atrium with a scattering of plants, and outside in the garden is a swimming pool.

7110 Hodgson Memorial Dr., Savannah, GA 31406. ⓒ 912/354-8560. Fax 912/356-1438. 51 units. $89–$99 double; $119 suite. Rates include continental breakfast. AE, DC, DISC, MC, V. **Amenities:** Pool; gym; Jacuzzi; sauna; room service; laundry service; dry cleaning; nonsmoking rooms; rooms for those w/limited mobility. *In room:* A/C, TV, Wi-Fi, microwave, fridge, coffeemaker, hair dryer, iron.

Wingate Inn   This is one of the newer and more comfortable hotels in the shopping-mall zone south of Savannah. Although the distance to the city's historic core is about 8 miles, part of the transit is via interstate highways, sometimes (if traffic is light) only about 18 minutes away. Built in a four-story brick-and-stucco format in 1999, with a bit of architectural flair, the inn offers comfortable, family-friendly rooms outfitted with modern furniture that carries no pretensions of Southern Colonial plantation life. (This might be a relief after a heavy dose of that style in other modern hotels nearby.)

11 Gateway Blvd. E., Savannah, GA 31419. ⓒ 800/228-1000 or 912/925-2525. Fax 912/925-7904. www.wingatehotels.com. 101 units. $79–$139 double. Rates include continental breakfast. AE, DC, DISC, MC, V. **Amenities:** Pool; gym; spa; Jacuzzi; nonsmoking rooms; rooms for those w/limited mobility. *In room:* A/C, TV, Wi-Fi, kitchenette, microwave, fridge, coffeemaker, hair dryer, iron, safe.

5

Where to Dine in Savannah

Savannah is known for the excellence of its seafood restaurants. They're among the best in Georgia, rivaled only by those in Atlanta. The best dining is in the Historic District, along River Street, bordering the water. However, locals also like to escape the city and head for the seafood places on Tybee and other offshore islands.

Some of Savannah's restaurants, like **Elizabeth on 37th,** are ranked among the finest in the South. And others, like **Mrs. Wilkes' Dining Room,** are places to go for real Southern fare—from collard greens and fried okra to fried chicken, cornbread, and hot biscuits.

1 Along or Near the Riverfront

EXPENSIVE

Chart House ⊛ STEAK/SEAFOOD   Overlooking the Savannah River and Riverfront Plaza, "the home of the mud pie" is part of a nationwide chain—and one of the better ones. It's housed in a building that predates 1790, reputed to be the oldest masonry structure in Georgia and once a sugar-and-cotton warehouse. You can enjoy a view of passing ships on the outside deck, perhaps ordering an appetizer and a drink before dinner. The bar is one of the most atmospheric along the riverfront. As in all Chart Houses, the prime rib is slow roasted and served au jus. The steaks from corn-fed beef are aged and hand cut on the premises before being chargrilled. The most expensive item is lobster. You may prefer one of the fresh catches of the day, which can be grilled to your specifications.

202 W. Bay St. © 912/234-6686. www.chart-house.com. Reservations recommended. Main courses $19–$47. AE, DC, DISC, MC, V. Mon–Fri 5–10pm; Sat 5–10:30pm; Sun 5–9pm.

MODERATE

Bistro Savannah ⊛⊛ SOUTHERN/FUSION   Cajun and Southern cuisine we're used to, but how many chefs prepare a Southern cuisine with Thai overtones? This is the most eclectic bistro in town, attracting serious Savannah foodies. Count on something different every night. Some readers of the Zagat Survey have even hailed this bistro as the number-one restaurant in Georgia, but that's going too far in enthusiasm for us. The chef does make the best coastal seafood bouillabaisse in town, and he excels in other specialties as well, namely crisp pecan chicken with blackberry bourbon sauce, one of the delights of Southern cuisine. On different occasions we've been impressed with the barbecued black grouper and the crispy roast duck with Bing cherries and orange marmalade, each dish perfectly seasoned. Naturally, being from Savannah, the cooks excel at shrimp 'n' grits. The atmosphere is cozy, with exposed brick and comfortable seating, and the service is among the best in town.

309 W. Congress St. ⓒ **912/233-6266.** Reservations required. Main courses $19–$27. AE, MC, V. Sun–Thurs 5–10:30pm; Fri–Sat 5–11pm.

Huey's ⓡ CAJUN/CREOLE At first glance, this casual place overlooking the Savannah River seems little different from the other restored warehouses. The chef even manages to please visitors from New Orleans—and that's saying a lot. The place is often packed. Breakfast begins with such dishes as a Creole omelet, followed by an oyster po'boy for lunch. It's at dinner, however, that the kitchen really shines, producing jambalaya with andouille sausage, crayfish étouffée, and crab-and-shrimp au gratin (with Louisiana crabmeat and Georgia shrimp). The soups are homemade and the appetizers distinctive. Breakfast can be ordered from 7am to 3pm daily. The bar next door offers live entertainment.

115 E. River St., in the River Street Inn. ⓒ **912/234-7385.** Reservations recommended. Sandwiches $8–$12; dinner main courses $14–$32. AE, DISC, MC, V. Mon–Thurs 7am–10pm; Fri 7am–11pm; Sat 8am–11pm; Sun 8am–10pm.

INEXPENSIVE

The Lady & Sons ⓡⓡ ⓕⓘⓝⓓⓢ SOUTHERN Paula Deen started this place in 1989 with $200, the help of her sons, and a 1910 structure. Today she runs one of Savannah's most celebrated restaurants. Her first cookbook, *The Lady & Sons Savannah Country Cookbook* (1998), is an ongoing bestseller (John Berendt wrote the introduction); and her second and third, *The Lady & Sons Too* and *Paula Deen's Kitchen Classics,* were published in 2000 and 2005, respectively. Paula also hosts a top-rated cooking show, *Paula's Home Cooking,* on the Food Network. One taste of the food and you'll understand the roots of her success. Menu items like crab cakes (one Maryland visitor claimed they were the best he'd ever eaten), crab burgers, and several creative varieties of shrimp best exhibit her style. The locals love her buffets, which are Southern to the bone. With fried chicken, meatloaf, collard greens, beef stew, creamed potatoes,

Where to Dine in Savannah

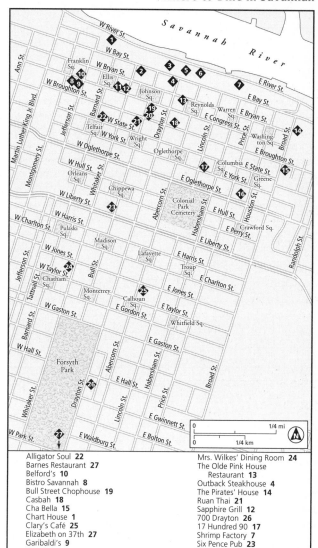

Alligator Soul **22**
Barnes Restaurant **27**
Belford's **10**
Bistro Savannah **8**
Bull Street Chophouse **19**
Casbah **18**
Cha Bella **15**
Chart House **1**
Clary's Café **25**
Elizabeth on 37th **27**
Garibaldi's **9**
Huey's **5**
Il Pasticcio **20**
Johnny Harris Restaurant **27**
The Lady & Sons **11**
Moon River Brewing Company **2**

Mrs. Wilkes' Dining Room **24**
The Olde Pink House
   Restaurant **13**
Outback Steakhouse **4**
The Pirates' House **14**
Ruan Thai **21**
Sapphire Grill **12**
700 Drayton **26**
17 Hundred 90 **17**
Shrimp Factory **7**
Six Pence Pub **23**
Toucan Café **27**
Tubby's Tank House **6**
Vic's on the River **3**
Wall's **16**

or macaroni and cheese, this buffet is more aptly described as "more-than-you-can-eat."

Lunches are busy with a loyal following; dinners are casual and inventive. The aphrodisiac dish has to be the oyster shooters—half a dozen raw oysters, each served in a shot glass ("It's like killing two birds with one stone"). Paula's signature dish, chicken potpie topped with puff pastry, looks so attractive you'll have reservations about eating it (maybe that's why *Southern Living* used a picture of it in their magazine). Other a la carte choices include fried green tomatoes with Vidalia onion relish and roasted red pepper sauce; peach-barbecued grouper; and Savannah-style crab cakes on a bed of black beans with fried collard greens and lemon-flavored dill sauce. Be careful not to fill up on the cheese biscuits and hoecakes that constantly land on your table. If for some reason you don't want a glorious glass of syrup-sweet tea, you'd better ask for unsweetened. But why rob yourself of the complete experience? In 2007, Paula Dean and Co. established a separately recommended cookware store in the space immediately adjacent to the restaurant.

120 W. Congress St. © 912/233-2600. www.ladyandsons.com. Reservations recommended for dinner. Main courses $6–$13 lunch, $18–$24 dinner; all-you-can-eat buffet $13 lunch, $18 dinner; Sun buffet $15. AE, DISC, MC, V. Mon–Thurs 11am–3pm and 5–9pm; Fri–Sat 11am–3pm and 5–10pm; Sun 11am–5pm (buffet only).

Shrimp Factory *(Value)* SEAFOOD   The exposed old brick and wooden plank floors form a setting for harborside dining in this former cotton warehouse (ca. 1850). Lots of folks drop in before dinner to watch the boats pass by, perhaps enjoying a Chatham Artillery punch in a souvenir snifter. Yes, the place is touristy, never more so than when it welcomes tour buses. A salad bar rests next to a miniature shrimp boat, and fresh seafood comes from local waters. A specialty, pine bark stew, is served in a little iron pot with a bottle of sherry on the side; it's a potage of five varieties of seafood simmered with fresh herbs but minus the pine bark. Other dishes include peeled shrimp, shucked oysters, live Maine lobsters, sirloin steaks, and various fish filets.

313 E. River St. (2 blocks east of the Hyatt). © 912/236-4229. www.theshrimp factory.com. Reservations not accepted. Main courses $7–$15 lunch, $21–$30 dinner. AE, DC, DISC, MC, V. Mon–Thurs 11am–10pm; Fri–Sat 11am–11pm; Sun noon–10pm.

Tubby's Tank House SEAFOOD   Hungry diners flock here for the fresh fish. This old-brick building has a nautical decor, a casual atmosphere, and an outdoor deck for river views. The menu is corny—appetizers, for example, are called "Tubby's Teasers"—but the food is affordable, good, and wholesome. Oysters Savannah is a favorite starter, baked with andouille sausage and Parmesan cheese. Lemon garlic shrimp is another savory opening. The chefs make the best crab stew along River Street. When we drop in, we generally opt for the fresh fish of the day. It's grilled to perfection over an open flame and served with fresh steamed vegetables and your choice of a starch such as fettuccine Alfredo. Families like to order the seafood baskets, or else one of the steam pots served with hush puppies. The most savory kettle of fish is the Low Country platter with steamed oysters, rock shrimp, steamed shrimp, snow crab, deviled crab, sausage, and corn on the cob. A limited number of steak and chicken dishes are offered, including charbroiled chicken breast and a 14-ounce rib-eye.

115 E. River St. ⓒ 912/233-0770. www.tubbystankhouse.com. Main courses $10–$20. AE, MC, V. Daily 11am–10pm. Closed Thanksgiving and Christmas.

2 In the Historic District
VERY EXPENSIVE

Bull Street Chophouse ⓡ STEAKS   This is the most talked-about and upscale restaurant in Savannah, the kind of two-fisted steakhouse where Frank Sinatra and his Rat Pack would have felt completely at home. Its location isn't immediately obvious, tucked away as it is on the second floor of a building that contains the also-recommended, and less-expensive, Il Pasticcio. An elevator will haul you up from street level to a mostly black-and-red enclave where an open-to-view kitchen shows something akin to Dante's fires of hell, out of which emerge superb versions of the best steaks in town. The portions are large—in some cases, a whopping 64 ounces (4 lb.) of meat on some of the platters prepared for two diners at a time. Begin with tuna or Kobe beef carpaccio, a spicy steak tartare, or perhaps a Caesar or spinach salad. Main courses include all manner of steaks and chops, as well as a limited array of seafood that includes lobster, platters of shellfish, and grilled ahi tuna with a slab of foie gras.

44 Bull St., upstairs from Il Pasticcio. ⓒ 912/232-2728. www.bullstreetchophouse. com. Reservations recommended. Main courses $30–$52. AE, DC, DISC, MC, V. Mon–Thurs 5:30–10:30pm; Fri–Sat 5:30–11:30pm.

Sapphire Grill ⓡ AMERICAN/LOW COUNTRY   One of the city's most consistently stylish restaurants evokes a low-key, counter-culture bistro, but its cuisine is grander and more cutting edge than its industrial-looking decor and its level of hipness would imply.

Christopher Nason is the owner and the most talked-about chef of the moment in Savannah, preparing what he defines as a "coastal cuisine" based on seafood hauled in, usually on the day of its preparation, from nearby waters. If you opt for a table here, you won't be alone: Scads of media and cinema personalities will have preceded you. Collectively, they add an urban gloss of the type you might expect to see in Los Angeles. Launch your repast with endive, rocket, and baby field lettuce with sesame cream sauce and confit of tomato and Stilton cheese, or barbecued wild halibut with sweet corn broth. Each day the chef serves a tasting menu—based on the market price—that includes an appetizer, salad, main course, and confections. Ask about it—it might be your best dining bet.

110 W. Congress St. ℂ **912/443-9962.** www.sapphiregrill.com. Reservations recommended. Main courses $23–$45; 6-course tasting menu $100. AE, DC, MC, V. Sun–Thurs 6–10:30pm; Fri–Sat 5:30–11:30pm.

700 Drayton ✸✸✸ INTERNATIONAL This is the culinary showplace of the most plush hotel to open in Savannah in years. It occupies the oldest section—a brick-built mansion from 1888—of the Mansion on Forsyth Park (p. 40). Inside, scattered over two floors of the echoing, high-ceilinged interior, are 150 seats and six dining rooms, each of which contains remnants and reminders (including the working fireplaces) of the building's original role as a private home. Some are convivial and public, others are suitable for everyone on the corporate board of your favorite bank, and still others are semiprivate hideaways, perfect for small, intimate gatherings.

The well-chosen menu is market inspired and one of the most seductive in Savannah, as evoked by the fried green tomatoes served with baked goat cheese, grilled pork chops stuffed with tomatoes and thyme, pecan-crusted rack of New Zealand lamb in a balsamic syrup or pan-roasted Gulf Coast grouper with a shrimp fricassee, and the most upscale version of tuna tartare we've seen. The steakhouse New York strip came as an imaginative and delightful surprise; it was Gorgonzola crusted with caramelized shallots and a blackberry compote. Skewered shrimp with grits are served in a saffron-flavored shellfish sauce. Desserts are among the more succulent in town, especially the Grand Marnier chocolate truffle mousse cake. Even if you're famished, we recommend a before-dinner drink at **Casimir's Bar,** which lies on the building's second floor.

700 Drayton St., in the Mansion on Forsyth Park. ℂ **912/238-5158.** www.700drayton. com. Reservations recommended. Main courses $11–$15 breakfast, $8–$16 lunch, $24–$35 dinner. AE, DC, DISC, MC, V. Daily 7am–2pm and 5–10pm.

EXPENSIVE

The Olde Pink House Restaurant 𝕮𝕮 SEAFOOD/SOUTH-
ERN   Built in 1771 and sheathed with a layer of pink stucco, this
house has functioned as a private home, a bank, a tearoom, and
headquarters for one of Sherman's generals. Today its interior is
severe and dignified, with stiff-backed chairs, bare wooden floors,
and an 18th-century aura similar to what you'd find in Williams-
burg, Virginia. In 2008, a renovation and enlargement added an
additional venue for lunch, within an antique cellar room outfitted
with a generously proportioned bar. Richly steeped in the traditions
of the Low Country, its cuisine includes sautéed local shrimp with
country ham and grits cake, crispy scored flounder with apricot
sauce, steak au poivre, black grouper stuffed with blue crab and
drenched in white onion and butter sauce, and grilled tenderloin of
pork served with collard greens and yams. You can enjoy your meal
in the rather formal and spartan-looking candlelit dining rooms or
within the more permissive, less formal decor of the Planters Tavern.

23 Abercorn St. ✆ 912/232-4286. Reservations recommended. Main courses $16–
$28. AE, MC, V. Sun–Mon 5–10:30pm; Tues–Thurs 11am–3pm and 5–10:30pm; Fri–
Sat 11am–3pm and 5–11pm.

17 Hundred 90 𝕮 INTERNATIONAL   In the brick-lined, low-
ceilinged cellar of Savannah's oldest inn, this place evokes a seafaring
tavern along the coast of New England. Many visitors opt for a drink
at the woodsy-looking bar in a separate back room before heading
down the slightly claustrophobic corridor to the nautically inspired
dining room. Students of paranormal psychology remain alert to the
ghost rumored to wander through this place, site of Savannah's most
famous 18th-century suicide. Lunch might include the quiche of the
day, Southern-style crab cakes, and a choice of salads and sandwiches. Dinners are more formal, featuring crab bisque, snapper
Parmesan, steaks, and bourbon-flavored chicken.

307 E. President St. ✆ 912/236-7122. www.17hundred90.com. Reservations recommended. Main courses $24–$36. AE, DISC, MC, V. Mon–Fri 11:30am–2pm and
6–10pm; Sat–Sun 6–10pm.

MODERATE

Casbah MOROCCAN   With its North African theme, this restaurant, a dining oddity for Savannah, offers a lush and sensual
atmosphere. Brocade tapestries on the walls and tented velvet ceilings create the aura; fortunetellers predict your future and belly
dancers entertain you. It has all that faux "Come with me to the Casbah" allure. You'll feast on exotic specialties. We like to start with a

festival of Moroccan salads. Ask your server about the day's selection. One tantalizing appetizer is cornish hen *Bastila*—served boneless and mixed with onions, parsley, spiced eggs, and toasted almonds in a pastry baked and garnished with cinnamon and powdered sugar. It's more economical to order the three-course Moroccan Diaffa dinner, in which you select your appetizer, main course, and dessert, finishing off with hot mint tea. For main courses you're taken on an "Arabian Nights" tour and can order such dishes as chicken and caramelized apricots dipped in a honey-nutmeg sauce. Our favorite is spicy roast lamb, served oven roasted and very tender with saffron rice and a choice of vegetables. If you like kabobs, you can opt for the Sultan's Feast, an assortment of chicken, beef, and lamb kabobs.

118 E. Broughton St. ℂ **912/234-6168.** Reservations recommended. Main courses $12–$25; 3-course menu $30. AE, DC, DISC, MC, V. Daily 5:30–10:30pm.

Cha Bella ✿ ORGANIC MEDITERRANEAN   Be prepared for pleasant surprises at this underpublicized dining venue. Set a few blocks east of historic Savannah's most-visited neighborhood, this avant-garde restaurant occupies a brick-built industrial structure with high ceilings, an appealingly macho-looking bar area, modern paintings, and a palette of yummy colors. New owners have breathed life into the cuisine. Very appealing starters include a peppery baby arugula salad, with spiced pecans, Gorgonzola cheese, and fresh raspberries, all bound together in a raspberry vinaigrette dressing. You could also try a salad of goat cheese, eggplant, and plum tomatoes flavored with fresh sweet basil. For a main course, you might select an 8-ounce filet of beef with a mushroom demi-glace, or else black grouper, freshly caught, and seared just right with a succotash of peas, sweet corn, and lump crabmeat. For dessert, you can sample such temptations as "Chocolate Fourways"—a chocolate hazelnut truffle, a chocolate mouse, a chocolate almond brownie, and a pair of chewy chocolate cookies.

102 E. Broad St. ℂ **912/790-7888.** www.cha-bella.com. Reservations recommended. Main courses $17–$29. AE, DC, MC, V. Daily 6–10pm.

Il Pasticcio NORTHERN ITALIAN   This restaurant is one of the city's most popular dining spots. In a postmodern style, with big windows and a high ceiling, it has a definite big-city style. A rotisserie turns out specialties. Many locals come here just for the pasta dishes, all homemade and served with savory sauces. Begin with carpaccio (thinly sliced beef tenderloin) or a tricolor salad of radicchio, endive, and arugula. Main dishes are likely to feature veal

Marsala, angel-hair pasta with shellfish, or a mixed-grill seafood platter or grilled fish steak with tricolor roasted sweet peppers. We also recommend the more upscale, much more expensive restaurant immediately upstairs from this place, the Steakhouse.

2 E. Broughton St. (corner of Bull and Broughton sts.). © **912/231-8888.** www. ilpasticciosavannah.com. Main courses $20–$36. AE, DC, DISC, MC, V. Mon–Thurs 5:30–10pm; Fri–Sat 5:30–11:30pm; Sun 5:30–9:30pm.

Outback Steakhouse STEAKS/SEAFOOD It's woodsy looking, comfortable, and well run and serves food that's tasty, well prepared, and a lot better than what's offered at some competing chains. This national chain has managed to elevate Australian pop culture into steakhouse glamour. Australians who visit invariably appreciate the food but can't help noting, for example, that "Alice Springs is a desert and doesn't produce chicken"—in reference to one of our favorite dishes, "Alice Springs chicken," which is slathered with cheese, sliced ham, mushrooms, and honey-mustard sauce. In truth, much of the food is all-American fare marketed with an Australian accent. The restaurant's focal point is the large, rectangular bar area where you might want to wait until your table becomes available. There's a sense of bustling popularity, high turnover, and (yes), charm in this place that has nothing to do with historic Savannah, but the food is affordable and good, including filets, prime rib, burgers, sirloins, pasta, chicken, shrimp, and lobster tail.

7 Drayton St. © **912/232-1611.** www.outback.com. Reservations recommended for dinner. Lunch sandwiches, salads, and platters $7–$12; dinner main courses $12–$29. AE, MC, V. Mon–Thurs 11:30am–10:30pm; Fri 11:30am–11:30pm; Sat 3–11:30pm; Sun noon–9:30pm.

Pearl's Saltwater Grille SEAFOOD/AMERICAN "Let's not cook tonight; let's go to Pearl's," is the nightly refrain often heard in local homes. Customers know they'll get good food and plenty of it, everything from fresh seafood to perfectly grilled steaks. Dress is casual, and service is good except when the waitstaff is overwhelmed by a packed house. "This is where I take my guests from the north to show them how we eat in Savannah," one patron informed us. The crowd is varied. Many diners arrive early for more than one drink at the bar before proceeding to a table. And on our last visit, we noticed many families dining here.

The cuisine may not be inspired here, but it's good and most filling, beginning with fresh hush puppies with sweetened butter. Southern-style vegetables—referred to as "sides" by the locals—accompany the main courses. Favorite dishes include shrimp and crab au gratin with a rich white sauce, and a shrimp trio—fried shrimp, garlic shrimp, and shrimp wrapped in bacon. Other good-tasting dishes include barbecued pork chops and pepper steak.

7000 La Roche Ave. ℂ **912/352-8221.** www.pearlssaltwatergrille.com. Reservations not accepted. Main courses $15–$25. AE, DC, DISC, MC, V. Sun–Thurs 5–10pm; Fri–Sat 5–10:30pm.

The Pirates' House AMERICAN/SOUTHERN   Positioned a few blocks east of the commercial bustle of the rest of Savannah, this is the most genuinely historic and atmospheric restaurant in town, complete with ghost sightings. It's also the most-touristy place to eat in Savannah. The Pirates' House incorporates a half-dozen antique houses and a relatively modern section, all conjoined into a labyrinth. You'll dine in a confusing but relentlessly atmospheric warren of 15 dining rooms, each sheathed in dark paneling, and each with a low ceiling. The floors and walls are a bit creaky and out of alignment. The spot that receives the highest number of ghost sightings (and the highest number of eerily overexposed photographs) is the Herb House. Dating from 1733, it was built for the caretaker of a state-sponsored experimental garden that used to grow here. Don't be surprised if, during the course of your drink or meal here, a tourist or two arrive, gawking in a kind of voyeuristic horror at the brick tunnels that honeycomb beneath this place, reacting to the statue of a (faux) prisoner's skeleton positioned at the bottom of a spooky-looking subterranean vault, or listening to the commentary about how Robert Louis Stevenson, who rented one of the rooms upstairs from time to time, was inspired by the place during his authorship of the world's most famous pirate epic, *Treasure Island.*

The food here is closely linked to Low Country traditions, and includes crab cakes, meal-size salads, various she-crab and shellfish gumbos and chowders, slow-cooked baby back ribs, steaks, and seafood. The Plantation Buffet, which includes the kind of traditional Southern food that might have been laid out in 1925 by the owner of a farmhouse to feed the field hands on a hot summer day, is the most popular choice here.

20 E. Broad St. ℂ **912/233-5757.** www.thepirateshouse.com. Reservations recommended for dinner. Lunch sandwiches, salads, and platters $10–$12; Low Country buffet lunch $14; dinner main courses $20–$25; Low Country buffet dinner $17. AE, DC, DISC, MC, V. Sun–Thurs 11:30am–10pm; Fri–Sat 11:30am–11pm.

Vic's on the River ⊛ MODERN SOUTHERN   This is one of the hottest and most appealing restaurants in Savannah, with award-winning food; a high-ceilinged and airy space that emulates a hip urban restaurant in, say, New York; and a gloss of historic authenticity that's Savannah all the way. It occupies the top floor of an antebellum cotton warehouse that was used by Sherman's troops during the Yankee occupation of Savannah. Even if you drop in here just for a drink, we urge you to wander past the sprawling cocktail bar into the dining room, where—adjacent to windows with high-altitude views over the Savannah River—you'll find the restaurant's pride and joy. It's a map that was painted by Union troops directly onto plaster, showing their idea of the layout of the juxtaposition of Georgia with Tennessee and South Carolina. Today it's preserved behind museum-quality Lucite, a historic holdover within an otherwise postmodern setting.

Culinary hip commingles with Southern pride on this menu. Lunch features sandwiches that are more creative than those at many competitors. Dinner might include a pulled-pork egg roll with barbecue sauce, hot mustard, and peach chutney; fried green tomatoes with goat cheese and tomato chutney; and popcorn grouper, served in a movie-palace cardboard popcorn box, with rémoulade sauce. The best main courses include braised shank of lamb with cherries; boneless filet of pork with butternut risotto; spicy wild Georgia shrimp over grits smothered in gravy made from andouille sausage and tasso ham (voted by a local newspaper as one of the 10 best main courses in Savannah); Black Angus filet mignon with roasted garlic demi-glace; and cornmeal-crusted grouper with citrus-flavored butter sauce and peach chutney.

26 E. Bay St. (main entrance) or via the elevator that's accessible through Vic's Coffeeshop at 15 E. River St. (✆) **912/721-1000**. www.vicsontheriver.com. Reservations recommended. Lunch sandwiches, salads, and platters $11–$16; dinner main courses $19–$29. AE, MC, V. Sun–Thurs 11am–10pm; Fri–Sat 11am–11pm.

INEXPENSIVE

Barnes Restaurant *⭐* *(Kids)* BARBECUE/LOW COUNTRY This casual, family-style restaurant is very affordable. Local hotels and B&Bs often refer their budget-minded guests to this joint for its generous helpings and good food. A tradition since 1975, it's typical of many eateries in the South, serving barbecue dinners, oyster po'boys, and fried catfish. "These dishes are popular," a waiter confided, "because it's what the customers want to eat day after day." From hand-cut and freshly battered onion rings to deviled and pan-seared crab cakes, the starters are spicy openings. The sandwiches are among the best in the area, including fish sandwiches, chicken sandwiches, and crab burgers. The spareribs are slowly smoked over oak

(Kids) Family-Friendly Restaurants

Barnes Restaurant (p. 65) This is an informal restaurant that feeds you well with large servings. The cooks are known for such offerings as onion rings fried quickly in a batter, or deviled crab that is fast-seared in a pan. The sandwiches are well stuffed and made with fresh ingredients, and a menu for the kiddies is also offered.

Mrs. Wilkes' Dining Room (p. 67) Since your kid didn't grow up in the era of the boardinghouse, here's a chance to experience a long-faded American dining custom. It's an all-you-can-eat, family-style place. Children might balk at the okra and collards but will go for the corn on the cob and barbecued chicken.

Wall's (p. 68) If your child is from the North and has never tasted Southern barbecue, come here. There is no finer introduction. Even the booths are plastic. Spareribs and barbecue sandwiches are the hearty fare, but there's also a vegetable plate for the nonmeat eater in the family.

or hickory wood, and the chicken is crispy and tasty outside, tender and moist inside, as it emerges from the rotisserie. A children's menu is also offered.

5320 Waters Ave. (at 68th St.). ⓒ **912/354-8745.** Main courses $7–$13. AE, DC, DISC, MC, V. Sun–Thurs 10:30am–10pm; Fri–Sat 10:30am–10:30pm. Closed Easter, Thanksgiving, and Christmas.

Clary's Café ⓚ (Value) AMERICAN Clary's Café has been a Savannah tradition since 1903, though the ambience today, under the direction of Jan Wilson, is decidedly 1950s. The place was famous long before it was featured in *Midnight in the Garden of Good and Evil* in its former role as Clary's drugstore, where regulars like eccentric flea-collar inventor Luther Driggers breakfasted and lunched. John Berendt is still a frequent patron, as is the fabled Lady Chablis. Begin your day with the classic Hoppel Poppel (scrambled eggs with chunks of kosher salami, potatoes, onions, and green peppers) and go on from there. Fresh salads, New York–style sandwiches, and stir-fries, along with Grandmother's homemade chicken soup and flame-broiled burgers, are served throughout the day, giving way in the evening to chicken potpie, stuffed pork loin, and planked fish (a fresh filet of red snapper—broiled, grilled, or blackened).

404 Abercorn St. (at Jones St.). ℂ 912/233-0402. Breakfast $4–$10; main courses $6–$11. AE, DC, DISC, MC, V. Mon–Fri 7am–4pm; Sat–Sun 8am–4pm.

Mrs. Wilkes' Dining Room 🞄 🇰ids SOUTHERN   Remember the days of the boardinghouse, when everybody sat together and belly-busting food was served in big dishes in the center of the table? Before her death in late 2002 at the age of 95, Sema Wilkes had served breakfast and lunch to locals and travelers in just that manner since the 1940s. Bruce Willis, Demi Moore, and Clint Eastwood are on the long list of celebrities who've dined here. The tradition continues. Expect to find a line of people patiently waiting for a seat at one of the long tables in the basement dining room of this 1870 brick house with curving steps and cast-iron trim.

Mrs. Wilkes believed in freshness and planned her daily menu around the seasons. Your food will be a reflection of the cuisine Savannah residents have enjoyed for generations—fried or barbecued chicken, red rice and sausage, black-eyed peas, corn on the cob, squash and yams, okra, cornbread, and collard greens.

107 W. Jones St. (west of Bull St.). ℂ 912/232-5997. www.mrswilkes.com. Lunch $16. No credit cards. Mon–Fri 11am–2pm.

Ruan Thai 🞄alue   This is the Savannah branch of a three-member chain which does a roaring business in other parts of coastal South Carolina and Georgia. It occupies a high-ceilinged former storefront along Savannah's main downtown shopping corridor—a welcome alternative to too constant a dose of regional Southern cuisine. Menu items come in whatever degree of spiciness you specify, and might include spring rolls, satay skewers with peanut sauce, and your choice of chicken, pork, beef, shrimp, tofu, or vegetables prepared with ginger sauce, garlic sauce, and/or various curries. An ongoing favorite is lemon-grass chicken topped with peanut sauce and served with rice.

17 W. Broughton St. ℂ 912/231-6667. Reservations not necessary. Main courses $11–$21. AE, MC, V. Mon–Thurs 11am–3pm and 4:30–9:30pm; Fri–Sat noon–3pm and 4:30–10pm; Sun 5–9pm.

Six Pence Pub AMERICAN   There's a lot about this woodsy-looking place that emulates an 18th-century pub in England, and, except for the (much-appreciated) air-conditioning, the Americanized menu, and the Southern accents of the staff, you might, for a moment or two, think you're in the U.K. It's always been popular as a centrally located neighborhood restaurant, but its main claim to fame comes from its inclusion as the set, several years ago, for a scene in *Something to Talk About,* when the character played by Julia Roberts (dressed in a nightgown) confronts the character played by Dennis Quaid about infidelity. As befits Savannah gossip, locals still talk about it.

The bar offers 37 kinds of beer, 10 of them on tap, and the salads served here are fresh, large, and big enough for a meal. Also look for juicy burgers, various kinds of spaghetti, fried fresh fish and shrimp, well-stuffed sandwiches, marinated pork roasts, and such old English staples as shepherd's pie and bangers and mash.

245 Bull St. ✆ **912/233-3151.** Reservations not necessary. Sandwiches, salads, and platters $7.50–$15. AE, MC, V. Daily 11:30am–midnight for food. Bar open 'til 12:30 or 1am, depending on business.

Wall's *Kids* BARBECUE   This is the first choice for anyone seeking the best barbecue in Savannah. Southern barbecue aficionados have built-in radar to find a place like this. Once they see the plastic booths, bibs, Styrofoam cartons, and canned drinks from a fridge, they'll know they've found home. Like all barbecue joints, the place is aggressively casual. Spareribs and barbecue sandwiches star on the menu. Deviled crabs are the only nonbarbecue item, though a vegetable plate of four nonmeat items is also served.

515 E. York Lane (btw. York St. and Oglethorpe Ave.). ✆ **912/232-9754.** Main courses $6.50–$10. No credit cards. Thurs–Sat 11am–9pm.

3 In & Around the City Market

EXPENSIVE

Alligator Soul ✿ NEW SOUTHERN   We have readers who adore this place, sinking right in to its agreeable bar area and cozy dining room. Others view it as a heavy-handed, theme-ridden, and overpriced bastion of Southern redneckism appealing shamelessly to local chauvinism and a yearning for The South the way it used to be. The best way to choose whether this place is for you involves dropping in for a cocktail at its bar, checking out the staff and the menu, and then moving on or not to other dining venues as the mood strikes you. Meals here mingle local ingredients with updated versions of time-tested recipes. Examples include fried green tomatoes with chipotle mayonnaise; bacon-flavored macaroni and cheese with shrimp. Main courses include all manner of oversize grilled steaks as well as "a big 'ol" grilled pork chop stuffed with apricot sausage and garnished with bourbon-braised Georgia peaches. A particularly scrumptious dessert is the house version of banana beignets served with roasted banana ice cream and candied pecans.

114 Barnard St. ℭ **912/232-7899.** Reservations recommended. Main courses $29–$45. AE, DC, DISC, MC, V. Mon–Sat 5:30–10pm; Sun 4:30–9pm.

Belford's ℛ LOW COUNTRY This restaurant keeps alive the tradition of offering good food in the area of the old City Market. The setting is nostalgic, with hardwood floors, brick walls, high ceilings, and a patio. The cooks prepare a daily crab stew that is excellent, along with such other favorites as fried green tomatoes, fried calamari, or crab cakes, the latter served with a spicy tomato jam and lemon aioli. A trio of pastas is featured daily, our favorite being the lobster and wild mushroom ravioli served with a spicy calamari salad and a balsamic brown butter sauce.

For your main course, the array of delights may include potato-wrapped grouper with a prosciutto-enhanced beurre blanc sauce. The hazelnut red snapper is also a temptation, served with prawns and lump crabmeat in a hazelnut-liqueur sauce and a side of apple chutney. Shrimp, greens, 'n' grits is a favorite, with smoked bacon, green onions, and a chardonnay butter sauce.

315 W. St. Julian St. ℭ **912/233-2626.** www.belfordssavannah.com. Reservations recommended. Breakfast buffet $8; main courses $5.50–$17 lunch, $18–$40 dinner; Sun brunch $6–$17. AE, DC, DISC, MC, V. Mon–Sat 8–11am, 11:30am–3pm, and 5:30–10pm; Sun 11:30am–3pm and 5:30–10pm. Closed Thanksgiving, Christmas Eve (night), and Christmas.

MODERATE

Garibaldi's SEAFOOD/ITALIAN Many of the city's art-conscious students appreciate this Italian cafe because of the fanciful murals adorning its walls. (Painted by the owner's daughter, their theme is "the jungles of Italy.") If you're looking for a quiet, contemplative evening, we advise you to go elsewhere—the setting is loud and convivial during the early evening and even louder later at night. Designed as a fire station in 1871, it boasts the original pressed-tin ceiling.

Menu items include roasted red peppers with goat-cheese croutons on a bed of wild lettuces, crispy flounder with an apricot-shallot sauce, artichoke hearts with aioli, about a dozen kinds of pasta, and a repertoire of Italian-inspired chicken, veal, and seafood dishes. Daily specials change frequently but sometimes include duck Garibaldi, king-crab fettuccine, and a choice of lusciously fattening desserts.

315 W. Congress St. ① **912/232-7118.** www.garibaldisavannah.com. Reservations recommended. Main courses $13–$40. AE, MC, V. Mon–Thurs 5–10:30pm; Fri–Sat 5pm–midnight; Sun 5–10:30pm.

INEXPENSIVE

Moon River Brewing Company AMERICAN/LOW COUNTRY This welcoming place, a local favorite, successfully combines a restaurant and a bar with a brewpub. You get a *Cheers*-like atmosphere as well as good food, affordable prices, and fresh ingredients. A local critic called the kitchen a "boiling pot of diversity," and so it is, offering a wide range of dishes. The atmosphere is pubby; the brewing company's dark woods and huge brewing tanks behind glass walls can be viewed by customers while they're eating or sampling the suds.

The restaurant is in the former City Hotel Building, where such notables as Gen. Winfield Scott, the Marquis de Lafayette, and John James Audubon have stayed. Audubon stayed here for 6 months after a gale marooned his boat, and it was at this site that he worked on his book, *Ornithological Biographies.*

The kitchen is big on crab, evoked by such appetizers as fried crabmeat or crab cakes. There is always a delectable array of soups, sandwiches, and salads made fresh daily. A perfectly seasoned, 16-ounce grilled rib-eye is served, as well as those local favorites: platters of fried catfish, shrimp 'n' grits, or chicken and sausage Creole. One reliable bet is the catch of the day. Ask the waiter what's on the grill, and tell him or her how you'd like it cooked.

21 W. Bay St. ① **912/447-0943.** www.moonriverbrewing.com. Reservations not required. Main courses $15–$18. AE, DC, DISC, MC, V. Mon–Thurs 11am–11pm; Fri–Sat 11am–midnight; Sun 11am–10pm.

4 In the Victorian District

VERY EXPENSIVE

Elizabeth on 37th ⓕⓕ MODERN SOUTHERN This restaurant is frequently cited as the most glamorous and upscale in town. It's housed in a palatial neoclassical-style 1900 villa ringed with semitropical landscaping and cascades of Spanish moss. The menu items change with the seasons and manage to retain their gutsy originality despite an elegant presentation. They may include roast quail with mustard-and-pepper sauce and apricot-pecan chutney, herb-seasoned rack of lamb, or broiled salmon with mustard-garlic glaze. You might begin with grilled-eggplant soup, a culinary first for many diners. There's also an impressive wine list. The desserts are the best in Savannah.

105 E. 37th St. ② **912/236-5547.** www.elizabethon37th.net. Reservations required. Main courses $25–$37; 7-course fixed-price menu $90. AE, DC, DISC, MC, V. Daily 6–10pm.

5 On the South Side

MODERATE

Johnny Harris Restaurant AMERICAN   Started as a roadside diner in 1924, Johnny Harris is Savannah's oldest continuously operated restaurant. The place has a lingering aura of the 1950s and features all that great food so beloved back in the days of Elvis and Marilyn: barbecue, charbroiled steaks, and seafood. The BBQ'd pork is especially savory, and the prime rib is tender. Colonel Sanders never came anywhere close to equaling the fried chicken here. Guests can dine in the "kitchen" (an area with a view into the slow-cooking barbecue pits) or in the main dining room, where you can dance under the "stars" (faux stars). The place will make you nostalgic.

1651 E. Victory Dr. (Hwy. 80). ② **912/354-7810.** Reservations recommended. Main courses $7–$12 lunch, $12–$23 dinner. AE, DC, DISC, MC, V. Mon–Thurs 11:30am–9:30pm; Fri–Sat 11:30am–10:30pm.

INEXPENSIVE

Toucan Café INTERNATIONAL/FUSION   This is one of the most sophisticated cafes in town, with a festive atmosphere that ranges in spirit from the Greek islands to the West Indies. You get everything here from down-home taste to exotic flavors. The cafe opened in 1994 in a hole in the wall and has been attracting a loyal following ever since. In 1998 the owners, Nancy and Steve Magulias, moved into larger quarters to better accommodate their growing number of fans. The decor alone sets the mood with its lime green, shocking pink, and bright yellow—very Jamaican.

The kitchen is known for turning out the best Havana black-bean soup in Savannah, and the salads are worth a visit here, especially the Toucan Caesar with tomatoes, red onions, and freshly grated Parmesan cheese topped with either chicken or salmon. Many dishes will appeal to the vegetarian, such as the black-bean burger. The lunch sandwiches are the best on the south side. The dinner menu is truly excellent if you launch yourself with the grilled eggplant with tomatoes, provolone, creamy feta, and mousalada over marinara, or the crayfish quesadilla. The Hellenic stuffed chicken with feta cheese and spinach is a main dish specialty, or you may prefer shrimp far-falle with mushrooms, artichokes, and tomatoes in a basil cream with bow-tie pasta. The sesame-encrusted tuna is presented atop soba noodles, and it's divinely wedded to shavings of marinated ginger in a lime beurre blanc sauce. Who can resist the coconut kiwi layer cake?

531 Stephenson Ave. (©) **912/352-2233.** www.toucancafe.com. Reservations rec-ommended. Main courses $7–$10 lunch, $12–$22 dinner. AE, DISC, MC, V. Mon 11:30am–2:30pm; Tues–Thurs 11:30am–2:30pm and 5–9pm; Fri–Sat 11:30am–2:30pm and 5–10pm.

6

Exploring Savannah

The very name evokes a romantic antebellum aura. Savannah is the city that General Sherman gave President Lincoln as a Christmas present. Crowds flock here to search for Forrest Gump's bench and other nonhistorical monuments, as well as to visit Juliette Gordon Low's Birthplace, now the National Center of the Girl Scouts of the U.S.A.

The city, founded in 1733 by James Oglethorpe as Georgia's first settlement, is located 18 miles inland from the Atlantic on the Savannah River at the South Carolina border. A deep channel connects Savannah to the ocean, attracting massive freighters to the terminals at the Georgia Ports Authority. Lined with classy nightspots and upscale restaurants, as well as a few rough pubs and artsy boutiques, cobblestone River Street has become a hub for visitors.

Savannah's historic sites rival those of Charleston, but paramount on the list are characters and dwellings from John Berendt's bestseller, *Midnight in the Garden of Good and Evil.* Ironically, a city that built its claim on historical prominence has become a gathering place for the curious, who flock to Club One, a popular gay nightspot that hosts a nightly transvestite show sometimes featuring Lady Chablis, one of Berendt's main characters. Visitors also dine at Clary's Café and gawk at the Mercer Williams House Museum, the house where the shooting described in Berendt's book took place.

SIGHTSEEING SUGGESTIONS

If You Have 1 Day

Don't set foot outside the Historic District—even there, you won't see it all. Go to the Savannah Visitor Information Center for a general orientation and a viewing of the 15-minute video presentation. Pick up a free map before going to an adjacent building to see the Savannah History Museum. Then set out on our Savannah's Historic Squares walking tour (see chapter 7), viewing sites like the Mercer Williams House Museum, which is the house featured in The Book and The Film. Later, dine along River Street and relax at one of the riverfront pubs or take a harbor cruise if it's offered.

If You Have 2 Days

Spend Day 2 exploring historic River Street, a 9-block plaza facing the Savannah River, with shops, restaurants, galleries, and pubs. Take our Riverwalk walking tour in chapter 7.

If You Have 3 Days

Spend Days 1 and 2 as above. On Day 3, stroll the Bull Street corridor with its shops, galleries, museums, and beautiful squares, and pay a visit to some of the elegant historic inns, all unique, perhaps deciding where you'd like to stay on your next visit to Savannah. Sit back and enjoy a leisurely horse-and-carriage tour to see Savannah in a different light. You'll especially enjoy this tour in the evening as the lights come on in the houses. Or you could opt for an evening ghost tour.

If You Have 4 Days

Spend Days 1, 2, and 3 as recommended above. On Day 4, start your morning at the Telfair Museum of Art, the oldest public art museum in the South. If you have time, walk about 6 blocks and also see the historic Owens-Thomas House and Museum, where Lafayette spent the night in 1825. In the afternoon, venture about 2 miles out of town to see Old Fort Jackson, Georgia's oldest standing fort. To top off your day, return to the city and enjoy a martini in Bonaventure Cemetery (take note—it closes at 5pm).

If You Have 5 Days

Spend Days 1, 2, 3, and 4 as recommended above. On Day 5, travel a little under 2 hours southeast of Savannah to Jekyll Island, where you can spend the day in the former playground of millionaires like the Vanderbilts, Rockefellers, Morgans, and Pulitzers. Stop by the Museum Visitors Center and learn about Jekyll Island's history through exhibits, artifacts, and displays. The museum's Historical Landmark District Tour begins here. You have a choice of several restaurants at the Jekyll Island Club Hotel—you can eat like the Rockefellers in the Grand Dining Room, or just grab a deli sandwich at Café Solterra. Specialty boat tours as well as carriage tours are available to enhance your day on the island.

1 Historic Homes

Andrew Low House   After her marriage, Juliette Gordon Low lived in this 1848 house, and it was here where she actually founded the Girl Scouts. She died on the premises in 1927. The classic mid-19th-century house facing Lafayette Square is of stucco over brick with elaborate ironwork, shuttered piazzas, carved woodwork, and

Savannah Attractions

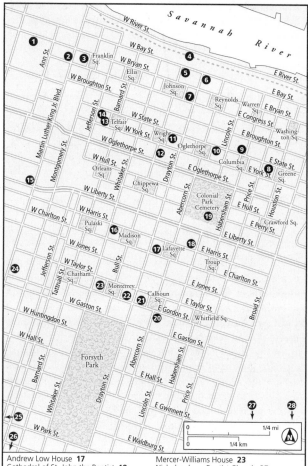

Andrew Low House **17**
Cathedral of St. John the Baptist **18**
Chamber of Commerce **6**
Christ Episcopal Church **7**
Colonial Park Cemetery **19**
Customs House **5**
Davenport House Museum **9**
Factors Walk **4**
First African Baptist Church **3**
First Bryan Baptist Church **1**
Green-Meldrim Home **16**
Juliette Gordon Low's Birthplace **12**
Laurel Grove-South Cemetery **26**
Lutheran Church of the Ascension **11**
Massie Heritage Interpretation Center **20**

Mercer-Williams House **23**
Nicholsonboro Baptist Church **27**
Owen-Thomas House and Museum **10**
Ralph Mark Gilbert Civil Rights Museum **24**
St. Phillip Monumental A.M.E. Church **25**
Savannah History Museum **15**
Savannah Visitor Center **15**
Second African Baptist Church **8**
Ships of the Sea Maritime Museum **2**
Telfair Mansion and Art Museum **14**
Temple Mickve Israel **22**
Trinity United Methodist Church **13**
Wesley Monumental
    United Methodist Church **21**
Wormsloe State Historical Site **28**

crystal chandeliers. William Makepeace Thackeray visited here twice (the desk at which he worked is in one bedroom), and Robert E. Lee was entertained at a gala reception in the double parlors in 1870.

329 Abercorn St. ℭ **912/233-6854.** www.andrewlowhouse.com. Admission $8 adults; $4.50 students, children 6–12, and Girl Scouts; free for children 5 and under. Mon–Wed and Fri–Sat 10am–4:30pm; Sun noon–4:30pm. Closed major holidays.

Davenport House Museum   This is where seven determined women started the whole Savannah restoration movement in 1954. They raised $22,500, a tidy sum back then, and purchased the house, saving it from demolition and a future as a parking lot. They established the Historic Savannah Foundation, and the whole city was spared. Constructed between 1815 and 1820 by master builder Isaiah Davenport, this is one of the truly great Federal-style houses in the United States, with delicate ironwork and a handsome elliptical stairway.

324 E. State St. ℭ **912/236-8097.** www.davenporthousemuseum.org. Admission $8 adults, $5 children 6–18, free for children 5 and under. Mon–Sat 10am–4pm; Sun 1–4pm. Closed major holidays.

Green-Meldrim House   This impressive house was built on Madison Square for cotton merchant Charleston Green, but its moment in history arrived when it became the Savannah headquarters of Gen. William Tecumseh Sherman at the end of his 1864 March to the Sea. It was from this Gothic-style house that the general sent his now infamous (at least, in Savannah) Christmas telegram to President Lincoln, offering him the city as a Christmas gift. Now the Parish House for St. John's Episcopal Church, the house is open to the public. The former kitchen, servants' quarters, and stable are used as a rectory for the church.

14 W. Macon St. ℭ **912/233-3845.** Admission $7 adults, $2 children. Tues and Thurs–Fri 10am–4pm; Sat 10am–1pm.

Juliette Gordon Low's Birthplace   Juliette Gordon Low—the founder of the Girl Scouts—lived in this Regency-style house. It's now maintained both as a memorial to her and as a national program center for the Girl Scouts. The Victorian additions to the 1818–21 house were made in 1886, just before Juliette Gordon married William Mackay Low.

142 Bull St. (at Oglethorpe Ave.). ℭ **912/233-4501.** www.girlscouts.org. Admission $8 adults, $7 children 6–18, free for children 5 and under. Mon–Sat 10am–4pm; Sun 11am–4pm. Closed major holidays and some Sun Dec–Jan.

2 Museums

Owens-Thomas House and Museum ℛ Famed as a place where Lafayette spent the night in 1825, this house evokes the hey-day of Savannah's golden age. It was designed in 1816 by English architect William Jay, who captured the grace of Georgian Bath in England and the splendor of Regency London. The place has been called a "jewel box." You can visit not only the bedchambers and kitchen, but also the garden and the drawing and dining rooms. Adapted from the original slave quarters and stable, the Carriage House Visitors' Center opened in 1995.

124 Abercorn St. ℂ **912/233-9743.** Admission $9 adults, $6 students, $3 children 6–12, free for children 5 and under. Tues–Sat 10am–5pm; Sun 2–5pm.

Savannah History Museum Housed in the restored train shed of the old Central Georgia Railway station, this museum is a good introduction to the city. In the theater, *The Siege of Savannah* is replayed. An exhibition hall displays memorabilia from every era of Savannah's history.

303 Martin Luther King Jr. Blvd. ℂ **912/651-6825.** www.chsgeorgia.org/shm. Admission $4.25 adults, $3.75 seniors and children 7–11, free for children 6 and under. Mon–Fri 8:30am–5pm; Sat–Sun 9am–5pm.

Ships of the Sea Maritime Museum This museum has intri-cately constructed models of seagoing vessels, from Viking warships to nuclear-powered ships. In models ranging from the size of your fist to 8 feet in length, you can see such famous ships as the *Mayflower* and the *Savannah,* the first steamship to cross the Atlantic. More than 75 ships are in the museum's ship-in-a-bottle collection, most of them constructed by Peter Barlow, a retired British Royal Navy commander.

41 Martin Luther King Jr. Blvd. ℂ **912/232-1511.** www.shipsofthesea.org. Admis-sion $8 adults, $6 children 8–12, free for children 7 and under. Tues–Sun 10am–5pm. Closed major holidays.

Telfair Museum of Art ℛ This is the oldest public art museum in the South, housing a collection of both American and European paintings. The building was designed and built by William Jay in 1818 as a home for Alexander Telfair, son of Edward Telfair, the governor of Georgia. Jay was a young English architect noted for introducing the Regency style to America. A sculpture gallery and rotunda were added in 1883, and Jefferson Davis attended the formal opening in 1886. William Jay's period rooms have been restored, and the Octagon Room and Dining Room are particularly outstanding.

121 Bernard St. © **912/232-1177**. www.telfair.org. Admission $10 adults, $6 students, $4 children 5–12, free for children 4 and under. Mon noon–5pm; Wed–Sat 10am–5pm; Sun 1–5pm.

3 Historic Churches & Synagogues

For other historic churches, see "Black History Sights," later in this chapter.

Cathedral of St. John the Baptist   This is the oldest Catholic Church in Georgia and the seat of the Diocese of Savannah. Organized in 1799, it was the first house of worship built on Liberty Square. In 1876 the first rendition of this current Victorian Gothic cathedral was constructed but it was destroyed by fire in 1898. Based on original designs, the cathedral was rebuilt. Over the past several years, the cathedral has undergone massive renovations. Today its twin spires and chiming bells make it one of Savannah's most notable landmarks. Inside you can view the marble railings, murals, Persian rugs, stained-glass windows from Austria, large carved wooden Stations of the Cross, and a 2,081-pipe Noack tracker organ.

222 E. Harris St. © **912/233-4709**. www.savannahcathedral.org. Self-guided tours Mon–Fri 9–11:30am and 12:30–5pm.

Christ Episcopal Church   Savannah was founded as a Church of England settlement, and its center of religious life was this church, the first established in the colony. It was known as the "Mother Church of Georgia." The present building on this site is in the style of an early Greek Revival public building, having been designed by James H. Cooper in 1838. The church was nearly destroyed by fire in 1898, but was rebuilt within its original walls. Famous clergy in the history of this church include John Wesley and George Whitehead. The first Sunday school conducted in Georgia was held here, as was the first hymnal in English. Its 1819 Revere Bell is one of the rarest in the country. The bell bears this ominous engraving: "THE LIVING TO THE CHURCH I CALL, AND TO THE GRAVE I SUMMON ALL."

28 Bull St. © **912/238-0434**. www.christchurchsavannah.org. Most Fri–Sat 10:30am–3pm.

Lutheran Church of the Ascension   Few churches in Georgia have had the bizarre history of this landmark. Its origins are in 1734, when Austrians emigrating from Salzburg founded the church. They came to settle in Savannah a year after Oglethorpe landed. Although most of the Salzburgers settled in a community called Ebenezer outside Savannah, not all of them did. The Reverend Johann Bolzius, who had created the Ebenezer New Jerusalem Lutheran Church, came back to Savannah in 1741 to create this church for the Salzburgers who had settled in the historic core. A wooden structure originally stood on this site, but in 1844 it was replaced by a Greek Revival church. Thirty-five years later, architect George B. Clarke added the second floor and the medieval-style turrets. Today it's a fine example of the Grecian-Doric style that swept eastern America.

When General Sherman invaded Savannah in 1864, the church pew cushions were used as beds by his soldiers, and the pews themselves were used as firewood. The church was turned into a hospital for the sick and wounded. Although the building was damaged, it was not destroyed. Today it's known for its spectacular "Ascension Window" inside the sanctuary behind the pulpit, and for its rose window featuring Martin Luther and his coat of arms in front of the building.

120 Bull St. on Wright Sq. (℗ **912/232-4151.** www.elcota.org. Mon–Fri 9am–1pm.

Temple Mickve Israel   At Monterey Square, this temple is home to Georgia's oldest Jewish congregation, the third-oldest congregation in the U.S. It is the nation's only Gothic synagogue (ca. 1878) and was designed by architect Henry G. Harrison, who had previously designed only Christian churches. Its founding members were Spanish, Portuguese, and German Jews who came to Savannah in 1733 to escape persecution in their homelands. With them, the group carried a precious relic, the Sepah Torah, the oldest Torah in America. The temple today houses a museum with more than 1,800 historical artifacts on view, including portraits, religious objects, documents, and letters to the congregation from presidents George Washington, Thomas Jefferson, and James Madison.

20 E. Gordon St. (on Monterey Sq.). (℗ **912/233-1547.** www.mickveisrael.org. $5 donation suggested. Tours and museum Mon–Fri 10am–1pm and 2–4pm. Closed major Jewish holidays.

Trinity United Methodist Church   This church, dedicated in 1848, is known as the "Mother Church of Savannah Methodism." It is hardly the most opulent church in Savannah, but it holds a fascination for students of architecture. It is known for its hand-hewn pine on its interior. It was constructed of stucco over Savannah gray brick, and its interior design is evocative of the Wesley Chapel in

Gateway to Historic Savannah

On a bluff above the river, **Factors Walk** and **Factors Row** are arrays of redbrick structures named for the brokers who graded cotton in these buildings in the heyday of the 19th-century King Cotton economy. The men who performed this duty were called "Factors." To build these structures, the architects had to contend with a bluff rising sharply from the river. On the bluff they designed a series of multitiered buildings of ballast stone and brick hauled across the Atlantic.

Rice and cotton were the main crops held in the warehouses along Factors Walk, both flourishing industries at the time. During Savannah's peak as a seaport, ships from all over the world docked adjacent to the row of warehouses so their exports could be directly loaded into their holds.

The rows of warehouses were made accessible by a network of iron bridgeways over cobblestone ramps. Today this section, lying between Bull and East Broad streets, is filled with many fine shops and restaurants. Ramps lead from the Bay Street level down the bluff to River Street, which you can promenade after checking out Factors Row and Factors Walk.

London. The formula for the Savannah gray brick is no longer in existence, having died with its inventor.

225 W. President St. © 912/233-4766. www.trinitychurch1848.org. Mon–Fri 9am–3pm.

Wesley Monumental United Methodist Church   Built between 1876 and 1890, this Gothic Revival church is a memorial to John and Charles Wesley, the founders of Methodism. It is based on designs for Queen's Kirk in Amsterdam and holds 1,000 parishioners surrounded by stained-glass windows dedicated to the historic figures of Methodism. The church took a long time to erect because of the financial problems in the Reconstruction era and a catastrophic outbreak of yellow fever in Savannah.

429 Abercorn St. © 912/232-0191. www.wesleymonumental.org. Mon–Fri 9am–5pm.

4 The Forts: Civil War Memories

Old Fort Jackson   About 2½ miles east of the center of Savannah via the Islands Expressway is Georgia's oldest standing fort, with a 9-foot-deep tidal moat around its brick walls. In 1775, an earthen battery was built here. The original brick fort was begun in 1808 and manned during the War of 1812. It was enlarged and strengthened between 1845 and 1860 and saw its greatest use as headquarters for the Confederate river defenses during the Civil War. Its arched rooms, designed to support the weight of heavy cannons mounted above, hold 13 exhibit areas.

1 Fort Jackson Rd. © **912/232-3945**. Admission $4.25 adults, $3.75 seniors and children 6–18, free for children 5 and under. Daily 9am–5pm.

Fort McAllister   Lying 10 miles southwest on U.S. 17, on the banks of the Great Ogeechee River, is a restored Confederate earthwork fortification. Constructed in 1861–62, it withstood nearly 2 years of bombardments before it finally fell on December 13, 1864, in a bayonet charge that ended General Sherman's infamous March to the Sea. There's a visitor center with historic exhibits and also walking trails and campsites.

Richmond Hill. © **912/727-2339**. Admission $4 adults, $3.50 seniors, $2.50 children 6 and over. Tues–Sat 8am–5pm.

Fort Pulaski   This national monument is 15 miles east of Savannah off U.S. 80 on Cockspur and McQueen islands at the very mouth of the Savannah River. It cost $1 million and took 25 tons of brick and 18 years of toil to finish. Yet it was captured in just 30 hours by Union forces. Completed in 1847 with walls 7½ feet thick, it was occupied by Confederate forces at the beginning of the war. However, on April 11, 1862, defense strategy changed worldwide when Union cannons, firing from more than a mile away on Tybee Island, overcame the masonry fortification. The effectiveness of rifled cannon (firing a heavier, bullet-shaped projectile with great accuracy at longer range) was clearly demonstrated. The new Union weapon marked the end of the era of masonry fortifications. The fort was pentagonally shaped, with galleries and drawbridges crossing the moat. You can still find shells from 1862 embedded in the walls. There are exhibits of the fort's history in the visitor center.

Cockspur and McQueen islands. © **912/786-5787**. Admission $3 adults, free for children 16 and under. Daily 9am–7pm. Closed Christmas.

Moments   **Martinis in the Cemetery**

All fans of *Midnight in the Garden of Good and Evil* must pay a visit to the now world-famous **Bonaventure Cemetery,** 330 Bonaventure Rd. (© **912/651-6843**), on the low-lying eastern edge of the city. Filled with obelisks and columns and dense shrubbery and moss-draped trees, it's open daily 8am to 5pm. You get here by taking Wheaton Street east out of downtown to Skidaway to Bonaventure Road.

This cemetery lies on the grounds of what was once a great oak-shaded plantation, built by Col. John Mulryne. In the late 1700s, the mansion caught fire during a formal dinner party; reportedly, the host quite calmly led his guests from the dining room and into the garden, where they settled in to finish eating while the house burned to the ground in front of them. At the end, the host and the guests threw their crystal glasses against the trunk of an old oak tree. It's said that on still nights you can hear the laughter and the crashing of the crystal. In The Book, Mary Harty calls the ruins the "scene of the Eternal Party. What better place, in Savannah, to rest in peace for all time—where the party goes on and on."

It is at the cemetery that John Berendt has martinis in silver goblets with Miss Harty, while they sit on the bench-gravestone

5 Cemeteries

Colonial Park Cemetery   The oldest burial ground (ca. 1750) in Savannah is filled with magnolia trees and is such a beautiful setting that the city turned it into a park in 1986. Many distinguished Georgians are buried here, none more famous than the two duelers who fought one of the most famous battles of insults in the state.

Button Gwinnett, one of the signers of the Declaration of Independence, is buried here. He died of wounds suffered in a duel with Gen. Lachlan McIntosh, another Georgia hero.

The feud between the two men stemmed from insults McIntosh leveled against Gwinnett after the abortive Georgia invasion of Florida in 1777. Infuriated, Gwinnett challenged McIntosh to a duel on what is now the cemetery grounds. Both men were shot in the thigh, at which point their seconds stopped the duel. McIntosh, though injured, had only sustained a flesh wound. Gwinnett's injury was far more serious, and he died 3 days after being taken to a of poet **Conrad Aiken.** She points out to the writer the double gravestone bearing the names of Dr. William F. Aiken and his wife, Anna, parents of Conrad. They both died on February 27, 1901, when Dr. Aiken killed his wife and then himself. The Aikens are buried in Lot #78H. Songwriter **Johnny Mercer** is buried in Lot #49H.

But not **Danny Hansford,** the blond hustler of the book. You can find his grave at Lot #6, Block: G-8 in the Greenwich Cemetery, next to Bonaventure. After entering Bonaventure, turn left immediately and take the straight path to Greenwich. Eventually, you'll see a small granite tile which says:

DANNY LEWIS HANSFORD
MARCH 1, 1960
MAY 2, 1981

Incidentally, **Jim Williams** is buried in Gordon, Georgia, a 3½-hour drive northwest of Savannah.

The "Bird Girl" statue, made famous by its appearance on the cover of The Book, now resides at the Telfair Museum of Art.

hospital. McIntosh was tried for murder but acquitted. Mrs. Gwinnett refused to condemn McIntosh for the death of her husband.

Nonetheless, other members of the Savannah colony turned on McIntosh, who left the city to take a command under George Washington.

In time, he redeemed himself by leading troops successfully at the Battle of Savannah in 1779. He became an esteemed citizen of Savannah in his later years. Those two enemies, Gwinnett and McIntosh, are buried very near each other.

201 E. Oglethorpe Ave. ℂ **912/651-6843**. www.ci.savannah.ga.us. Free admission. Daily 9am–5pm.

Laurel Grove South Cemetery   Many of the city's most prominent African Americans are buried in this cemetery, one of the oldest black cemeteries in America. Both antebellum plantation slaves and free blacks during the Reconstruction era were buried here, including Andrew Bryan (1716–1812), a pioneer Baptist preacher in the area.

802 W. Anderson St. ✆ **912/651-6772**. www.ci.savannah.ga.us. Free admission. Daily 8am–5pm.

6 Black History Sights

For a preview of a famous cemetery of African Americans, see "Cemeteries," above.

First African Baptist Church   This was the first African Baptist church built in America. It was established by George Leile, a slave whose master allowed him to preach to other slaves when they made visits to plantations along the Savannah River. Leile was granted his freedom in 1777 and later raised some $1,500 to purchase the present church from a white congregation. The black congregation rebuilt the church brick by brick, and it became the first brick building in Georgia to be owned by African Americans. The pews on either side of the organ are the work of African slaves.

23 Montgomery St., Franklin Sq. ✆ **912/233-2244**. www.firstafricanbc.org. Sun worship 8:30am and 11:30am.

First Bryan Baptist Church   A congregation of slaves purchased a lot on Bryan Street to build this place of worship. The land is the oldest parcel of real estate in America to be owned by blacks. As such, it has figured greatly over the years into the history of Savannah. In 1788 Rev. Andrew Bryan, a slave, was ordained as minister. With his preaching, Bryan aroused the fear of plantation owners, who tried to prevent him from holding meetings. Somehow Bryan managed to hold his devout group of followers together.

A slave insurrection in Haiti set off fears in Low Country plantations. Bryan and his brother, Sampson, were beaten savagely and imprisoned, and their meetinghouse was taken away. Sympathetic white preachers intervened and secured their release. After Bryan's owner, Jonathan Bryan, died, Andrew Bryan was able to purchase his freedom for 50 pounds sterling. He and his brother restored their church for African Americans. The former slave lived until 1812. In 1873 his church was torn down, and John Hogg designed a new church for the site.

559 W. Bryan St. ✆ **912/232-5526**. Free tours by appointment only.

Nicholsonboro Baptist Church   This church serves as a monument to an African-American community founded during the

Reconstruction days by 200 former slaves who relocated to Nicholsonboro from St. Catherine's Island. Eighteen settlers signed a $5,000 mortgage for 200 acres of land, paying it off in 5 years and receiving title. For a time they thrived as a fishing and farming community before falling on hard times. Eventually their economic base all but disappeared. Today this small clapboard church serves as a memorial to those early settlers. Some of the original pews and a porcelain doorknob remain from the original church, which had no electricity but was warmed by a wood-burning stove. In 1978 the church was placed on the National Register of Historic Places. The current Nicholsonboro Baptist Church (ca. 1890) is adjacent to the original structure and holds weekly services.

13319 White Bluff Rd. *C* **912/921-0566.** Tours available by appointment only. Take Bull St. south until it runs into White Bluff Rd.

Ralph Mark Gilbert Civil Rights Museum   Close to the Savannah Visitor Information Center, this pioneer museum opened in 1996. It's dedicated to the life and service of African Americans and their contributions to the civil rights movement in Savannah. Dr. Gilbert died in 1956 but was a leader in early efforts to gain educational, social, and political equity for African Americans in Savannah.

460 Martin Luther King Jr. Blvd. *C* **912/231-8900.** Admission $4 adults, $3 seniors, $2 children. Mon–Sat 9am–5pm.

St. Phillip Monumental A.M.E. Church   This was the first African Methodist Church to be established in Savannah. It was organized by Rev. A. L. Stanford in June 1865, the year the Civil War ended. The original church was destroyed by a storm in 1896, but was rebuilt into the church standing today.

1112 Jefferson St. *C* **912/233-8547.** Mon–Fri 9am–5pm.

Second African Baptist Church   This early African-American church (ca. 1802) was known for training more ministers—black or white—than any other church in the country. Two historic events took place here. In 1864 Gen. William Tecumseh Sherman read the Emancipation Proclamation to Savannah citizens, promising the newly freed slaves 40 acres and a mule. Dr. Martin Luther King, Jr., proclaimed his "I have a dream" sermon here before the famous march on Washington in 1963.

123 Houston St. *C* **912/233-6163.** www.secondafrican.org. Mon–Fri 10am–2pm.

A Visit to the Murder House

The Mercer Williams House, paid for by Gen. Hugh W. Mercer, great-grandfather of Johnny Mercer, was completed around 1868. It became known as "the envy of Savannah." Decades later, it was rumored that Jacqueline Onassis wanted to purchase it for use as a private home.

Mostly its fame was promulgated by the John Berendt book *Midnight in the Garden of Good and Evil*. It was here, in May 1981, as related in the book, that the wealthy homosexual antiques dealer Jim Williams fatally shot his lover, that blond "walking streak of sex," Danny Hansford, age 21. The house was also the setting where Williams gave his legendary Christmas parties each year. In January 1991, Williams died of a heart attack at the age of 59 in the same room where he'd shot Hansford.

For years, heirs to Williams's estate have been downplaying its prurience and emphasizing, with much justification, Williams's role as a bon vivant and the savior of at least 60 historic houses in and around Savannah.

The Mercer Williams House is open for tours. Buy your ticket in the carriage house behind the Mercer Williams House, inside a gift shop loaded with objects of which Jim, the decorator, might have approved, and a few that he might have found sappy and sentimental. You'll be ushered into one of an ongoing series of tours, each lasting about 30 or 35 minutes. Tours depart from the Carriage House Shop, at the compound's back entrance (430 Whitaker St.).

7 Literary Landmarks

Long before John Berendt's *Midnight in the Garden of Good and Evil*, there were other writers associated with Savannah. Chief of these is **Flannery O'Connor** (1924–64), one of the South's greatest writers, author of *Wise Blood* (1952) and *The Violent Bear It Away* (1960). She is also known for her short stories, including the collection *A Good Man Is Hard to Find* (1955). She won the O. Henry Award three times. You can visit the **Flannery O'Connor Childhood Home,**

Don't think for a second that questions about Williams's sexuality, his promiscuity, or his murder will be engaged. Guides firmly advise before tours even begin that these are AAA tours (including only questions about art, architecture, and antiques). Photos are rigidly forbidden, and a strong-willed guide will emphatically urge you "not to touch, drool on, dribble on, or engage the furniture or art objects in any way."

You'll learn that the Mercer family commissioned the design of the house but no member ever actually lived here; that a dry moat surrounds the house, allowing for light and air to enter the lower floors; that there's a ballroom on the second floor, but because of fire codes, no one is allowed upstairs.

The house has been used as the setting for movies, including Clint Eastwood's film of the book, *Swamp Thing*, and *Return of Swamp Thing*. It is gorgeously furnished in a style that befits a sophisticated millionaire. It is not an authentic re-creation of a Federal or mid-Victorian home, thanks to the presence of comfortable 20th-century sofas, personalized photos, and art objects, and the eclectic vision of its style setter.

The tour's main benefit is that it makes you realize that Jim Williams was a helluva benefactor to the Savannah that has so richly profited from his efforts ever since.

The Mercer Williams House Museum is at 429 Bull St. (© **912/236-6352**). Admission is $13 for adults and seniors and $8 for students with ID (both college and grad school). Tours run every 40 minutes daily from 10:30am to 4:30pm.

207 E. Charlton St. (© **912/921-5618**). The house is open only Saturday and Sunday from 1 to 4pm. Admission is free.

Conrad Aiken (1889–1973), the American poet, critic, writer, and Pulitzer Prize winner, was born in Savannah. He lived at 228 (for the first 11 years of his life) and also at 230 E. Oglethorpe Ave. (for the last 11 years of his life). In *Midnight in the Garden of Good and Evil*, Mary Harty and author John Berendt sip martinis at the bench-shaped tombstone of Aiken in Bonaventure Cemetery (see "Martinis in the Cemetery," above).

8 Especially for Kids

Much of Savannah is kid friendly, including walks along the waterfront and across the cobblestones of the Historic District. Kids particularly enjoy such attractions as the **Ships of the Sea Maritime Museum** and the **Civil War forts** on the outskirts. They're especially fond of the beaches at Tybee Island; see chapter 10. Here's one more sight of interest.

Massie Heritage Interpretation Center *(Kids*   Here's a stop in the Historic District for the kids. Geared to school-age children, this center features various exhibits about Savannah, including such subjects as the city's Greek, Roman, and Gothic architecture; the Victorian era; and a history of public education. Other exhibits include a period costume room and a 19th-century classroom, where children can experience a classroom environment from days gone by.

207 E. Gordon St. ℂ 912/201-5070. Admission $3 for all ages. Mon–Fri 9am–4pm.

A Visit to the U.S. Custom House

The U.S. Custom House is a Greek Revival building, designed by John Norris and completed in 1852. It is the oldest federal building in Georgia. It is an austere granite temple with a "Tower-of-the-Winds" portico. It lies on historic ground: James Edward Oglethorpe lived in the area, and John Wesley delivered his first sermon in Savannah on this site. Today, if you look across Bay Street near Savannah City Hall, you'll see cannons that were presented to the Chatham Artillery in 1791 by George Washington.

A one-story frame house originally stood on the site in 1733 and was rented by Oglethorpe. All the granite in the present building was brought down from New England by sea or rail. The granite columns out front weighed 15 to 20 tons each; it took 30 days to transport each column up the 30-foot bluff from the river to the site of the Customs House. Once there, it took yet another month to move the mammoth pillars into place. The carved capitals were modeled from the pattern of a tobacco leaf.

The U.S. Custom House stands at 1 E. Bay St. (ℂ 912/652-4264), and can be viewed at any time.

9 Organized Tours

If it's a *Midnight in the Garden of Good and Evil* tour you seek, then you've obviously come to the right place. Virtually every tour group in town offers tours of the *Midnight* sites, many of which are included on their regular agenda. Ask any of the tour groups. Note that some tour outfits will accommodate only groups, so if you're traveling alone or as a pair, be sure to make that known when you make your tour reservations.

A delightful way to see Savannah is by horse-drawn carriage. An authentic antique carriage carries you over cobblestone streets as the coachman spins a tale of the town's history. The 1-hour tour ($20 for adults, $10 for children 5–11) covers 15 of the 20 squares. Reservations are required, so contact **Carriage Tours of Savannah** at ℂ **912-236-6756** or www.carriagetoursofsavannah.com.

Old Town Trolley Tours (ℂ **912/233-0083;** www.trolleytours. com) operates tours of the Historic District, with pickups at most downtown inns and hotels ($23 for adults, $10 for children 4–12), as well as a 1-hour **Haunted History** tour detailing Savannah's ghostly past (and present). Call to reserve for all tours.

Savannah Walks, Inc., from a headquarters at Abercorn Street just south of Reynolds Square (ℂ **912/238-9255;** www.savannah walks.com), offers well-orchestrated walks for three distinct moods and manifestations of Savannah's illustrious past. The most mainstream of the walks is the *Savannah Stroll,* a well-articulated ramble through the city's most central parks and thoroughfares—an anecdotal introduction to the city's history, lore, and legend. There is also a tour focusing on Savannah's triumphs, torments, and despair during the War between the States. Both of these tours last 90 minutes, and are offered twice daily, at 10am and 1pm. After dark, the venue gets more mystical and spookier, with the Savannah Ghost Tour, a 90-minute exposure to the city's flair for the macabre, with departures at 7:30pm and 9:30pm. When business warrants, there is a tour at 5:30pm as well. Each of the above-mentioned tours requires an advance reservation, and costs $15 for adults, and $7 for children 6 to 14. Your guide might be a part-time student at Savannah College of Art and Design (SCAD) or an older, long-term resident of the city, but the likelihood is high that he or she will have some dramatic flair and a gift for oratory as well.

Gray Line Savannah Tours (ℂ **866/374-8687**) has joined forces with **Historic Savannah Foundation Tours** to feature narrated bus tours of museums, squares, parks, and homes. Reservations must be made for all tours, and most have starting points at the visitor center and pickup points at various hotels. Tours cost $10 per person.

Riverboat cruises are offered aboard the *Savannah River Queen,* operated by the River Street Riverboat Co., 9 E. River St. (*©* **800/786-6404** or 912/232-6404; www.savannah-riverboat.com). You get a glimpse of Savannah as Oglethorpe saw it back in 1733. You'll see the historic cotton warehouses lining River Street and the statue of *Savannah's Waving Girl* as the huge modern freighters see it when they arrive daily at Savannah. The fare is $18 for adults and $11 for children 12 and under.

Ghost Talk Ghost Walk takes you through Colonial Savannah on a journey filled with stories and legends based on Margaret Debolt's book *Savannah Spectres and Other Strange Tales.* If you're not a believer at the beginning of the guided tour, you may be at the end. The tour starts at Reynolds Square. For information, call *©* **912/233-3896.** Hours for tour departures can vary. The cost is $10 for adults and $5 for children 12 and under.

Low Country River Excursions offers narrated nature cruises, departing from the Bull River Marina, 8005 Old Tybee Rd. (U.S. 80 E.). Call *©* **912/898-9222** for more information. Passengers are taken on a 40-foot pontoon boat, *Natures Way,* for an encounter with friendly bottle-nosed dolphins. Both scenery and wildlife unfold during the 90-minute cruise down the Bull River. Trips are offered daily noon, 2pm, and sunset spring through fall, weather permitting. The fare is $25 for adults, $12 for seniors, and $10 for children 11 and under. There's a 30-passenger limit.

10 Sports & Outdoor Activities

Recreational opportunities abound, and many outfitters in the Savannah area stand ready to hook you up with the action.

BIKING   Savannah doesn't usually have a lot of heavy traffic except during rush hours, so you can bicycle up and down the streets of the Historic District, visiting as many of the green squares as you wish (note that you must *walk* your bike across the squares). There's no greater city bicycle ride in all of Georgia. The best outfitter is **Bicycle Link,** at 408 Martin Luther King Jr. Blvd. (*©* **912/355-4771**), which rents bikes for $15 per half-day, or $20 per full day. Hours are Monday to Saturday 10am to 6pm. Many inns and hotels also provide bikes for their guests.

CAMPING   The **Savannah Oak RV Resort,** 805 Fort Argyle Rd. (*©* **912/748-4000**), is 2½ miles west of I-95, 4½ miles west of

Exploring the Savannah National Wildlife Refuge

A 10-minute drive across the river from downtown Savannah delivers you to the wild, even though you can see the city's industrial and port complexes in the background. The **Savannah National Wildlife Refuge** ✿ (✆ **912/652-4415**; www.fws.gov/savannah), which overflows into South Carolina, was the site of rice plantations in the 1800s and is today a wide expanse of woodland and marsh, ideal for a scenic drive, a canoe ride, a picnic, and most definitely a look at a variety of animals.

From Savannah, get on U.S. Hwy. 17A, crossing the Talmadge Bridge. It's about 8 miles to the intersection of highways 17 and 17A, where you turn left toward the airport. You'll see the refuge entrance, marked LAUREL HILL WILDLIFE DRIVE, after going some 2 miles. Inside the gate to the refuge is a visitor center that distributes maps and leaflets.

Laurel Hill Wildlife Drive goes on for 4 miles or so. It's possible to bike along this trail. People come here mainly to spy on the alligators, and sightings are almost guaranteed. However, other creatures in the wild abound, including bald eagles and otters. Hikers can veer off the drive and go along Cistern Trail, leading to Recess Island. Because the trail is marked, there's little danger of getting lost.

Nearly 40 miles of dikes are open to birders and backpackers. Canoeists float along tidal creeks, which are fingers of the Savannah River. Fishing and hunting are allowed under special conditions and in the right seasons. Deer and squirrels are commonplace; rarer is the feral hog known along coastal Georgia and South Carolina.

Visits are possible daily from sunrise to sunset. For more information, go to **www.fws.gov/savannah** or write to the Savannah National Wildlife Refuge, U.S. Fish & Wildlife Service, Savannah Coastal Refuges, PO Box 8487, Savannah, GA 31412.

U.S. 17, and 12 miles from the Savannah Historic District on the banks of the Ogeechee River. Facilities include full hookups, LP gas service, a store, self-service gas and diesel fuel, a dump station, hot showers, laundry facilities, and a pool. The rate is $39 for an RV hookup.

Open year-round, **Skidaway Island State Park** (✆ **912/598-2300;** www.gastateparks.org/info/skidaway) offers 88 camping sites with hookups, costing $25. On arrival, you purchase a $3 parking pass valid for your entire stay. The grounds include 1- and 3-mile nature trails, grills, picnic tables, a pool, a bathhouse, and laundry facilities. Also open year-round, the **River's End Campground and RV Park,** Polk Street, Tybee Island (✆ **912/786-5518;** www.rivers endcampground.com), consists of 128 sites featuring full hookups, with groceries and a beach nearby. Tent sites cost $34 to $39 per day and RV sites $45 to $55 per day.

DIVING The **Diving Locker-Ski Chalet,** 74 W. Montgomery Cross Rd. (✆ **912/927-6604;** www.divinglockerskichalet.com), offers a wide selection of equipment and services for various water-sports. Scuba classes cost $225 for a series of weekday evening les-sons and $240 for a series of lessons beginning on Friday evening. A full scuba-gear package, including a buoyancy-control device, tank, and wet suit, is included. It's open Monday to Friday 10am to 6pm and Saturday 10am to 5pm.

FISHING **Amick's Deep Sea Fishing,** 6902 Sand Nettles Dr. (✆ **912/897-6759;** www.amicksdeepseafishing.com), offers daily charters featuring a 41-foot 1993 custom-built boat. The rate is $156 per person and includes rod, reel, bait, and tackle. Bring your own lunch, though beer and soda are sold on board. Reservations are recommended, but if you show up 30 minutes before the scheduled departure, there may be space available. The boat departs at 7am and returns at 5pm.

GOLF **Bacon Park,** Shorty Cooper Drive (✆ **912/354-2625;** www.baconparkgolf.com), is a 27-hole course with greens fees of $21 to $23 for an 18-hole round, including carts. Golf facilities include a lighted driving range, putting greens, and a pro shop. It's open daily dawn to dusk.

Henderson Golf Club, 1 Henderson Dr. (✆ **912/920-4653;** www.hendersongolfclub.com), includes an 18-hole championship course, a lighted driving range, a PGA professional staff, and golf instruction and schools. The greens fees are $39 Monday to Friday and $44 Saturday and Sunday. It's open daily 7am to 10pm.

Or try the 9-hole **Mary Calder,** West Congress Street (✆ **912/238-7100**), where the greens fees, including cart, are $27 per day

Monday to Friday and $39 per day Saturday and Sunday. It's open daily 7:30am to 7pm (to 5:30pm in winter).

JOGGING   "The most beautiful city to jog in"—that's how the president of the Savannah Striders Club characterizes Savannah. He's correct. The historic avenues provide an exceptional setting for your run. The Convention & Visitors Bureau can provide you with a map outlining three of the Striders Club's routes: Heart of Savannah YMCA Course, 3 miles; Symphony Race Course, 5 miles; and Children's Run Course, 5 miles.

NATURE WATCHES   Explore the wetlands with **Palmetto Coast Charters,** Lazaretto Creek Marina, Tybee Island (© 912/786-5403). Charters include trips to the Barrier Islands for shell collecting and watching for otter, mink, birds, and other wildlife. The captain is a naturalist and a professor, so he can answer your questions. Palmetto also features a dolphin-watch usually conducted daily 4:30 to 6:30pm, when the shrimp boats come in with dolphins following behind. The cost is $150 for up to six people for a minimum of 2 hours, plus $50 for each extra hour.

RECREATIONAL PARKS   **Bacon Park** (see "Golf," above, and "Tennis," below) includes 1,021 acres, with archery, golf, tennis, and baseball fields. **Daffin Park,** 1500 E. Victory Dr. (© 912/351-3851), features playgrounds, tennis, basketball, baseball, a pool, a lake pavilion, and picnic grounds. Both parks are open daily May to September 8am to 11pm and October to April 8am to 10pm.

Located at Montgomery Cross Road and Sallie Mood Drive, **Lake Mayer Park** (© 912/652-6780) consists of 75 acres featuring a multitude of activities, such as public fishing and boating, lighted jogging and bicycle trails, a playground, and pedal-boat rentals.

SAILING   **Sail Harbor,** 618 Wilmington Island Rd. (© 912/897-2896; www.sailharbormarina.com), features the Catalina 25 boat, costing $150 per full day, with an extra day costing $125. It's open Tuesday to Saturday 10am to 6pm and Sunday 12:30 to 5:30pm.

TENNIS   **Bacon Park** (see "Golf," above; © 912/351-3850) offers 16 lighted courts open Monday to Thursday 9am to 9pm, Friday 9am to 4pm and 5 to 8pm, and Saturday 9am to 1am. **Forsyth Park,** at Drayton and Gaston streets (© 912/351-3850), has four courts open daily 7am to 9pm. Both parks charge $5 per hour. The use of the eight lighted courts at **Lake Mayer Park,** Montgomery Cross Road, costs nothing. They are open daily 8am to 11pm.

7

Savannah Strolls

The only real way to discover Savannah is in your walking shoes. Be sure to wear sturdy ones along the often-cobbled streets. Walking is a fun way to encounter the city up close.

| | SAVANNAH'S HISTORIC |
| WALKING TOUR 1 | SQUARES |

Start:	City Hall.
Finish:	Whitefield Square.
Time:	2½ hours.
Best Times:	Any day from 9am to 5pm, when there's less traffic.
Worst Times:	Between 5 and 6:30pm, when stores are closing and traffic is heavier. Also after dark.

Much of the charm of Savannah's historic core derives from the layout of the city. The series of verdant and rhythmically ordered squares was mapped out by Oglethorpe in the early 18th century. This tour exposes you to the allure of at least a dozen of these squares, with historic highlights en route.

Begin at the corner of Bay Street and Bull Street, directly at the foundation of:

1 City Hall
Completed in 1906, City Hall is one of the grandest civic buildings in the country. Its gilt-clad copper dome is designed in the neo-Renaissance style. The two floors of this building open onto the spot where, on May 22, 1819, the SS *Savannah* set sail, becoming the first steamship to cross the Atlantic.

Turn your back to it and walk along Bull Street. Within 2 very short blocks, you'll be at **Johnson Square,** the center of which is marked with a soaring obelisk commemorating Nathanael Greene, and the edges of which are almost entirely lined with banks and insurance companies.

Walking Tour: Savannah's Historic Squares

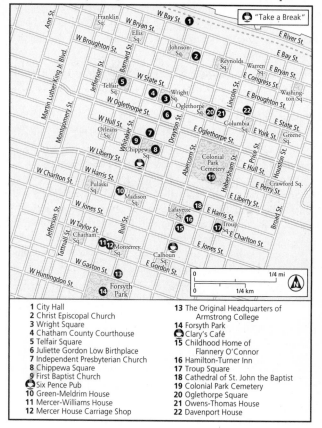

"Take a Break"

1 City Hall
2 Christ Episcopal Church
3 Wright Square
4 Chatham County Courthouse
5 Telfair Square
6 Juliette Gordon Low Birthplace
7 Independent Presbyterian Church
8 Chippewa Square
9 First Baptist Church
   Six Pence Pub
10 Green-Meldrim House
11 Mercer-Williams House
12 Mercer House Carriage Shop

13 The Original Headquarters of
    Armstrong College
14 Forsyth Park
   Clary's Café
15 Childhood Home of
    Flannery O'Connor
16 Hamilton-Turner Inn
17 Troup Square
18 Cathedral of St. John the Baptist
19 Colonial Park Cemetery
20 Oglethorpe Square
21 Owens-Thomas House
22 Davenport House

A noteworthy exception to this is on the square's eastern edge:

2 Christ Episcopal Church

Established in 1733, it is separately recommended under "Historic Churches & Synagogues." See p. 78.

Cross over Broughton Street, downtown Savannah's main shopping street, and continue walking south on Bull Street.

After Bull Street's intersection with State Street, you'll enter:

3 Wright Square

The square is named for Sir James Wright, the third and last colonial governor of Georgia. A large boulder marks the grave of

Tomochichi, the Yamacraw Indian chief who befriended Oglethorpe's colonists. A monument here honors William Washington Gordon I, early Georgia financier and founder of the Central Georgia Railway.

The glistening neo-Renaissance bulk that rises from the western edge of Wright Square is:

❹ The Chatham County Courthouse

Much modified from its original design, the courthouse is evocative of the civic pride Savannah exhibited around the turn of the 19th century.

From Wright Square walk west along State Street for 2 blocks to:

❺ Telfair Square

In distinct contrast to the stately grandeur of Wright Square and Johnson Square, Telfair Square is relatively unadorned—it's basically a patch of manicured greenery, inhabited by squirrels and a distinct sense of residential, rather than "official," neighborhood life.

Located between York and State streets, the square was originally called St. James's Square but was renamed for the Telfair family in 1883. Modern federal buildings are located on two sides of the square. It's also home to the **Telfair Museum of Art,** the royal governor's residence from 1760 until the end of the Revolutionary War. Today it's a museum of the arts. See p. 77.

Exit from Telfair Square by walking for 2 blocks east along West York Street until you return once again to Wright Square. At Wright Square, turn south on Bull Street and walk for 2 blocks until you reach Oglethorpe Street, a street you'll recognize by the strip of greenery running down its middle.

Turn left on Oglethorpe for a half-block until you reach:

❻ Juliette Gordon Low's Birthplace

Many informed locals describe this elegant stone mansion at 10 E. Oglethorpe St. as one of the two or three best-furnished historic houses in Savannah. See p. 76 for more information.

Retrace your steps along Oglethorpe Street to Bull Street and continue walking south.

Within a few steps, on your left, you'll see the classical white bulk of the:

❼ Independent Presbyterian Church

This church's New England–born organist and music director, Lowell Mason (1792–1872), wrote at least three hymns that are among the best known of any Christian liturgy, including "My Faith Looks Up to Thee" and "Nearer, My God to Thee," the melody that was played by the *Titanic's* orchestra as the ship sank into the depths of the North Atlantic.

Continue walking south along Bull Street to:

⑧ Chippewa Square

Located along Bull Street, between Perry and Hull streets, this square holds a bronze figure immortalizing General Oglethorpe, done by Daniel Chester French, dean of America sculptors. The square is visited today by hordes wanting to see not Georgia's founder but the bench where Tom Hanks sat in *Forrest Gump.* Unfortunately, the movie bench isn't here—it was only a prop—but plop yourself down somewhere on the square anyway and have a few minutes of relaxation.

On the west side of Chippewa Square stands:

⑨ First Baptist Church

This church was established in 1800, although the limestone facade you see today dates from 1922. This was one of the very few churches to remain open throughout the course of the Civil War.

After passing through Chippewa Square, continue walking south along Bull Street. On the right, at 245 Bull St., immediately adjacent to an old-fashioned, red-painted replica of a London phone booth, you'll find your first place to:

TAKE A BREAK
Cozy, pine-paneled, and (mercifully) air-conditioned against the sometimes staggering heat, the **Six Pence Pub**, at 245 Bull St. (🕾 **912/233-3151**), is a fine choice for salads, sandwiches, hot or iced tea, pastries, shepherd's pie, and bangers and mash. In its quirky way, the pub is famous in Savannah for its role as a movie location. It is here that the character played by Julia Roberts confronts her husband, the philandering character played by Dennis Quaid, in *Something to Talk About.* For more on this cheerful pub, see p. 67.

After your refueling, continue walking south along Bull Street 'til you reach Madison Square, site of:

⑩ Green-Meldrim House

This house functioned as Sherman's headquarters during the Civil War. Built for a total cost of $93,000 in the Gothic Revival style in the early 1850s for an English-born merchant, it was, at the time of construction, one of the most expensive houses ever built in Georgia. See p. 76 for more information.

At Madison Square, turn right onto West Harris Street for 2 blocks 'til you reach Pulaski Square. Walk to its southernmost edge (Charlton St.), heading east along Charlton Street until you find yourself once again in Madison Square. From here, turn south (right) onto Bull Street once again, walking for 4 blocks to Monterey Square. There, on the west side of the square is the:

⓫ Mercer Williams House Museum

This splendid Italianate redbrick mansion at 429 Bull St. was built around 1860. It was here in May 1981 that wealthy antiques dealer Jim Williams, about 50, fatally shot his lover-assistant, blond "walking streak of sex" Danny Hansford, age 21. Williams claimed that he'd shot Danny in self-defense because Danny was waving a gun around and taking shots. Williams was tried three times in Savannah. He was found guilty twice, though each conviction was overturned; the third time was declared a mistrial because of a hung jury. He finally was acquitted at a fourth trial, held in Augusta, far removed from the intrigues of the Savannah swamps. As a result, Jim Williams became the first person in Georgia to be tried four times for murder.

Mercer Williams House is also where each year Williams gave his legendary Christmas parties: Friday night for the cream of society and Saturday night "for gentlemen only." Note the lavender interior shutters on the second story's right-hand window. They shield from the sun what Williams called his "playroom," site of *trompe l'oeil* baroque-style frescoes and one of Savannah's most valuable pipe organs. The shooting occurred (as you face the house) in Williams's study, illuminated by the ground floor's right-hand window.

In January 1990, Jim Williams died of a heart attack at 59. As recounted in the book *Midnight in the Garden of Good and Evil,* a strange coincidence occurred at this time: Williams died in the room where he'd killed Hansford, and his body was found behind his desk in the exact spot where his body would have been found in 1981 if Hansford had shot at him and not missed.

Though Jacqueline Kennedy Onassis reportedly once offered Williams $2 million for the house, it's today inhabited by Williams's sister, Dorothy Williams Kingery, who allowed Clint Eastwood's film crew complete access—all for a price, mind you, despite her condemnation of the "circus atmosphere" surrounding her brother's trials and the publication of The Book.

And, no, Johnny Mercer never lived in this house, though his great-grandfather built it.

Monterey Square itself is one of the most beautiful in Savannah. The statue in this square represents Lady Liberty atop a stone plinth, and is dedicated to Casimir Pulaski, the gallant Polish military officer of Revolutionary War fame. He looks back archly over his shoulder at Mercer Williams House. During production of The Film, the statue was removed for restoration, so Clint Eastwood had a copy constructed of plywood, Styrofoam, and plastic.

In the back of the Mercer Williams House still stands:

⑫ The Carriage House Shop

It was here, in Mercer Williams House's detached carriage house at 430 Whitaker St., that Williams offered for sale some of the South's finest antiques, lovely pieces that he'd discovered and restored. He even managed to run this business while he was in jail after his second trial. The property is now a gift shop where you can buy souvenirs related to The Book and Savannah, as well as tickets to tour Mercer Williams House Museum.

From Monterey Square, continue your southbound trajectory on Bull Street. Within 2 short blocks, at the corner of Gaston Street, on the west side of the street stands:

⑬ The Original Headquarters of Armstrong College

Conceived in 1919 as the home of a local millionaire, and built of white brick and granite, it functioned as the headquarters of Armstrong College between 1935 and 1966. Today, it contains the offices of a local law firm.

Bull Street's run through the Historic District comes to an end at:

⑭ Forsyth Park

This park is the largest swath of greenery in historic Savannah. From your perspective at the southern terminus of Bull Street, you can see, in the middle distance, the sprays of what is the most-photographed fountain in the South.

Now, turn left (eastward) along East Gaston Street to the corner of Abercorn Street, and then turn left (northward), and walk for 2 short blocks 'til you reach Calhoun Square. The sprawling brownish-pink building that dominates its southern edge is the **Massie Community School House.** Also opening onto this square is the cathedral-like **Wesley Monumental United Methodist Church** (p. 80). Continue walking northward on Abercorn Street. On the right-hand side of the street is Clary's Café, one of the most famous coffee shop–luncheonettes in the South. See p. 66 for a full review.

Time to:

TAKE A BREAK
Savannah has been enjoying great food and conversation at Clary's Café, 404 Abercorn St., at Jones Street (② 912/233-0402), since 1903. Today, along with flame-broiled burgers, the store carries souvenirs of The Book, not only T-shirts but also postcards of Lady Chablis. Both Chablis ("My mama took my name from a wine bottle") and author John Berendt have frequented the place for its good-tasting food. When we last encountered her ladyship here, she informed us that all this "fuss about The Book is helping [her] save up the big ones for [her] retirement one day."

After your refueling, continue walking north on Abercorn Street 'til you reach Lafayette Square. When you get here turn right onto Charlton Street 'til you reach the square's southeast corner. At 207 E. Charlton St. is the:

⓯ Childhood Home of Flannery O'Connor

The author of such classics as *Wise Blood* and *The Violent Bear It Away* is one of the South's greatest writers. When in Savannah, she lived at this address; for more details, see p. 86.

On the east side of Lafayette Square is the:

⓰ Hamilton-Turner Inn

Built in the 1870s for the then-astronomical sum of $100,000, almost obscenely ostentatious at the time, this building is featured as the notorious home of two of the characters (Joe and Mandy Odum) in John Berendt's *Midnight in the Garden of Good and Evil*. Since 1997, it's been operated as a respectable and very elegant B&B. It's separately recommended in chapter 4, "Where to Stay in Savannah."

Now, turn right (eastward) on Charlton Street (it's the one that separates the Flannery O'Connor home from the Hamilton-Turner Inn) and walk for 2 blocks to:

⓱ Troup Square

Entirely surrounded by historic private homes, this is considered by many aficionados to be the most beautiful and architecturally perfect of the Savannah squares. From its center rises an astrolabe.

Walk to the north end of Troup Square, then turn left (westward) onto Harris Street, which will bring you back to the northern edge of the previously visited Lafayette Square. Immediately on your right are the soaring twin Victorian Gothic needles of the oldest Catholic Church in Georgia.

⓲ Cathedral of St. John the Baptist

Organized in 1799, this is the seat of the Diocese of Savannah. See p. 78 for more information.

Turn right (northward) onto Abercorn Street, and walk for a few blocks until, on your right, behind an iron fence, you'll see:

⑲ Colonial Park Cemetery

It functioned as Savannah's burial ground from 1750 to 1853, and as such, it's loaded with the graves of and memorials to many heroes of the American Revolution. In 1896, it was designated a city park. See p. 82.

Cross over the double traffic lanes of East Oglethorpe Avenue, and continue walking north along Abercorn Street until you reach:

⑳ Oglethorpe Square

Mapped out in 1742, the square between State and York streets honors, of course, Gen. James Oglethorpe, founder of Georgia.

Rising on the northeastern edge of the square is the:

㉑ Owens-Thomas House

This is the most historically intriguing and most lavishly and authentically furnished historic home in Savannah, with strong links to the 18th-century aristocracy of England and to the Marquis de Lafayette (p. 77). From here, walk 2 blocks east along either East State Street or East President's Street. Within 2 short blocks, you'll find yourself in Columbia Square.

From its northwest edge rises the elegant outlines of:

㉒ Davenport House

This is the building that caused all the ruckus back in the days when historic Savannah risked being torn down. It's more famous for its exterior, whose proportions are believed to be "perfect," than for the quality of its interior furnishings. (It has a worthy collection of porcelain, but the furniture is nowhere near the equal of that in the Owens-Thomas House.) See p. 76. Your visit to Davenport House marks the end of this walking tour.

WALKING TOUR 2   THE RIVERWALK

Start:	Bull Street.
Finish:	The Riverfront.
Time:	2 hours.
Best Times:	Any day from 9am to 5pm.
Worst Times:	Between 5 and 6:30pm.

Begin your tour at the northernmost terminus of Bull Street, at the corner of
Bay Street, at:

❶ City Hall

Built between 1903 and 1906, City Hall is capped with a soaring
cupola in the Renaissance Revival style. You can enter the lobby of
this monument Monday to Friday 8am to 5pm for a view of its elaborate mosaics and a three-tiered row of circular balconies that extend
upward to an elaborate circular stained-glass skylight at the top. In
the lobby is a small-scale exhibit of the role that the building has
played in the region's history. Between 1986 and 1987, an anonymous philanthropist paid $200,000 to have the copper-clad cupola
of the building clad in gold leaf. Films that have been shot in or
around the building include the 1962 version of *Cape Fear,* with
Gregory Peck and Robert Mitchum, as well as *The Gingerbread Man*
(1998) and *The Legend of Bagger Vance* (2000).

After you exit City Hall, take a very short detour to the west to a
point directly in front of the Hyatt Regency Savannah Hotel.

A large bronze plaque lies very close to both a granite marker and a marble
bench from around 1906 that commemorate:

❷ Yamacraw Bluff

It was here, in 1733, that Oglethorpe pitched his tent after his long
sea-and-land voyage from England. Today, it's credited as the site
where the fledgling colony of Georgia began. Now, retrace your
steps back to the entrance to City Hall, and continue walking left
(eastward).

Immediately across Bay Street, on the southeast corner of Bull Street, rises the
granite, Grecian-style portico of the:

❸ U.S. Custom House

Its six soaring columns have "Temple of the Winds" capitals, a style
that's rare in Savannah. Its interior can't be visited, so remain on the
same side of Bay Street as City Hall, and continue walking eastward.

Within about 30 paces, you'll see a covered, open-air pavilion containing:

❹ The Washington Guns

Captured by George Washington during the Revolutionary War's
Battle of Yorktown, these guns were donated by him to the Savannah militia after they feted him lavishly during his visit to Savannah
several years after the end of the American Revolution. Since then,
they've been fired as a welcome gesture to VIPs who have included
James Monroe, the Marquis de Lafayette, James Polk, Millard Fill-
more, Chester A. Arthur, Jefferson Davis, Grover Cleveland,
William McKinley, William H. Taft, and FDR. Interestingly, one of

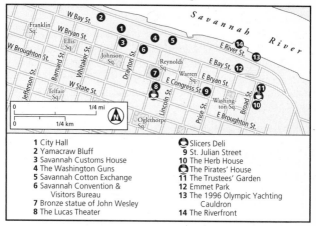

1 City Hall
2 Yamacraw Bluff
3 Savannah Customs House
4 The Washington Guns
5 Savannah Cotton Exchange
6 Savannah Convention &
  Visitors Bureau
7 Bronze statue of John Wesley
8 The Lucas Theater

🍴 Slicers Deli
9 St. Julian Street
10 The Herb House
🍴 The Pirates' House
11 The Trustees' Garden
12 Emmet Park
13 The 1996 Olympic Yachting
  Cauldron
14 The Riverfront

the two guns bears the insignia of English king George III, the other, the coat of arms of the French king Louis XIV.

Now, continue walking eastward along the north side of Bay Street.

Within about 30 more paces, you'll see a fountain spewing water from the mouth of a terra-cotta gryphon (a lion with wings), marking the rust-colored brick facade of the:

⑤ Savannah Cotton Exchange

The former exchange building now houses the Solomon's Lodge Number 1 of the Free Masons. When it was built it 1887, it was the major center for cotton trading. An example of the Romantic Revival period, it became one of the first buildings in America to use "air rights" and was erected completely over a public street. Its wrought-iron railing honors famous writers and politicians.

Immediately across the roaring traffic of Bay Street rises the severely dignified Doric portico of the:

⑥ Savannah Convention & Visitors Bureau

At 101 E. Bay St. you'll find the most complete and comprehensive array of printed information, often in the form of brochures, in town. The building's soaring and stately looking interior was originally conceived in the 20th century as a bank.

Leave the shade of the live oak trees that rise above you on Bay Street and turn right onto Abercorn Street.

Within 2 very short blocks, you'll reach Reynolds Square, which is dominated by a:

➐ Bronze Statue of John Wesley

This monument honors the founder of Methodism and a figure pivotal to the history of Savannah. Wesley is dressed in the vestments of his former role as a minister of the Church of England. On the western edge of the square, notice the Planters Inn and the Olde Pink House Restaurant, separately recommended in chapters 4 and 5, respectively.

On the south side of Reynolds Square is:

➑ The Lucas Theater

This Art Deco movie palace is now used as a performance-art showcase by the Savannah College of Art and Design, among others.

A few paces to the south, if you're hungry, consider a stop to:

TAKE A BREAK
Slicers Deli, at 42 Abercorn St. (© **912/236-1458**), is open Monday to Friday 7:30am to 3pm and Saturday and Sunday 10:30am to 3pm. It's the most recent incarnation of Beth Bolton's locally popular deli. Its predecessor, established in 1984 in a location a few blocks away, is cited as one of downtown Savannah's first New York–style delis. Don't expect anything fancy: The format is heavy on plastic, and you'll place your order for breakfast or lunchtime salads and sandwiches directly at the counter. But the service is cheerful and the prices are relatively affordable.

Now, return to the Lucas Theater and turn eastward onto East Congress Street. Within 2 short blocks, you'll find yourself in Warren Square. Pass through Warren Square, noting how the neighborhood has become more stately looking, more residential, and more architecturally "important." Depart from Warren Square at the eastern (most distant) end from where you entered, taking care to exit from:

➒ St. Julian Street

The short length of houses, about 2 blocks, lining St. Julian Street between Warren and Washington squares is particularly rich in Federal and mid-19th-century architecture, much of it restored by early pioneers during the early 1980s after the neighborhood had devolved into a virtual slum. Don't be shy about wandering through the surrounding streets for more insights into this, one of downtown Savannah's loveliest and most elegantly understated neighborhoods. Also note the pavement along this stretch of St. Julian Street: It's one of the few remaining oyster-shell pavements left in a city where many equivalent sections have been covered with more modern building materials.

Continue your eastbound walk through Washington Square, which competes with Troup Square (to the south, and visited as part of our Walking Tour 1) as the most beautiful square in Savannah. Pass through Washington Square, admiring the architecture along it and its side street, until you come to the wide asphalt thoroughfare of East Broad Street, where you turn left.

At 25 E. Broad St. is the crazed and skewed facade of what's believed to be the oldest house in Georgia:

🔟 The Herb House

This house was built as the private residence of the caretaker to a garden that stood on this site in the early 18th century. Today, it's connected architecturally to the Pirates' House, a public bar and restaurant.

Now is a good time to:

> **TAKE A BREAK**
> The **Pirates' House**, at 20 E. Broad St. (📞 **912/233-5757**), contains a bar that doubles as a cafe. Its labyrinthine interior, more like a maze really, has 15 different dining rooms formed by the interconnection of at least six antique buildings, some of which many Savannahians believe to be haunted. For more on the rich and sometimes bizarre history of this place, which often functions as a tourist attraction in its own right, see p. 64. If you're in the mood for a drink (and if you are, cheer up, because this tour is almost over), the house specialties include a "Skullcrusher," composed of three different kinds of rum and three different fruit juices, and a "Chatham Artillery Runner," made with gin, brandy, rum, Benedictine, and fruit juices. You get to keep the glass as a souvenir.

In the parking lot that flanks the Pirates' House are a bronze plaque and the ruins of a low redbrick wall. They are all that remain of:

1️⃣1️⃣ The Trustees' Garden

This was the first public agricultural experimental garden in America, modeled after the Chelsea Physic Garden in London. From here were sown the upland cotton and peach trees that later become indelibly associated with Georgia. Queen Caroline sometimes dressed in silk derived from this garden as a gesture of public support for the entrepreneurial efforts of its researchers. Alas, the experiments in the manufacture of both silk and wine failed, and the garden's patrons in faraway London, not realizing the benefits that might have come from experimentation with other crops, ended all funding for the garden in 1755. More recently, the historic 10-acre garden was paved over for parking and building sites.

After your refreshment, turn northward on East Broad Street, then cross Bay Street at any point that's reasonably safe. (There's a crosswalk directly in front of the Mulberry Inn, a few paces to the west.) You'll find yourself on the verdant lawns of:

🄓 Emmet Park

You can pass quickly through this park (we suggest that you descend the curved iron-railed stone steps at the park's most easterly end, close to the point where you initially entered the park). Or you can stop and admire the park's individual monuments. Moving from east to west (about 50 paces apart from one another), they include **Harbor Light,** an ornate cast-iron Victorian column at the tip of which perches a light that once guided ships in and out of Savannah Harbor. It's flanked with five antique iron anchors. The **Vietnam War Veterans Memorial** contains the names of local soldiers killed during that conflict, with a reflecting pool and a replica of a rifle, boots, and helmet. A stone replica of a **Celtic Cross** was erected in honor of Savannah's Irish community, as represented by the park's 19th-century namesake (Mr. Emmet). A small-scale **obelisk** is engraved with the names of soldiers from Savannah's 10th Infantry Division during the Korean War.

At the bottom of the curved stone stairs, clutch the railing carefully. It, like all of the stairs leading from Emmet Park down to the Savannah riverfront, is steep and narrow.

Directly in front of you you'll see two nearly side-by-side bronze memorials:

🄔 The 1996 Olympic Yachting Cauldron

A bronze replica of the eternal Olympic flame is perched atop four bronze columns. It commemorates the yachting competitions that were conducted here in 1996 as part of the Atlanta-based Olympics. A few steps to the west, in a miniplaza surrounded by evergreen shrubs, stands the statue, *Savannah's Waving Girl.* It honors Florence Martus (1869–1943), who rushed to the riverbank waving a white cloth countless times to welcome sailors into Savannah. Cynics (and some bona fide historians) cite her as a symbol of the hordes of prostitutes who welcomed sailors, one way or another, into Savannah's Riverfront District during its heyday as a maritime center.

In any event, the statue is an appropriate symbol for the final phase of your walking tour, an east-to-west ramble along:

⑭ The Riverfront

It's the single most-visited neighborhood in Savannah, the subject of thousands of tales of euphoria and sorrow. In the 19th century, slaves toiled and sweated, loading bales of cotton onto ships and barges bound for Liverpool and Boston, and merchants made and lost fortunes erecting the brick-and-stone warehouses that line the river's banks. Today, the Riverfront is the closest thing to a New Orleans series of honky-tonk bars, seafood and steak restaurants, and souvenir shops—some of them tacky, all of them colorful. Meander along the riverfront for as long as you'd like, bottling yourself up at any bar you feel comfortable in, or perhaps planning a return later during the cocktail hour.

8

Shopping in Savannah

While you may not be in Savannah solely for the shopping, you'll discover some unique shops to browse (especially if you're looking for antiques) and several excellent galleries. Of course, the popular chains and several department stores are represented at the major malls, and outlet shopping is available as well.

River Street is a shopper's delight, with some 9 blocks (including Riverfront Plaza) of interesting shops, offering everything from crafts to clothing to souvenirs. The **City Market,** between Ellis and Franklin squares on West St. Julian Street, boasts art galleries, boutiques, and sidewalk cafes along with a horse-and-carriage ride. Bookstores, boutiques, and antiques shops are also located between Wright Square and Forsyth Park.

Oglethorpe Mall, at 7804 Abercorn St., has more than 100 specialty shops, four major department stores, a Barnes & Noble, and a selection of restaurants and fast-food outlets. The **Savannah Mall,** 14045 Abercorn St., is Savannah's newest shopping center, offering two floors of shopping. Included on the premises is a food court with its own carousel. The anchor stores are Dillard's, Target, and Bass Pro Shops Outdoor World.

Some 30 manufacturer-owned "factory direct" stores offer savings up to 70% at the **Savannah Festival Factory Stores,** Abercorn Street at I-95 (© **912/925-3089;** www.savannahfestival.com). Shops feature name brands of shoes, luggage, gifts, cosmetics, household items, toys, and clothing. Shops include the Bass Outlet, Carter's, Dress Barn, and Samsonite.

Most shops are open Monday to Saturday 10am to 6pm. Only a few also open on Sunday, mainly noon to 5pm.

1 Shopping A to Z

ANTIQUES

Abercorn Antique Village   Savannahians come here to shop in a self-described setting of "shabby chic." Vendors featuring some 50 dealers and designers are set up in a historic house, a cottage, and an adjacent carriage house. The "village" is strong on vintage silver, crystal, furniture, linens, clocks, and paintings from the 18th to the 20th centuries. 201 E. 37th St. ℭ **912/233-0064.** www.abercornantiques.com.

Alex Raskin Antiques   This shop offers a wide array of antiques of varying ages. The selection includes everything from accessories to furniture, rugs, and paintings. 441 Bull St. (in the Noble Hardee Mansion), Monterey Sq. ℭ **912/232-8205.**

Clipper Trading Company   This store imports antique furnishings and decorative accent pieces from Southeast Asia, including China, Myanmar (Burma), and Thailand. To make it easier for you, the collection is arranged by country. Vendors sell rare pieces such as Han dynasty burial urns (206 B.C.–A.D. 220), Song dynasty bowls (A.D. 960–1279), and Ming and early Qing dynasty furniture. Other items of interest are woodcarvings, alabaster Buddha statues, ancestral paintings, and temple objects. 201 W. Broughton St. ℭ **912/238-3660.** www.clippertrading.com.

J.D. Weed & Co.   This shop prides itself on providing "that wonderful treasure that combines history and personal satisfaction with rarity and value." If you're looking for a particular item, let the staff know and they'll try to find it for you. 102 W. Victory Dr. ℭ **912/234-8540.** www.jdweedco.com.

ART & SCULPTURE

Compass Prints, Inc./Ray Ellis Gallery   From 1998 to 2000, Ray Ellis was the artist chosen to paint the official White House Christmas card. All three of his original paintings are part of the permanent White House collection of art. This gallery features Ellis's original watercolors, oils, and bronzes, as well as limited-edition prints, reproductions, art books, and other gift items. 205 W. Congress St. ℭ **912/234-3537.** www.rayellis.com.

Gallery 209   Housed in an 1820s cotton warehouse, this gallery displays two stories of original paintings by local artists, sculpture, woodworking, fiber art, gold and silver jewelry, enamels, photography, batiks, pottery, and stained glass. You'll also find a wide selection of limited-edition reproductions and notecards of local scenes. 209 E. River St. ℭ **912/236-4583.** www.gallery209.com.

John Tucker Fine Arts ℛ   This gallery offers museum-quality pieces by local artists as well as artists from around the world, including Haitian and Mexican craftspeople. The restored 1800s home features 19th- and 20th-century landscapes, marine-art paintings, portraits, folk art, and still lifes. 5 W. Charlton St. ℭ **912/231-8161.** www. johntuckerfinearts.com.

Morning Star Gallery   This gallery features the works of more than 80 artists. Pieces include handthrown pottery, metalwork, paintings, prints, woodworks, jewelry, and glass (handblown and leaded). 8 E. Liberty St. © **912/233-4307.**

Village Craftsmen   This collective of artisans offers a wide array of handmade crafts, including handblown glass, needlework, folk art, limited-edition prints, restored photographs, and handthrown pottery. 223 W. River St. © **912/236-7280.** www.thevillagecraftsmen.com.

BAKED GOODS

Baker's Pride Bakery   If it's baked, it's here: a wide range of pastries, rich-tasting cookies, and the town's most delectable and aromatic muffins fresh from the oven. The leading family bakery in Savannah since 1982, the establishment has been expanded to include a dining section for those who want to consume the baked goods on-site. Gathering the makings for a party, we loaded up on such desserts as cream puffs, both Key lime and pecan squares, coconut tarts, date bars, assorted rugelach, éclairs, strawberry tarts, and strudel. Kids love the store's gingerbread men, and who can fault the superb macaroons? 840 E. DeRenne Ave. © **912/355-1155.** www.savannah bakery.com.

BOOKS

Barnes & Noble   This superstore is located in the Oglethorpe Mall. The store holds many events, including a regular open mic night for poetry readings. 7804 Abercorn St. © **912/353-7757.** www.barnes andnoble.com.

Books-a-Million   This enormous store is located in the Abercorn Plaza. 8108 Abercorn St. © **912/925-8112.** www.booksamillioninc.com.

Book Warehouse   This store offers more than 75,000 titles, including fiction, cookbooks, children's books, computer manuals, and religious tomes. Prices begin at less than a dollar, and all proceeds are donated to Emory University for cancer research. 11 Gateway Blvd. © **912/927-0824.**

E. Shaver, Bookseller   Housed on the ground floor of a Greek Revival mansion, E. Shaver features 12 rooms of tomes. Specialties include architecture, decorative arts, regional history, and children's books as well as 17th-, 18th-, and 19th-century maps. 326 Bull St. © **912/234-7257.**

CANDY & OTHER FOODS

Byrd Cookie Company   Located 6 miles from the historic center, this store started as a small, family-run local bakery in 1924. Today it's one of Georgia's leading manufacturers in the gourmet industry. Its retail store and showplace, the mammoth Gourmet Marketplace, has it all, including a complete floral design department, daily in-store sampling displays, custom designs such as gift baskets, nautically themed merchandise and, of course, the entire Byrd Cookie line of products—which includes not only cookies and candy, but relishes, jams, preserves, salsas, salad dressings, and other specialty items. 6700 Waters Ave. ✆ **912/355-1716**. www.byrdcookiecompany.com.

Plantation Sweets Vidalia Onions   Outside Savannah, check out the Vidalia onion specialties offered by the Collins family for more than 50 years. Sample one of the relishes, dressings, or gift items. Call for directions. Rte. 2, Cobbtown. ✆ **800/541-2272**. www.plantationsweets.com.

River Street Sweets   Begun more than 20 years ago as part of the River Street restoration project, this store offers a wide selection of candies, including pralines, bear claws, fudge, and chocolates. Included among the specialties are more than 30 flavors of taffy made on a machine from the early 1900s. 13 E. River St. ✆ **800/793-3876** or 912/233-6220. www.riverstreetsweets.com.

Savannah's Candy Kitchen   Chocolate-dipped Oreos, glazed pecans, pralines, and fudge are only a few of the delectables at this confectionery. Staff members are so sure you'll be delighted with their offerings that they offer a full money-back guarantee if you're not satisfied. 225 E. River St. ✆ **800/443-7884** or 912/233-8411. www.savannah candy.com.

COOKWARE

The Paula Deen Store   In 2007, the Paula Deen group took over what had previously functioned as a pub and transformed it into a retail outlet selling the cookbooks and gadgets you'll need to cook like a pro and emulate the award-winning TV technique of Savannah's most famous chef. It's located immediately adjacent to Ms. Deen's also-recommended restaurant, within tempting view of the lines that form prior to mealtimes. 108 W. Congress St. ✆ **912/233-2600**.

GIFTS & COLLECTIBLES

The Book Gift Shop   At Calhoun Square, this store is the official memorabilia headquarters for *Midnight in the Garden of Good and Evil.* Just about anything you can think of that has to do with The Book can be found here, including The Book (of course), coasters,

T-shirts, charms, earrings, golf towels, statues, cookies, bookmarks, music, and DVDs. 127 E. Gordon St. ℂ **912/233-3867.** www.midnightin savannah.com.

Charlotte's Corner   Featuring local items, this shop offers a wide array of gifts and souvenirs. The selection encompasses children's clothing, a few food items, Sheila houses, and Savannah-related books, including guidebooks and Southern cookbooks. 1 W. Liberty St. (at Bull St.). ℂ **912/233-8061.**

The Christmas Shop   This shop keeps the Christmas spirit alive all year with a large selection of ornaments, Santas, nutcrackers, and collectibles. Collectors will appreciate the various featured lines, including Department 56, Polonaise, Christina's World, and Patricia Breen. 307 Bull St. ℂ **912/234-5343.** www.thechristmasshop.homestead.com.

A Fine Choice   This is one of the best places for high-quality gifts in Savannah. In its gifts and collectibles category, it carries more than 20 different lines of merchandise. Among them are paperweights from Scotland and America, Polish hand-carved wooden boxes, Polish mouth-blown glass, Italian porcelains, Celtic pieces, lead glass "fairies" and angels, and art reproductions. 10 W. State St. ℂ **912/650-1845.**

True Grits   Located along River Street, this outlet welcomes you aggressively to the land of cotton. Civil War books, a display of Civil War swords, even authentic Civil War artifacts keep alive the memory of "the War of Northern Aggression." Naturally, there are Confederate T-shirts and such "fun" items as 10-gauge blank-firing cannons. The shop is strong on nautical accessories, including ship bells and models. It also features Southern gourmet food items. 107 E. River St. ℂ **912/234-8006.**

JEWELRY & SILVER

Levy Jewelers   Located downtown, this boutique deals mainly in antique jewelry. It offers a large selection of gold, silver, gems, and watches. Among its other items are crystal, china, and gift items. 101 E. Broughton St. ℂ **800/237-5389.** www.levyjewelers.com.

Simply Silver   The specialty here is sterling flatware, ranging from today's designs to discontinued items of yesteryear. The inventory includes new and estate pieces along with a wide array of gift items. 236 Bull St. ℂ **912/238-3652.**

9

Savannah After Dark

River Street, along the Savannah River, is the major after-dark venue. Many night owls stroll the waterfront until they hear the sound of music they like, then follow their ears inside.

In summer, concerts of jazz, Big Band, and Dixieland music fill downtown **Johnson Square** with foot-tapping sounds that thrill both locals and visitors. Some of Savannah's finest musicians perform regularly at this historic site.

1 The Performing Arts

The **Savannah Symphony Orchestra,** one of two fully professional orchestras in the state of Georgia, presents its regular nine-concert masterworks series in the Savannah Civic Center's **Johnny Mercer Theatre,** Orleans Square (© **912/651-6557;** www.savannahcivic. com), which is also home to ballet, musicals, and Broadway shows. Call to find out what's being presented at the time of your visit. Tickets range from $15 to $100.

Savannah Theatre, Chippewa Square (© **912/233-7764;** www. savannahtheatre.com), presents contemporary plays. Tickets are usually $33 for regular admission, $31 for seniors and students, and $16 for those 17 and under.

Late September brings the 5-day **Savannah Jazz Festival** (© **912/ 675-5419;** www.savannahjazzfestival.org), with nationally known musicians appearing around the city.

2 Live Music Clubs

Deja Groove   The setting is a severe-looking 19th-century warehouse perched on soaring bulwarks on the sloping embankment between Riverwalk and the busy traffic of Bay Street. Inside, you'll find an intriguing blend of exposed brick and timber, psychedelic artwork, and a youthful (under 35-ish) sense of hip. There's a dance floor featuring dance music from the '70s and '80s, at least two sprawling bar areas, video games, and about a dozen pool tables, priced at $1 per game. Entrance is usually free, but sometimes a $3 cover charge is levied after 10pm. Hours are Tuesday through Thursday 8:30pm to 3am and Friday and Saturday 8pm to 3am. 301 Williamson St. ℂ **912/644-4566.**

Jinxed 🔊 This is Savannah's number-one live music venue, as noted in the city's *Creative Loafing* magazine. It's known as punk-rock heaven to its hundreds of local fans, with a battered but prominent stage for live bands, and a wraparound collection of rock-'n'-roll memorabilia and kitsch. Until its current manifestation, it was a hippie-style junk store; now you're likely to find such visiting luminaries as Kevin Spacey, John Cusack, and Tracey Cunningham. Hours are Monday through Saturday from 5pm to 3am. 127 W. Congress St. ℂ **912/ 236-2281.** Cover for live music $4–$10, depending on the band.

3 Bar Hoppin' & Pub Crawlin'

Bernie's River Street This bar and grill, conveniently located on the riverfront, lies in one of the city's pre–Civil War cotton warehouses and has the ambience of an old portside pub. The bar offers live music, televised sports, and extended late weekend hours. The bartenders claim their bloody mary, which is presented in a Mason jar and topped with pickled okra, is the best on River Street. If you're hungry, a light menu features seafood, burgers, and sandwiches. It's open Monday to Thursday 11am to midnight, Friday to Saturday 11am to 3am, and Sunday noon to midnight. 115 E. River St. ℂ **912/ 236-1827.** www.berniesriverstreet.com.

Café Ambrosia This hangout evokes Starbucks in some ways, offering cakes, pastries, exotic coffees, and a variety of food for snacking. Revelers often stop in here to tank up before beginning their nightly rounds of the pubs. Coffee, depending on the size of the cup and the brand, costs from $1.85 to $4.50. Open Monday to Thursday 8am to 8pm, Friday and Saturday 8am to 10pm, and Sunday 10am to 4pm. 202 E. Broughton St. (at the corner of Abercorn). ℂ **912/ 443-0909.**

Churchill's Pub & Restaurant If you like a cigar with your martini (the pub has a large selection), this is the place for you. Once the oldest bar in Savannah, it was originally built in England in 1860, dismantled, and shipped to Savannah in the 1920s. A fire in 2003 forced it to move to this new location. On tap are such imported beers as John Courage, Guinness, Dry Blackthorn, and Bass Ale. You can also order pub grub like fish and chips, homemade bangers

(English sausage), or shepherd's pie. The pub is open Sunday to Friday 5pm to 2am and Saturday noon to 2am. 13–17 W. Bay St. ⓒ 912/232-8501: www.thebritishpub.com.

Gallery Espresso Facing Chippewa Square, occupying the site of what used to be a Victorian storefront, this is an artsy, New Age, bohemian enclave evoking the hippie heyday of the 1960s. If you can find an available seat on any of the battered, artfully mismatched sofas and armchairs, you might be tempted to remain in place a long, leisurely time. There's no waiter service—you'll order your espresso, salads, desserts, pastries, and ice cream directly from the countertop and display cases in back. Some of the macramé, weavings, and ceramics are for sale, and throughout are scattered free copies of the city's various student magazines and culture guides. The only alcohol served is wine, priced at $6 to $8 per glass. Open Monday to Friday 7:30am to 8pm and Saturday and Sunday 8am to 11pm. 234 Bull St. ⓒ 912/233-5348.

Jazz'd Tapas Bar ⓐ It's hip, it's cool, and it's happening here, in City Market, at the bottom of an unlikely-looking cement staircase that descends from the sidewalk into a venue that looks a bit spooky until you actually enter. There you'll find low-slung leather sofas and bar stools that seem to show off clients' miniskirts to their best advantage; a stage where singers croon melodies that emulate latter-day versions of Frank Sinatra and Tony Bennett; and wild, large-scale paintings in tones of deep green and maroon. Choose from a wide selection of cocktails (its martinis were voted the best in the city in 2006 by *Savannah Magazine*) and tapas, small platters inspired by the traditions of Spain—or, in this instance, the cuisines of the world. As the menu says, "to eat tapas style is to eat by whim, free from rules and schedules," and that's exactly what the staff here encourages you to do. Select from an extensive menu that includes asparagus wrapped in prosciutto baked with béarnaise sauce and served on a bed of braised leeks; grilled baby lamb chops garnished with garlic and rosemary; Asian-style ahi tuna, encrusted with sesame coriander, poppy seed, and lime zest; or a potato-leek frittata with fig chutney. Tapas cost from $6.50 to $12, and hours are Sunday to Thursday 4:30pm to midnight and Friday and Saturday 4:30pm to 2am. 52 Barnard St. ⓒ 912/236-7777. www.jazzdsavannah.com.

Kevin Barry's Irish Pub The place to be on St. Patrick's Day, this waterfront pub rocks all year. Irish folk music will entertain you as you choose from a menu featuring such Irish fare as beef stew, shepherd's pie, and corned beef and cabbage. Many folks come here just to drink, often making a night of it in the convivial atmosphere. It's open Monday to Saturday 11am to 3am and Sunday 12:30pm to 2am. 117 W. River St. ℂ **912/233-9626.** www.kevinbarrys.com.

Mellow Mushroom   Don't expect grandeur here. A member of a Georgia-based restaurant chain, it appeals to a funky, irreverent, and sometimes raucous crowd of college students and faded counterculture aficionados from yesterday. Decor includes rambling murals painted with an individualized—and subjective—iconography that might require an explanation from a member of the cheerful waitstaff. There's the cut-off front end of a VW Beetle near the entrance; a limited menu that focuses almost exclusively on pizzas, salads, and calzones; and a die-hard emphasis on cheap beer, especially Pabst Blue Ribbon, which sells by the pitcher. Expect lots of SCAD (Savannah College of Art and Design) students, a battered and dimly lighted interior, recorded (not live) music, and a vague allegiance to the hard-rock, hard-drugs, and hard-sex fantasies of the early 1970s. Open daily 11am to 11pm. 11 W. Liberty St. ℂ **912/495-0705.** www.mellow mushroom.com.

Mercury Lounge   The venue is as hip, counterculture, and artfully kitsch as anything you might have expected in Manhattan, with the added benefit of a reputation for the biggest martinis (10 oz.) in town. You'll find the most comfortable bar stools anywhere (they're covered in faux leopard or zebra), live music most nights, and, when a band is not performing, a jukebox. Everything is congenially battered, with enough rock music memorabilia to please the curators of a rock-'n'-roll hall of fame. It's open daily from 3pm to 3am. 125 W. Congress St. ℂ **912/447-6952.**

Savannah Smiles   Near River Street and in back of the Quality Inn, this piano bar not only encourages audience participation, it requires it. A pair of talented musicians duels for the audience's attention as they play old-time favorites. Request a song, and the musicians will do the rest. Savannah Smiles won city awards for best new bar in 2001 and best overall bar in 2002. There are several shows of the "dueling pianos" Wednesday to Saturday, and a karaoke night (featuring a live pianist) on Sunday. The bar is open Wednesday through Saturday 7pm to 3am and Sunday 7pm to 2am. 314 Williamson St. ℂ **912/527-6453.** Cover varies from $5; free for ladies Wed.

17 Hundred 90 Lounge   This is Savannah's haunted pub. The ghost of Anna Powers, who killed herself by jumping out of the third-floor window onto a brick courtyard, has been spotted wandering about at night. She committed suicide after falling in love with a married sea captain who sailed away. If you don't mind ghosts, this is a cozy bar attached to one of Savannah's most acclaimed restaurants. Happy hour with hors d'oeuvres lasts from 4:30 to 7pm Monday to Friday. It's open Monday through Friday 11am to closing, and Saturday and Sunday from 6 to 10pm. 307 E. President St. ℭ 912/236-7122. www.17hundred90.com.

Wet Willie's   Few other nightspots in Savannah seem to revel so voluptuously in the effects produced by 190-proof grain alcohol. If you want to get falling-down drunk in a setting that evokes the more sociable aspects of a college fraternity/sorority bash, this is the place. When it's busy, it's loaded with the young, the nubile, and the sexually accessible—a worthy pickup joint if you're straight and not particularly squeamish. If you aren't sure what to order, consider such neon-colored head-spinners as Call-a-Cab, Polar Cappuccino, Monkey Shine, or Shock Treatment. Karaoke is the main attraction every Monday and Tuesday night; otherwise, it's something of a free-for-all with a Southern accent. Hours are Monday to Thursday 11am to 1am, Friday and Saturday 11am to 2am, and Sunday 12:30pm to 1am. 101 E. River St. ℭ 912/233-5650. www.wetwillies.com.

4 Gay & Lesbian Bars

Chuck's Bar   Most of the bars along Savannah's River Street are mainstream affairs, attracting goodly numbers of tourists, some of whom drink staggering amounts of booze and who seem almost proud of how rowdy they can get. In deliberate contrast, Chuck's usually attracts local members of Savannah's counterculture, including lots of gay folk, who rub elbows in a tucked-away corner of a neighborhood rarely visited by locals. The setting is a dark and shadowy 19th-century warehouse, lined with bricks, just a few steps from the Jefferson Street ramp leading down to the riverfront. Hours are Monday to Wednesday from 8pm to 3am and Thursday to Saturday 7pm to 3am. 305 Wet River St. ℭ 912/232-1005.

Club One 𝒦𝒦   Club One defines itself as the premier gay bar in a town, priding itself on a level of decadence that falls somewhere between New Orleans's and Key West's, and it's the hottest and most amusing spot in town. Patrons include lesbians and gays from the coastal islands, visiting urbanites, and cast and crew of whatever film is being shot in Savannah at the time (Demi Moore and Bruce Willis showed up here when they were still a couple). There's also likely to be a healthy helping of voyeurs who've read *Midnight in the Garden of Good and Evil.*

You pay your admission at the door, showing ID if the attendant asks for it. Wander through the street-level dance bar, trek down to the basement-level video bar for a (less-noisy) change of venue, and (if your timing is right) climb one floor above street level for a view of the drag shows. There, a bevy of black and white *artistes* lip-sync the hits of Tina Turner, Gladys Knight, and Bette Midler. The bar is open daily 5pm to 3am. Shows are nightly at 10:30pm and 12:30am. 1 Jefferson St. © **912/232-0200.** www.clubone-online.com. Cover (after 9:30pm) $10 for those 18–20, $5 for those 21 and older.

5 Dinner Cruises

The **Savannah River Queen,** a replica of the boats that once plied this waterway, is a 350-passenger vessel operated by the River Street Riverboat Co., 9 E. River St. (© **800/786-6404** or 912/232-6404; www.savannah-riverboat.com). It offers a 2-hour cruise with a prime rib or fish dinner and live entertainment. Reservations are necessary. The fare is $45 for adults and $28 for children 12 and under. Departures are usually daily at 7pm, but the schedule might be curtailed in the colder months.

10

Day Trips & Overnights from Savannah

You can use Savannah as a base, returning to your lodging after local excursions, or embarking from the city to nearby points of interest, including South Carolina's Hilton Head and Daufuskie islands and the quaint Southern town of Beaufort.

   We'll start off with a day trip and then move on to travel at greater distances, including a stop at one of Georgia's "Golden Isles."

1 Tybee Island ☆☆

14 miles E of Savannah

For more than 150 years, **Tybee Island** has lured those who want to go swimming, sailing, fishing, and picnicking. Pronounced "*Tie-bee*," an Euchee Indian word for salt, the island offers 5 miles of unspoiled sandy beaches, only 14 miles east of Savannah. From Savannah, take U.S. 80 until you reach the ocean.

VISITOR INFORMATION

The **Tybee Island Visitors Information Center** (© 800/868-2322 or 912/786-5444; www.tybeevisit.com) provides complete information if you plan to spend some time on the island, as opposed to a day trip. It is open daily 9am to 5:30pm.

SEEING THE SIGHTS

Consisting of 5 square miles, Tybee was once called the "Playground of the Southeast," hosting millions of beach-loving visitors from across the country. In the early 1900s, Tybrisa Pavilion, on the island's south end, became one of the major summer entertainment pavilions in the South. Benny Goodman, Guy Lombardo, Tommy Dorsey, and Cab Calloway all played here. It burned down in 1967 and was rebuilt in 1996.

   Over Tybee's salt marshes and sand dunes have flown the flags of pirates and Spaniards, the English and the French, and the Confederate States of America. A path on the island leads to a clear pasture

Finds   Strolling Around Isle of Hope

About 10 miles south of downtown Savannah is the charming community of **Isle of Hope** ⭐. First settled in the 1840s as a summer resort for the wealthy, it's now a showcase of rural antebellum life. To reach Parkersburg (as it was called in those days), citizens traveled by steamer down the Wilmington River or by a network of suburban trains. Today you can reach Isle of Hope by driving east from Savannah along Victory Drive to Skidaway Road. At Skidaway, go right and follow it to LaRoche Avenue. Take a left and follow LaRoche until it dead-ends on Bluff Drive.

This is the perfect place for a lazy afternoon stroll. The short path is home to authentically restored cottages and beautiful homes, most enshrouded with Spanish moss cascading from the majestic oaks lining the bluff. A favorite of many local landscape artists and Hollywood directors, Bluff Drive affords the best views of the Wilmington River.

As you head back toward Savannah, drive down Skidaway Road. On your left is **Wormsloe Plantation,** 7601 Skidaway Rd. (© **912/353-3023;** www.wormsloe.org). Wormsloe, the home of Noble Jones, isn't much more than a ruin. After you enter the gates, you proceed down an unpaved oak-lined drive, and the ruins lie less than half a mile off the road. Dr. Jones was one of Georgia's leading Colonial citizens and a representative to the Continental Congress. Wormsloe was also home to forts and garrisons during the Civil War and the Spanish-American War. It's open Tuesday to Saturday 9am to 5pm and Sunday 2 to 5:30pm. Admission is $2.50 for adults and $1.50 for students 6 to 18; children 5 and under are admitted free.

where John Wesley, founder of the Methodist Church, knelt and declared his faith in the new land.

Fort Screven, on the northern strip, began as a coastal artillery station and evolved into a training camp for countless troops in both world wars. Remnants of wartime installations can still be seen. Also in the area is the **Tybee Museum,** housed in what was one of the fort's batteries. Displayed is a collection of photographs, memorabilia, art, and dioramas depicting Tybee from the time the Native

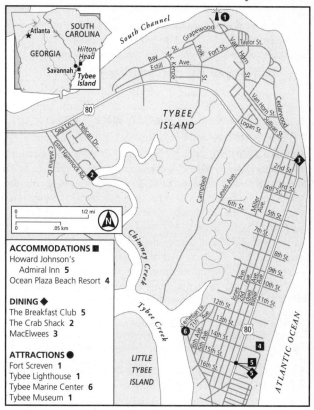

Tybee Island

ACCOMMODATIONS ■
Howard Johnson's
  Admiral Inn **5**
Ocean Plaza Beach Resort **4**

DINING ◆
The Breakfast Club **5**
The Crab Shack **2**
MacElwees **3**

ATTRACTIONS ●
Fort Screven **1**
Tybee Lighthouse **1**
Tybee Marine Center **6**
Tybee Museum **1**

Americans inhabited the island through World War II. Across the street is the **Tybee Lighthouse** (www.tybeelighthouse.org), built in 1742 and the third-oldest lighthouse in America. It's 154 feet tall, and if you're fit, you can climb 178 steps to the top. From the panoramic deck you get a sense of the broad and beautiful marshes.

For information about the museum and lighthouse, call ℂ **912/ 786-5801.** Both are open Wednesday to Monday 9am to 5:30pm. Admission is $6 for adults and $5 for seniors 62 and older and for children 6 to 17. Kids 5 and under enter free. The site has picnic tables, and access to the beach is easy.

Tybee Marine Center, in the 14th Street parking lot (ℂ **912/ 786-5917;** www.tybeemarinescience.org), has aquariums with species indigenous to the coast of southern Georgia. Also on display is the usual cast of marine mammals, sharks, and other creatures. Hours are daily 9am to 5pm (closes at noon on Tues). Admission is $4 for adults, $3 for children, and free for children 4 and under.

WHERE TO STAY ON TYBEE ISLAND

If you're interested in daily or weekly rentals of a condo or beach house (one or two bedrooms), contact **Tybee Beach Rentals,** PO Box 2802, Tybee Island, GA 31328 (© **800/967-4433** or 912/786-0100; www.renttybee.com).

Howard Johnson's Admiral Inn (Kids)   Set within a mixed commercial and residential neighborhood, about a block from the beach, this is a clean, well-managed hotel. With only 41 units, the inn conveys a sense of intimacy. Guest rooms are chain-motel uncontroversial, with the kind of blandly international contemporary furniture you might expect in, say, Florida. The units are large enough to accommodate families. Some have microwaves and minirefrigerators. Some have whirlpool bathtubs. There's no restaurant, but lots of options lie within a short drive.

1501 Butler Ave. (U.S. 80 E.), Tybee Island, GA 31328. © **800/793-7716** or 912/786-0700. Fax 912/786-0399. www.tybeehowardjohnson.com. 41 units. $59–$170 double. Off-season discounts available. Children 16 and under stay free in parent's room. AE, DC, DISC, MC, V. **Amenities:** Outdoor pool; Jacuzzi; room service; babysitting; laundry service; dry cleaning; nonsmoking rooms; rooms for those w/limited mobility. *In room:* A/C, TV, Wi-Fi, microwave (in some), fridge (in some), hair dryer.

Ocean Plaza Beach Resort (F)   This hotel has more direct exposure to the beach than any other hotel or motel on Tybee Island. As such, it considers itself among the upscale of the island's resorts, a bit more plush than, say, the also-recommended Howard Johnson's Admiral Inn. Its bar-lounge and restaurant—added in 1999—boast big-windowed views of the sea. Guest rooms are a bit larger than those in some of the hotel's competitors, with bland furnishings and sliding glass doors that open onto private balconies. The hotel has a number of suites, each with a microwave and refrigerator.

1401 Strand Ave., Tybee Island, GA 31328. © **800/215-6370** or 912/786-7777. Fax 912/786-4531. www.oceanplaza.com. 200 units. $99–$149 double. Off-season discounts available. Children 12 and under stay free in parent's room. AE, DC, DISC, MC, V. **Amenities:** Restaurant; bar; 2 pools; room service; nonsmoking rooms; rooms for those w/limited mobility. *In room:* A/C, TV, Wi-Fi, microwave, fridge, coffeemaker, hair dryer.

WHERE TO DINE ON TYBEE ISLAND

The Breakfast Club (F) (Value) AMERICAN   Established in 1976, this restaurant was selected to cater the wedding of the late John

Kennedy, Jr., on Cumberland Island. It's become so successful that lines form around the block daily, and it has won Savannah's "Best Place to Eat Breakfast" contest 11 times. What's the big attraction? The food and the affordable prices. The omelets are the best in the area, including a Philly steak omelet with top sirloin tips, sautéed onions, mushrooms, and cream cheese. The waffles are superb; most guests prefer the ones with pecans, although toppings are varied enough to include corned beef hash. If you drop in for lunch, know that the joint has consistently won "Best Burger in Savannah" awards. Expect a half pound of lean ground beef grilled to perfection and served on a freshly baked bun. Hot daily specials are also featured, including shrimp 'n' grits.

1500 Butler Ave. ℂ **912/786-5984.** Main courses $9. DISC, MC, V. Daily 6:30am–12:30pm. Closed Christmas.

The Crab Shack ℱ *Kids* SEAFOOD   This local joint advertises itself as "where the elite eat in their bare feet." Your lunch or dinner might have just arrived off the boat after swimming in the sea only an hour or so earlier. Fat crab is naturally the specialty. It's most often preferred in cakes or can be blended with cheese and seasonings. Boiled shrimp is another popular item. Kids delight in selecting their crabs from a tank. A Low Country boil (a medley of seafood) is a family favorite. The jukebox brings back the 1950s.

40 Estill Hammock Rd. ℂ **912/786-9857.** www.thecrabshack.com. Reservations not accepted. Main courses $8–$35. MC, V. Mon–Thurs 11:30am–10pm; Fri–Sun 11:30am–11pm.

MacElwee's Seafood House ℱℱ SEAFOOD   This restaurant was voted number one in Chatham County by *Food & Wine* magazine. Established in 1982, it is imbued with a nautical theme and opens onto ocean views from its location along Hwy. 80 at the big curve on Tybee Island. It is famous locally for its beer-battered shrimp and raw and steamed oysters. It's also known for grilling the best chicken and serving the best Angus beef on the island. The chef's special appetizer is oysters MacElwee on the half shell, topped with melted cheese, diced onions, bell peppers, and bacon. The crab soup is also an island favorite. The chef does perfectly grilled filet mignon and rib-eye; his specialty is a 10-ounce rib-eye, steak Tybrisa, cooked to your specifications and smothered with fresh crabmeat, scallions, and mushrooms in a peppercorn demi-glace. The kitchen also turns out succulent pastas such as fettuccine Diane made with shrimp and scallops in a lobster brandy cream sauce.

101 Lovel Ave. ⓒ **912/786-8888**. www.macelweesontybee.com. Main courses $9–$28. AE, MC, V. Tues–Fri 4–11pm; Sat noon–10pm. Closed Easter, Thanksgiving, and Christmas.

2 Hilton Head ★★

41 miles NE of Savannah

The largest sea island between New Jersey and Florida and one of America's great resort meccas, Hilton Head is surrounded by the Low Country, where much of the romance, beauty, and graciousness of the Old South survives. Broad white-sand beaches are warmed by the Gulf Stream and fringed with palm trees and rolling dunes. Palms mingle with live oaks, dogwood, and pines, and everything is draped in Spanish moss. Graceful sea oats, anchoring the beaches, wave in the wind. The subtropical climate makes all this beauty the ideal setting for golf and for some of the Southeast's finest saltwater fishing. Far more sophisticated and upscale than Myrtle Beach and the Grand Strand, Hilton Head's "plantations" (as most resort areas here call themselves) offer visitors something of the traditional leisurely lifestyle that's always held sway here.

Although it covers only 42 square miles (it's 12 miles long and 5 miles wide at its widest point), Hilton Head feels spacious, thanks to judicious planning from the beginning of its development in 1952. And that's a blessing, because about 2.3 million resort guests visit annually (the permanent population is about 35,000). The broad beaches on its ocean side, sea marshes on the sound, and natural wooded areas of live and water oak, pine, bay, and palmetto trees in between have all been carefully preserved amid commercial explosion. This lovely setting attracts artists, writers, musicians, theater groups, and craftspeople. The only city (of sorts) is Harbour Town, at Sea Pines Resort, a Mediterranean-style cluster of shops and restaurants.

ESSENTIALS
GETTING THERE

It's easy to fly into Savannah, rent a car, and drive to Hilton Head. From Savannah, take I-95 North to U.S. 278 East, which leads directly into Hilton Head. If you're driving from other points south or north, exit I-95 to reach the island (exit 28 off I-95 South, exit 5 off I-95 North). U.S. 278 leads over the bridge to the island. It's 52 miles northeast of Savannah and located directly on the Intracoastal Waterway.

VISITOR INFORMATION

The official **Welcome Center** of the Hilton Head Island–Bluffton Chamber of Commerce (© **800/523-3373** or 843/785-3673; www.hiltonheadisland.org) is located at 100 William Hilton Pkwy. and is open daily 8:30am until 5:30pm. You can pick up free vacation guides (or order them from the website) and free maps of the area. The staff can assist you in finding places of interest and activities and also offers video tours in several languages.

GETTING AROUND

U.S. 278 is the divided highway that runs the length of the island.

Yellow Cab (© **843/686-6666**) has two-passenger flat fares determined by zone, with an extra $2 charge for each additional person.

SPECIAL EVENTS

Scattered cultural events in February, including basket-weaving classes, art exhibitions, and storytelling, showcase the island's mysterious Gullah heritage as part of the annual **Gullah Celebration.** For more information call © **843/689-9314** or visit www.gullahcelebration.com. During the first week of March, the Hilton Head Hospitality Association sponsors **Winefest** (© **800/424-3387**; www.hiltonhead hospitalityassociation.com), an annual outdoor wine tasting—the largest of its kind on the East Coast—that transforms even the most devoted beer drinkers into oenophiles and connoisseurs. Outstanding PGA golfers descend on the island in mid-April for the **Verizon Heritage PGA Tour and Tournament** at the Harbour Town Golf Links at the Sea Island Resort (© **800/243-1107**; www.verizon heritage.com). To herald fall, the **Hilton Head Celebrity Golf Tournament** (© **843/842-7711**; www.hhcelebritygolf.com) is held on Labor Day weekend at various island golf courses. For 3 days straddling Halloween, Hilton Head's Concours d'Elegance and Motoring Festival (© **843/785-7469**; www.hhiconcours.com) provides a venue for some of the most sought-after antique automobiles in the world.

BEACHES, GOLF, TENNIS & OTHER OUTDOOR PURSUITS

You can have an active vacation here any time of year; Hilton Head's subtropical climate ranges in temperature from the 50s (teens Celsius) in winter to the mid-80s (around 30 Celsius) in summer. And if you've had your fill of historic sights in Savannah or Charleston, don't worry—the attractions on Hilton Head mainly consist of nature preserves, beaches, and other places to play.

The Gullah Heritage of Hilton Head

Tours that take a journey back in time are offered through **Gullah Heritage Trail Tours** (www.gullaheritage.com). Arrangements can be made by callling (✆ **843/681-7066.** Gullah culture is a West African–based system of traditions, art forms, customs, and beliefs. A 2-hour narrated tour takes you through the hidden paths of Hilton Head, where you'll meet a fourth-generation Gullah family, relating firsthand stories of their traditions and even speaking Gullah for you. The tour also takes you to ruins or remnants of Hilton Head of yesterday, including a visit to a one-room schoolhouse, plantation tabby ruins, and a historic marker of the First Freedom Village. Tours depart at 10am and 2pm Wednesday to Saturday and at 2pm on Sunday, costing $25 for adults and $12 for children 11 and under. Tours depart from the Coastal Discovery Museum at 70 Honey Horn Dr.

The **Coastal Discovery Museum,** at historic Honey Horn, 70 Honey Horn Dr. (✆ **843/689-6767;** www.coastaldiscovery.org), provides a concentrated dose of information about the Low Country's ecology, history, and sociology. In 1990, the Town of Hilton Head bought 68 acres of landlocked flatlands (Honey Horn) historically used to grow cash crops such as rice and indigo, as a means of protecting it from development as a shopping center. The site contains about a dozen historic buildings, a few of them from before the Civil War. Today, the site is used for municipally sponsored events such as picnics, concerts, charity drives, and sporting events. It's administered by the Coastal Discovery Museum, whose mission involves teaching and celebrating the history and culture of Low Country South Carolina. A focal point for local volunteers, with adult and children's education programs and several ongoing lecture series, it sponsors guided tours focusing on the parcel's ecology and history. Tours go along island beaches and salt marshes or stop at Native American sites and the ruins of old forts or long-gone plantations. Children can search for sharks' teeth with an identification chart. The nature, beach, and history tours generally cost $12 for adults and $7 for children 4 to 12. The dolphin and nature cruise costs $19 per adult and $13 per child, and a kayak trip goes for $27 per adult and $25 per child. Hours are Monday to Saturday 9am to 4:30pm and Sunday 11am to 3pm. There is also an older and still active branch of the museum at 100 William Hilton Pkwy.

BEACHES

Travel + Leisure ranked Hilton Head's **beaches** ⭐⭐⭐ as among the most beautiful in the world, and we concur. The sands are extremely firm, providing a sound surface for biking, hiking, jogging, and beach games. In summer, watch for the endangered loggerhead turtles that lumber ashore at night to bury their eggs.

All beaches on Hilton Head are public, but land bordering the beaches is private property. Most beaches are safe, although there's sometimes an undertow at the northern end of the island. Lifeguards are posted only at major beaches, and concessions are available to rent beach chairs, umbrellas, and watersports equipment.

Most frequently used are **North** and **South Forest** beaches, adjacent to Coligny Circle (enter from Pope Ave. across from Lagoon Rd.). You'll have to use the parking lot opposite the Holiday Inn, paying a $4 daily fee until after 4pm. The adjacent beach park has toilets and a changing area, as well as showers, vending machines, and phones. It's a family favorite.

There are a number of public-access sites to popular beach areas. **Coligny Beach** at Coligny Circle at Pope Avenue and South Forest Beach Drive is the island's busiest strip of sand with toilets, sand showers, a playground, and changing rooms. **Alder Lane,** entered along South Forest Beach Road at Alder Lane, offers parking and is less crowded. Toilets are also found here. Off the William Hilton Parkway, **Dreissen Beach Park** at Bradley Beach Road has toilets, sand showers, and plenty of parking as well as a playground and picnic tables. Of the beaches on the island's north, we prefer **Folly Field Beach.** Toilets, changing facilities, and parking are available.

BIKING

Enjoy Hilton Head's 25 miles of bicycle paths. There are even bike paths running parallel to U.S. 278. Beaches are firm enough to support wheels, and every year, cyclists delight in dodging the waves or racing fast-swimming dolphins in the nearby water.

Most hotels and resorts rent bikes to guests. If yours doesn't, try **Hilton Head Bicycle Company,** off Sea Pines Circle at 112 Arrow Rd. (🕐 **800/995-4319** or 843/686-6888; www.hiltonheadbicycle. com). The cost starts at $27 per week. Baskets, child carriers, locks, and headgear are supplied. The inventory includes cruisers, BMXs, mountain bikes, tandems, and bikes for kids. Hours are daily 9am to 5pm. The company also offers free delivery and pickup.

Another rental place is **Peddling Pelican** (🕐 **843/785-3546;** www.pelicancruiser.com), offering beach cruisers, tandems, child carriers, and bikes for kids. There's free delivery to any area hotel or resort. Cost is $15 for a full day or $25 for 3 days. Hours are 9am to 6pm daily.

CRUISES & TOURS

To explore Hilton Head's waters, contact **Adventure Cruises, Inc.,** Shelter Cove Harbour, Ste. G, Harbourside III (*©* **843/785-4558**). Outings include a 1¾-hour dolphin-watch cruise, which costs $20 for adults and $11 for children 3 to 12.

Another outfitter, **Drifter & Gypsy Excursions,** South Sea Pines Drive, South Beach Marina (*©* **843/363-2900;** www.hiltonhead boattours.com), takes its 65-foot *Gypsy,* holding 89 passengers, on dolphin-watches, sightseeing cruises, and nature cruises. A 1-hour dolphin cruise costs $14 for adults and $7 for children 12 and under. Call for more information and to see what's happening at the time of your visit.

FISHING

No license is needed for saltwater fishing, although freshwater licenses are required for the island's lakes and ponds. The season for fishing offshore is April through October. Inland fishing is good between September and December. Crabbing is also popular; crabs are easy to catch in low water from docks, boats, or right off banks.

Off **Hilton Head** *⍟*, you can go deep-sea fishing for amberjack, barracuda, shark, and king mackerel. Many rentals are available; we've recommended only those with the best track records. The previously recommended **Drifter & Gypsy Excursions** (*©* **843/363-2900**) features a 50-passenger, 60-foot drifter vessel that offers 3- to 5-hour offshore and inshore fishing excursions ranging in price from $53 to $63. The 32-foot *Boomerang* fishing boat is available for private offshore and inshore custom fishing charters lasting up to 8 hours.

Harbour Town Yacht Basin, Harbour Town Marina (*©* **843/ 671-2704**), has five boats of various sizes and prices, each available for rentals. *The Hero* and *The Echo* are 32-foot ships. Their rates for a group of six are $450 for 4 hours, $675 for 6 hours, and $900 for 8 hours. A smaller four-passenger inshore boat is priced at $390 for 4 hours, $585 for 6 hours, and $780 for 8 hours. A pair of 6-passenger boats is also available for rent, *The Proving Ground* and *The Judith E,* costing $525 to $800 for 4 hours, $775 to $1,200 for 6 hours, and $1,000 to $1,600 for 8 hours.

A cheaper way to go deep-sea fishing—only $47 per person—is aboard *The Drifter* (© **843/363-2900**), a party boat that departs from the South Beach Marina Village. Ocean-bottom fishing is possible at an artificial reef 12 miles offshore.

GOLF

With more than 20 highly challenging **golf courses** ৫৫৫ on the island itself, and an additional 16 within a 30-minute drive, this is heaven for both professional and novice golfers. Some of golf's most celebrated architects—including George and Tom Fazio, Robert Trent Jones, Pete Dye, and Jack Nicklaus—have designed championship courses on the island. Wide, scenic fairways and rolling greens have earned Hilton Head the reputation of being the resort with the most courses on any number of the "World's Best" lists. To receive a copy of the island's *Golf Planner,* a guide to the golf courses and golf packages on Hilton Head Island, call © **888/465-3475.** For additional information about golf on Hilton Head, go to **www. golfisland.com**.

Most of Hilton Head's championship courses are open to the public, including the **George Fazio Course** ৫ at Palmetto Dunes Oceanfront Resort (© **843/785-1130**), an 18-hole, 6,534-yard, par-70 course that *Golf Digest* ranked in the top 50 of its "75 Best American Resort Courses." The course has been cited for its combined length and keen accuracy. The cost is $58 to $125 for 18 holes, and hours are daily from 6:30am to 6pm.

Old South Golf Links ৫৫৫, 50 Buckingham Plantation Dr., Bluffton (© **800/257-8997** or 843/785-5353; www.oldsouthgolf. com), is an 18-hole, 6,772-yard, par-72 course, open daily from 7:30am to 7pm. It was recognized in 1992 as one of the "Top 10 New Public Courses" by *Golf Digest,* which cites its panoramic views and setting ranging from an oak forest to tidal salt marshes. Greens fees range from $55 to $95. The course lies on Hwy. 278, 1 mile before the bridge leading to Hilton Head.

Hilton Head National Golf Club, Hwy. 278 (© **843/842-5900**), is a Gary Player Signature Golf Course, including a full-service pro shop and a grill and driving range. It's a 27-hole, 6,779-yard, par-72 course with gorgeous scenery that evokes Scotland. Greens fees range from $55 to $95, and hours are daily 7am to 6pm.

Island West Golf Club, Hwy. 278 (© **843/689-6660**), was nominated in 1992 by *Golf Digest* as the best new course of the year. With its backdrop of oaks, elevated tees, and rolling fairways, it's a challenging but playable 18-hole, 6,803-yard, par-72 course. Greens fees range from $37 to $68, and hours are daily from 7am to 6pm.

Robert Trent Jones Ocean Course at the Palmetto Dunes Oceanfront Resort (© **843/785-1138**) is an 18-hole, 6,710-yard, par-72 oceanfront course. The greens fees are $89 to $165 for 18 holes, and hours are daily from 7am to 6pm.

HORSEBACK RIDING

Riding through beautiful maritime forests and nature preserves is reason enough to visit Hilton Head. We like **Lawton Stables,** 190 Greenwood Dr., the Sea Pines Resort (© **843/671-2586;** www.lawtonstableshhi.com), which offers trail rides for both adults and kids (kids 7 and under ride ponies instead of horses) through the Sea Pines Forest Preserve. The cost is $60 per person for a ride that lasts somewhat longer than an hour. Riders must weigh under 250 pounds. The stables are open Monday to Saturday 7:30am to 5:30pm. Reservations are necessary.

JOGGING

Our favorite place for jogging is Harbour Town at the Sea Pines Resort. Go for a run through the settlement just as the sun is going down. Later, you can explore the marina and have a refreshing drink at one of the many outdoor cafes. In addition, the island offers lots of paved paths and trails that cut through scenic areas. Jogging along U.S. 278, the main artery, can be dangerous because of heavy traffic, however.

KAYAK TOURS

Few other venues provide as close a view of the flora and fauna of the salt marshes as a kayak. **Outside Hilton Head** (© **800/686-6996** or 843/686-6996; www.outsidehiltonhead.com) offers well-orchestrated kayak tours of various Low Country waterways and salt marshes from at least two locations on island. Their busiest location is at 32 Shelter Cove Lane, Hilton Head, close to Shelter Cove Marina. Their 2-hour Dolphin Nature Kayak Tour costs $40 (half price for children 11 and under). The tour takes you through the salt-marsh creeks of the Calibogue Sound or Pinckney Island National Wildlife Refuge. The trip begins with instructions on how to control your boat.

A worthy competitor is **Marshgrass Adventures** (© **843/684-3296;** www.marshgrassadventures.com), featuring sailing and kayak tours from a base at Broad Creek Marina. Every day between April and October, an experienced guide takes participants out on 2-hour kayak tours for sightings of egrets, herons, fish, crabs, and all manner of crawling critters. There's even the occasional spotting of dolphins from the low-slung, waterfront seat of your oared craft. The cost is $30 for adults and $20 for children 12 and under.

NATURE PRESERVES

The **Audubon-Newhall Preserve,** Palmetto Bay Road (no phone), is a 50-acre preserve on the south end of the island. Here you can walk along marked trails to observe wildlife in its native habitat. Guided tours are available when plants are blooming. Except for a scattered handful of public toilets, there are no amenities. The preserve is open from sunrise to sunset; admission is free, and it's likely that your entire time within these laissez-faire acres will be unsupervised.

The second-leading preserve is also on the south end of the island. **Sea Pines Forest Preserve** 𝒦𝒦, the Sea Pines Resort (② 843/ 363-4530), is a 605-acre public wilderness with marked walking trails. Nearly all the birds and animals known to live on Hilton Head can be seen here. (Yes, there are alligators, but there are also less fearsome creatures, such as egrets, herons, ospreys, and white-tailed deer.) All trails lead to public picnic areas in the center of the forest. The preserve is open from sunrise to sunset year-round. Maps and toilets are available.

The **Pinckney Island National Wildlife Refuge** 𝒦 is protected land with 115 prehistoric and historic sites. French and Spanish settlers inhabited the island back in the 1500s, with the first permanent settlement occurring in 1708. The island is named for Gen. Charles Cotesworth Pinckney, a signer of the U.S. Constitution. By 1818 more than 200 slaves were used to harvest Sea Island cotton here. In 1975 the refuge was donated to the U.S. Fish and Wildlife Service.

Today it comprises four islands, including Corn, Little Harry, Big Harry, and Pinckney Island, the latter the largest of the islands with 1,200 acres. The islands are riddled with hiking and biking trails, and are home to large concentrations of white ibis, herons, and egrets, even osprey nests. Two of the island's freshwater ponds are ranked among the top 20 wading bird colony sites of the South Carolina coastal plain. Alligators are also a common sight.

Take I-95 to S.C. exit 8 and go east on U.S. Hwy. 278 toward Hilton Head for 18 miles to the refuge entrance. From Hilton Head itself, exit the island via U.S. 278 west. The refuge, which can be visited during daylight hours, is on your right after a half-hour ride.

SAILING

Advanced Sail, Inc., Palmetto Bay Marina (© **843/686-2582;** www. hiltonheadisland.com/sailing), is a two-catamaran charter operator piloted by Captain John and his mate Jeanne. You can pack a picnic lunch and bring your cooler aboard for a 2½-hour trip—in the morning but more often during either the afternoon or at sunset. The cost for an excursion aboard the 53-foot-long *Pau Hana* is $32 for adults and $20 for children 11 and under. *Flying Circus,* measuring 30 feet in length, offers private 2-hour trips for up to six people priced at $220. Call for daytime special rates for fewer than six people.

H2O Sports, Harbour Town Marina (© **843/671-4386**), offers jet-skiing, parasailing, eco-tours, and water-skiing. We especially recommend their eco-tours (or "enviro," as they are called). Passengers head out on Zodiac inflatable boats for close encounters with wildlife, including dolphins and birds. Rates are $24 to $51 for adults and $24 to $44 for kids 12 and under.

SPA TREATMENTS

Hilton Head Island boasts a denser concentration of spas than virtually anywhere else in South Carolina. As such, you might be confronted with a barrage of publicity and brochures touting the virtue of various health-and-beauty farms, each offering a staggering array of treatments. They don't come cheaply—we urge you to compare prices and treatment options, and then, if it's possible, to reserve your spa session as far in advance as possible, since space in each of them is limited. Your choices include the **Heavenly Spa** within the Westin (© **843/681-4000;** www.westin.com/hiltonhead); and the **Spa Soleil** within the Marriott (© **843/686-8400;** www.hiltonhead marriott.com). Both of these accept bookings from nonresidents of the hotels that contain them. Spas more geared to in-and-out traffic without priority for clients of any particular hotel or resort include **Faces Day Spa** (© **843/785-3075;** www.facesdayspa.com); and the **Sanctuary Day Spa** (© **843/842-5999;** www.sanctuaryeurospa.com).

TENNIS

Tennis magazine ranked Hilton Head among its "50 Greatest U.S. Tennis Resorts." No other domestic destination can boast such a concentration of **tennis facilities** ⭐⭐⭐: more than 300 courts that are ideal for beginning, intermediate, and advanced players. The island has 19 tennis clubs, seven of which are open to the public. A wide variety of tennis clinics and daily lessons are available.

Sea Pines Racquet Club ✦✦✦, the Sea Pines Resort (✆ 843/
363-4495), has been ranked by *Tennis* magazine as a top-50 resort
and was selected by the *Robb Report* as the best tennis resort in the
United States. The club has been the site of more nationally televised
tennis events than any other location. Two hours per day of tennis
are complimentary for guests of the resort; otherwise, there's a $25-
per-hour charge. The club has 23 Har-Tru courts (2 are lighted for
night play). Sea Pines's most visible competitor, with a long history
of teaching tennis techniques, an equivalent number of courts, and
equivalent prices, is the **Van Der Meer Shipyard Tennis Resort,**
116 Shipyard Dr. (✆ **800/845-6138** or 843/686-8804; www.vdm
tennis.com).

Port Royal Racquet Club, Port Royal Plantation (✆ **843/686-
8803**), offers 10 clay and 4 hard courts. Charges range from $20 to
$32 per hour, and reservations should be made a day in advance.
Clinics are $20 per hour for adults and $15 for children. Private lessons are available.

Palmetto Dunes Tennis Center, Palmetto Dunes Resort (✆ **843/
785-1152;** www.palmettodunes.com), has 23 clay and 2 hard courts
(some lighted for night play). Hotel guests pay $25 per hour; other-
wise, the charge is $30 per hour.

WINDSURFING

Hilton Head is not recommended as a windsurfing destination.
Finding a place to windsurf is quite difficult, but with the plethora
of other sporting activities available, no one seems to mind. One
windsurfer warns that catching a tailwind at the public beaches at
the airport and the Holiday Inn could land you at the bombing
range on Parris Island, the Marine Corps' basic-training facility.

SHOPPING

Hilton Head is browsing heaven, with more than 30 shopping centers spread around the island. Chief shopping sites include **Pineland
Station** (Matthews Dr. and U.S. 278), with more than 30 shops and
half a dozen restaurants; and **Coligny Plaza** (Coligny Circle), with
more than 60 shops, food stands, and several good restaurants. We've
found some of the best bargains in the South at **Tanger Outlet
Stores I and II** (✆ 843/837-4339), on U.S. Hwy. 278 at the gateway to Hilton Head. The outlet has more than 45 factory stores,
including Ralph Lauren, Brooks Brothers, and J. Crew. The hours of
most shops are Monday to Saturday 10am to 9pm and Sunday 11am

An Excursion to Sleepy but Historic Bluffton

Despite the deep appeal of the area's sports and outdoor cur-riculums, history buffs might want a morning's diversion into a Low Country venue that's older and more historic than what's available within the relatively modern resorts of Hilton Head. If that's the case, consider a few hours' excur-sion to a 19th-century riverfront community that time has almost literally passed by: historic Bluffton, a town perched on the South Carolina mainland within a short drive of Hilton Head.

Bluffton's historic core remains about the way it looked in 1901. Be warned in advance not to expect palatial, aristo-cratic homes open to the public. Some of those were burned in 1863 during the Civil War. Most of those that remain are private, closed to the public, and relatively small, collectively reflecting the mercantile society of river traders who occu-pied them. The most impressive of the buildings is the much-weathered, carpenter Gothic Episcopal Church of the Cross, 110 Calhoun St., at the edge of the May River.

Calhoun Street has the community's densest concentration of historic homes. But for a deeper insight into just how slow and sleepy this town really is, drop into the **Heyward House,** 70 Boundary St. at the corner of Bridge Street (© **843/757-6293**). The low-slung farmhouse design of Heyward House, originally built in 1840 and later enlarged prior to 1900, was inspired by earlier planters' homes in the British West Indies. It's open for guided tours Monday through Friday 10am to 3pm and Saturday 11am to 2pm. Tours are free, but dona-tions to the upkeep of the house are appreciated. A care-taker here will give you a free map for a self-guided walking tour of the town as well. Depending on the season there may or may not be a kitschy collection of battered memorabilia for sale somewhere along the length of Calhoun Street.

For information about the somewhat limited appeal of Bluffton, contact the **Old Town Bluffton Merchant Society** at © **843/815-9522** or visit www.oldtownbluffton.com.

to 6pm. Another desirable gaggle of upscale boutiques is the **Village at Wexford,** on Hilton Head Island's south end. Within, you'll find one of the most comprehensive purveyors of kitchen tools and table-ware in the Low Country, **Le Cookery,** B-3 Wexford Village (© **843/785-7171**).

WHERE TO STAY ON HILTON HEAD

Since its debut, Hilton Head tended to specialize in the rental of upscale, ocean-fronting luxury homes and villas, and prices are higher than what's available in less-desirable parts of South Carolina. In recent years, however, the roster of lodgings has expanded to include some simplified economy lodgings as well. The resort boasts more than 6,000 villas, 3,000 hotel or motel rooms, and at least 1,000 timeshare units. Most facilities offer discount rates between November and March, and golf and tennis packages are available year-round.

VERY EXPENSIVE

Hilton Head Marriott Resort & Spa 🏨🏨   Set on 2 acres of landscaped grounds and bordering the oceanfront, this supremely comfortable hotel is surrounded by the much more massive acreage of the Palmetto Dunes Oceanfront Resort (p. 143) and is just 10 minutes from the Hilton Head airport. The hotel's 10-story tower of rooms dominates everything around it. Thanks to an elaborate $28-million renovation in 2007 and 2008, things here are looking spiffy, indeed. Rooms are smaller and less opulent than you might expect of such a well-rated hotel, but all are comfortably furnished. Most rooms open onto small balconies overlooking the garden or the ocean. The hotel's program of sports and recreation is among the best on the island, and the island's state-of-the-art spa (Soleil) is the largest on Hilton Head Island.

In the Palmetto Dunes Oceanfront Resort, Hilton Head Island, SC 29938. © **800/228-9290** or 843/686-8400. Fax 843/686-8450. www.hiltonheadmarriott.com. 513 units. $179–$229 double; $435–$725 suite. AE, DC, DISC, MC, V. Valet parking $18; self-parking $10. **Amenities:** Restaurant; 2 bars; coffee shop; 3 pools (1 indoor); 3 18-hole golf courses; 25 tennis courts nearby; health club; full spa; sauna; gift shop; hair salon; room service; babysitting; laundry service; dry cleaning; nonsmoking rooms; rooms for those w/limited mobility. *In room:* A/C, TV, Wi-Fi, minibar, coffeemaker, hair dryer, iron, safe, bathrobe.

The Inn at Palmetto Bluff 🏨🏨🏨 *(Kids)*   A jewel in the crown of the world-renowned Auberge Resorts, the Inn at Palmetto Bluff is an elegant, peaceful, relentlessly upscale resort located on the May River. With the South Carolina Low Country as a backdrop, guests can walk through the beautiful gardens, play golf on the Jack Nicklaus signature course, relax in the full-service spa, enjoy watersports like kayaking and fishing, enroll children in the kids' camp, take art classes, or enjoy a beach excursion. There is a $25-per-day service fee per guest room to be able to use the fitness center, kayaks, canoes,

Hilton Head

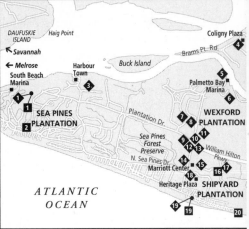

and outdoor lap pool. Guest room choices include cottages, cottage suites, and village homes. Exquisitely appointed, the cottages and cottage suites have vaulted ceiling and hardwood pine floors, fireplaces, and screened porches. Both choices open onto water views. You can also choose to rent one of the village homes. With two to four bedrooms, full kitchens, screened porches, and luxury bed linens, the village homes are ideal for families. The Inn at Palmetto Bluff offers four dining options: the elegant **River House Restaurant,** with river views; the **May River Grill** at the May River Golf Club; **Buffalo's,** centrally located in the Village; or dining in your own cottage.

476 Mount Pilla Rd., Bluffton, SC 29910. © **866/706-6565** or 843/706-6500. Fax 843/706-6550. www.palmettobluffresort.com. 77 units (42 cottages, 8 cottage suites, 27 village homes). $475–$850 cottage; $700–$1,100 cottage suite; from $1,100 village home. AE, DC, DISC, MC, V. **Amenities:** 3 restaurants; outdoor heated pool; fitness center; spa; boating activities; kids' camp; nonsmoking rooms; rooms for those w/limited mobility. *In room:* A/C, TV, Wi-Fi, kitchen (in village home), fridge.

The Westin Hilton Head Island Resort & Spa ☆☆ Set near the relatively isolated northern end of Hilton Head Island on 24

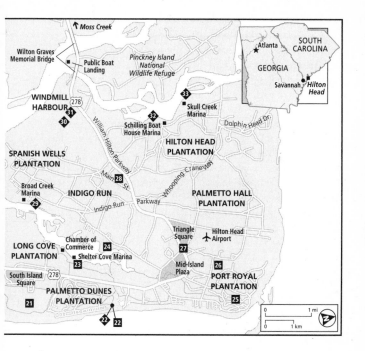

landscaped acres, this hotel stands out as the most child- and pet-friendly blockbuster hotel on the island. Its Disneyesque design, including cupolas and postmodern ornamentation that looks vaguely Moorish, evokes fanciful Palm Beach hotels. If there's a drawback, it's the fact that it is so obviously geared to families with children that romantically inclined couples without children in tow might not be thrilled. Fortunately, there's an active and much-respected children's camp on-site for the care and attention of young'uns. Most of the guest rooms have ocean views, and are outfitted in modernized interpretations of the Low Country plantation style.

2 Grasslawn Ave., Hilton Head Island, SC 29928. © **800/937-8461** or 843/681-4000. Fax 843/681-1096. www.starwoodhotels.com. 412 units. $169–$429 double; $450–$1,900 suite. Children 17 and under stay free in parent's room; children 4 and under eat free. Special promotions available. AE, DC, DISC, MC, V. **Amenities:** 3 restaurants; bar; 3 pools; 3 18-hole golf courses; 16 tennis courts; full-service health spa; Jacuzzi; room service; laundry service; dry cleaning; nonsmoking rooms; rooms for those w/limited mobility. *In room:* A/C, TV, Wi-Fi, minibar, coffeemaker, hair dryer, iron, safe.

EXPENSIVE

Crowne Plaza Hilton Head Island Beach Resort ⟨⟨   Tucked
away in the Shipyard Plantation and designed as the centerpiece of
that plantation's 800 acres, this five-story inn gives its primary competitor, Westin Resort, stiff competition. Today the hotel has the
island's most dignified lobby: a mahogany-sheathed postmodern
interpretation of Chippendale decor. The golf course associated with
the place has been praised by the National Audubon Society for its
respect for local wildlife. Guest rooms are nothing out of the ordi-
nary, with simple furnishings; yet the sheer beauty of the landscaping, the attentive service, the omnipresent nautical theme, and the
well-trained staff (dressed in nautically inspired uniforms) go a long
way toward making your stay memorable. On the premises are three
restaurants. The most glamorous is **Portz,** off the establishment's
main lobby. A good middle-bracket choice is **Brella's,** serving both
lunch and dinner. Certain nights in the premier bar, **Signals,** feature
line dancing and shag dancing.

130 Shipyard Dr., Shipyard Plantation, Hilton Head Island, SC 29928. ⟨⟩ **800/334-
1881** or 843/842-2400. Fax 843/785-8463. www.cphiltonhead.com. 340 units.
$199–$399 double; from $400 suite. AE, DC, DISC, MC, V. Free parking. **Amenities:**
2 restaurants; bar; 2 pools (1 indoor); fitness center; Jacuzzi; bikes; room service;
laundry service; dry cleaning; nonsmoking rooms; rooms for those w/limited mobility. *In room:* A/C, TV, Wi-Fi, minibar, coffeemaker, hair dryer, iron, safe.

Disney's Hilton Head Island Resort ⟨⟨ *Kids*   This medium-
scale, cost-effective, family-conscious resort is on a 15-acre island,
inland from the coast, that rises above Hilton Head's widest estuary,
Broad Creek. When it opened in 1996, it was the only U.S.-based
Disney resort outside of Florida and California. About 20 woodsy-
looking buildings are arranged into a compound. Expect lots of pine
trees and fallen pine needles, garlands of Spanish moss, plenty of
families with children, and an ambience that's several notches less
intense than that of hotels in Disney theme parks. Don't expect the
scale or the cast you've been conditioned to expect thanks to Disney's
more visible megaresorts in Orlando. As stated by a member of the
youthful and buoyant staff, "Mickey is on holiday," just like the
guests here. In lieu of that, references are made to Shadow the Dog
(a golden retriever that is the resort's mascot) and Blue Crab, a mul-
tifunctional storyteller, fisherman, and musician who provides at
least some of the resort's entertainment. Part of the fun, if you like
this sort of thing in concentrated doses, is the many summer-camp-
style·activities for kids with or without their parents. Public areas

have outdoorsy colors (forest green and cranberry), stuffed game fish, and varnished pine. Guest rooms usually contain minikitchens, suitable for feeding sandwiches and macaroni to the kids. **Tide Me Over** is a walk-up window serving Carolina cookery for breakfast and lunch. The resort runs a shuttle to and from a nearby beach at 15-minute intervals daily between 10am and 5pm.

22 Harbourside Lane, Hilton Head Island, SC 29928. *©* **407/939-7540** or 843/341-4100. Fax 843/341-4130. www.dvc.disney.go.com. 123 units. $165–$330 studio; $260–$920 villa. AE, DC, DISC, MC, V. **Amenities:** 2 restaurants; bar; 3 outdoor pools; fitness center; Wi-Fi in public areas; babysitting; laundry service. *In room:* A/C, TV, kitchenette (in most), coffeemaker, hair dryer, iron, safe.

Hilton Oceanfront Resort *⚓*   This award-winning property isn't the most imposing on the island. Many visitors, however, prefer the Hilton because of its hideaway position: tucked at the end of the main road through Palmetto Dunes and because its rooms are, on average, a bit larger than those within any other resort on the island. In addition, a $4-million renovation, completed in 2008, added to its appeal. The low-rise design features hallways that open to sea breezes at either end. Balconies angle out toward the beach allowing sea views from all guest rooms. **HH Prime,** an upmarket steakhouse that looks a lot more glamorous at night than during the day, is the resort's premier restaurant, although an on-site Pizza Hut serves less-expensive fare. In 2007, the resort inaugurated a glossy, urban-looking bar and lounge, with live music.

23 Ocean Lane (PO Box 6165), Hilton Head Island, SC 29938. *©* **866/625-2496** or 843/842-8000. Fax 843/341-8033. www.hiltonoceanfrontresort.com. 323 units. $139–$349 double; $299–$609 suite. AE, DC, DISC, MC, V. Parking $8–$12. **Amenities:** 4 restaurants; 2 bars; 2 outdoor pools; fitness center; spa; room service; laundry service; dry cleaning; coin-op laundry; nonsmoking rooms; rooms for those w/limited mobility. *In room:* A/C, TV, Wi-Fi, kitchenette, coffeemaker, hair dryer, iron, safe.

The Inn at Harbour Town *⚓⚓⚓*   Set within the boundaries of the Sea Pines Resort, this postmodern and upscale inn provides the only conventional hotel accommodations within a resort that's otherwise devoted to rentals of villas and condominiums. In its development of this inn, Sea Pines demanded an exceptionally high staff-to-client ratio. The building's exterior (ca. 2001) is high style, buff colored, and postmodern. Inside, there's a richly upholstered, lushly paneled replica of an English-inspired country house, with heart pine floors. Although the inn isn't positioned directly beside the sea, shuttle buses haul guests back and forth, and its location within a very short walk from the waterways, restaurants, shops, and entertainment of Harbour Town and its marina more than make up for it. The hotel is proud of its status as an AAA Four Diamond Award resort.

7 Lighthouse Lane, in the Sea Pines Resort, Hilton Head Island, SC 29928. ℂ **800/ 732-7463** or 843/363-8100. Fax 843/363-8155. www.seapines.com. 60 units $99– $349 double. AE, DISC, MC, V. **Amenities:** Bar; outdoor pool; 3 tennis courts; exercise area; spa; bikes; private butler and concierge services; business center; room service; laundry service; dry cleaning; nonsmoking rooms. *In room:* A/C, TV, Wi-Fi, fridge, hair dryer, iron, safe, fax machine.

Main Street Inn ★★★ *(Finds)* Don't expect cozy Americana from this small, luxurious inn, as it's grander and more European in its motifs than its name would imply. Designed like a small-scale villa that you might expect to see in the south of France, it was built in 1996 in a format that combines design elements from both New Orleans and Charleston, including cast-iron balustrades and a formal semitropical garden where guests are encouraged to indulge in afternoon tea. Inside, you'll find artfully clipped topiary, French Provincial furnishings, and accommodations that are more luxurious and more richly appointed than those of any other hotel in Hilton Head. Overall, despite a location that requires a drive to the nearest beach, the hotel provides a luxe alternative to the less personalized megahotels that lie nearby.

2200 Main St., Hilton Head Island, SC 29926. ℂ **800/471-3001** or 843/681-3001. Fax 843/681-5541. www.mainstreetinn.com. 33 units. $159–$249 double. $35 surcharge for 3rd occupant of double room. Rates include breakfast. AE, DISC, MC, V. Free parking. **Amenities:** Breakfast room; outdoor pool; spa; massage; laundry service; dry cleaning; nonsmoking rooms; rooms for those w/limited mobility. *In room:* A/C, TV, Wi-Fi, minibar, coffeemaker, hair dryer, iron.

Royal Dunes Resort ★ Comfortable and clean, but blandly standardized and somewhat anonymous, this is a compound of three-bedroom, three-bathroom apartments, occupancy of which has been aggressively marketed to independent investors as a timeshare. Whenever the investors aren't in residence, the apartments become available for rent on the open market. They occupy a quartet of four-story buildings located on the Port Royal Plantation. Each has a washer and dryer; a durable collection of wicker, rattan, and Southern Colonial furniture; and tub/shower combinations. The compound's location is at the edge of a forested greenbelt, within a 10-minute walk from the beach.

8 Wimbledon Court, Hilton Head, SC 29928. ℂ **843/681-9718.** Fax 843/681-2003. www.spmresorts.com. 56 units. $175–$235 double. AE, MC, V. **Amenities:** 2 pools; children's wading pool; gym; bike rentals; barbecue area; sporting activities. *In room:* A/C, TV, kitchen, iron, washer/dryer.

MODERATE

Holiday Inn Oceanfront 👫 *(Kids)*   The island's leading moderately priced hotel, and its oldest, with a history going back to 1970, this sprawling five-story building opens onto a crowded stretch of beach on the southern side of the island, directly across the road from the fast-food joints and souvenir shops of Coligny Plaza. The rooms are spacious and informally but comfortably furnished with rattan furniture and pastel colors, but the balconies are generally too small to actually walk out onto. Only a few of the rooms have actual sea views—most of them overlook parking lots and trees. In summer, planned children's activities are offered. Don't expect glamour, as the place is comfortable, crowded, and family invasive, with a crowded pool and barely enough parking. The staff, despite the many demands on their time, is genuinely concerned and helpful.

1 S. Forest Beach Dr. (PO Box 5728), Hilton Head Island, SC 29938. © **800/465-4329** or 843/785-5126. Fax 843/785-6678. www.holiday-inn.com. 202 units. $99–$249 double. AE, DC, DISC, MC, V. Free parking. **Amenities:** Restaurant; outdoor bar; outdoor pool; exercise room; room service; laundry service; nonsmoking rooms; rooms for those w/limited mobility. *In room:* A/C, TV, Wi-Fi, coffeemaker, hair dryer, iron, safe.

Park Lane Hotel Suites   Set on the eastern edge of Hilton Head's main traffic artery, midway between the Palmetto Dunes and Shipyard plantations, this is a three-story complex of functionally furnished but comfortable one-bedroom suites. The setting is wooded and parklike, and both cost-conscious families and business travelers on extended stays appreciate the simple cooking facilities in all suites.

12 Park Lane (in Central Park), Hilton Head Island, SC 29938. © **877/247-3431** or 843/686-5700. Fax 843/686-3952. www.hiltonheadparklanehotel.com. 156 units. $89–$100 suite. Rates include continental breakfast. AE, DC, DISC, MC, V. **Amenities:** Breakfast room; outdoor pool; 2 tennis courts; basketball court; fitness center; Jacuzzi; laundry service; dry cleaning; coin-op laundry; nonsmoking rooms; rooms for those w/limited mobility. *In room:* A/C, TV, Wi-Fi, kitchenette, coffeemaker, hair dryer, iron.

The South Beach Marina Inn 👫 *(Finds)*   Of the dozens of available accommodations within the Sea Pines Resort, this 1986 clapboard-sided complex of marina-front buildings is the only place offering traditional, by-the-night rooms. With lots of nautical, seafaring charm, the inn meanders over a labyrinth of catwalks and stairways above a complex of shops, souvenir kiosks, and restaurants. It is especially known for its location immediately adjacent to the Salty Dog Cafe—one of the island's most popular eateries. Each guest room is cozily outfitted with country-style braided rugs, pinewood floors, and homespun-charm decor celebrating rural 19th-century America.

232 S. Sea Pines Dr. (in the Sea Pines Resort), Hilton Head Island, SC 29920. © **800/ 367-3909** or 843/671-6498. www.sbinn.com. 17 units. $65–$179 1-bedroom apt; $87–$186 2-bedroom apt. AE, DISC, MC, V. Free parking. **Amenities:** Outdoor pool; nonsmoking rooms. *In room:* A/C, TV, kitchenette, coffeemaker, hair dryer, iron.

INEXPENSIVE

Days Inn   The Days Inn provides easy access to the beach, golf, tennis, marinas, and shopping. The rooms are wheelchair accessible and, although unremarkable, they are a good value for expensive Hilton Head. Families save money by using one of the grills outside for a home-style barbecue, to be enjoyed at one of the picnic tables.

9 Marina Side Dr., Hilton Head Island, SC 29928. © **800/329-7466** or 843/842-4800. Fax 843/842-5388. www.daysinn.com. 119 units. $89–$189 double; $201 suite. Rates include continental breakfast. Senior discounts available. AE, DISC, MC, V. Free parking. **Amenities:** Breakfast room; lounge; outdoor pool; coin-op laundry; nonsmoking rooms; rooms for those w/limited mobility. *In room:* A/C, TV, Wi-Fi, hair dryer, iron, safe.

Hampton Inn Hilton Head Island   This is one of the two or three most sought-after motels on Hilton Head, especially by families and business travelers who don't mind its lack of resort-style amenities and its straightforward, cost-effective simplicity. It's 5 miles from the Graves bridge and the closest motel to the airport. Rooms in pastel pinks and greens are quite comfortable and well maintained. Some rooms have refrigerators. Local calls are free, and continental breakfast is included in the rates. A renovation in 2007 added to its appeal.

1 Dillon Rd., Hilton Head Island, SC 29926. © **800/426-7866** or 843/681-7900. Fax 843/681-4330. www.hamptoninnhiltonhead.com. 125 units, 11 with kitchenette. $129–$189 double. Children 17 and under stay free in parent's room. Rates include continental breakfast. AE, DC, DISC, MC, V. **Amenities:** Breakfast room; outdoor pool; putting green; fitness center; coin-op laundry; nonsmoking rooms; rooms for those w/limited mobility. *In room:* A/C, TV, Wi-Fi, kitchenette (in some), fridge (in some), coffeemaker, hair dryer, iron, safe.

Hilton Head Metropolitan *(Kids)*   Affordable and favored by families with children, this 1970s-era hotel is a five-story, white-concrete hotel set directly across from the island's premier beach. Rooms are outfitted with contemporary-looking furniture and the kind of amenities that can make a stay here comfortable and convenient. But don't expect cutting-edge style: Each room is configured in a bland, generic style duplicated in motels throughout the world. Virtually everything on Hilton Head is within a 15-minute drive. Expect lots of families with children, especially during the peak holiday months of midsummer.

36 S. Forest Dr., Hilton Head, SC 29928. (℗ **800/535-3248** or 843/842-3100. Fax 843/785-6928. www.hiltonheadmetropolitan.com. 140 units. $49–$139 double. Rates include continental breakfast. AE, DC, DISC, MC, V. **Amenities:** Outdoor pool; gym; game room; all nonsmoking rooms; rooms for those w/limited mobility. *In room:* A/C, TV, kitchenette (in some), coffeemaker, hair dryer, iron.

VILLA RENTALS

With thousands of available villas for rent on an island whose construction boom almost seems to never end, you'd be well advised to contact an expert. The **Vacation Company** (℗ **800/845-7018;** www.vacationcompany.com) has been in business for almost a quarter-century and specializes in the rental of homes and villas throughout the region. Its leading competitors include **Beach Properties of Hilton Head** (℗ **800/671-5155** or 843/671-5155; www.beach-property.com); **Hilton Head Vacation Rentals** (℗ **800/732-7671;** www.800beachme.com); and **ResortQuest Vacation Home Network** (℗ **800/448-3408** or 843/686-8124; www.resortquesthilton head.com).

Two developments that we consider especially appealing are the following:

Palmetto Dunes Oceanfront Resort 🐾 🄺ids   This relaxed and informal enclave of privately owned villas is set within the sprawling 1,800-acre complex of Palmetto Dunes Plantation, 7 miles south of the bridge. Accommodations range all the way from one-bedroom condos, booked mostly by groups, to four-bedroom villas, each of the latter furnished in the owner's personal taste. This is the place for longer stays, ideal for families who want a home away from home when they're traveling. In fact, in 2003 it was ranked as the number-one family resort in the continental U.S. and Canada by *Travel + Leisure Family* and is still listed among the top 10. Villas are fully equipped and receive housekeeping service; they're located on the ocean, fairways, or lagoons. Each villa comes with a full kitchen, washer and dryer, living room, dining area, and balcony or patio.

Palmetto Dunes (PO Box 5606), Hilton Head Island, SC 29938. (℗ **800/827-3006.** www.palmettodunes.com. 500 units. $575–$3,500 per week condo or villa. Golf and honeymoon packages available. 2-night minimum stay. 50% deposit for reservations. AE, DC, DISC, MC, V. Free parking. **Amenities:** 20 restaurants; 12 bars; 28 pools; 3 18-hole golf courses; 25 tennis courts; 200-slip marina; nonsmoking rooms; rooms for those w/limited mobility. *In room:* A/C, TV, safe (in some).

The Sea Pines Resort 🐾🐾🐾   Since 1955, this has been one of the leading condo developments in America, sprawling across 5,500 acres at the southernmost tip of the island. Don't come to Sea Pines looking for quick overnight accommodations. The entire place encourages stays of at least a week. Lodgings vary—everything from one- to four-bedroom villas to opulent private homes that are available when the owners are away. An additional option is the separately recommended Inn at Harbour Town, a 60-room inn, which offers the only venue at Sea Pines Resort for renting a conventional hotel room. The clientele here includes hordes of golfers because Sea Pines is the home of the Verizon Heritage golf tournament, a major stop on the PGA tour. If you're not a Sea Pines guest, you can eat, shop, or enjoy aspects of its nightlife.

Sea Pines (PO Box 7000), Hilton Head Island, SC 29938. ✆ **888/807-6873** or 843/785-3333. Fax 843/842-1475. www.seapines.com. 400–500 units. $170–$280 1-bedroom villa; $290–$365 2-bedroom villa; $305–$550 3-bedroom villa. Rates are daily, based on 3-night stay. AE, DC, DISC, MC, V. **Amenities:** 12 restaurants; 12 bars; 2 outdoor pools; 3 18-hole golf courses; 28 tennis courts; fitness center; spa; watersports; massage; babysitting; horseback riding; nonsmoking rooms; rooms for those w/limited mobility. *In room:* A/C, TV, Wi-Fi, kitchenette or kitchen, washer/dryer.

WHERE TO DINE ON HILTON HEAD

Hilton Head has the dubious distinction of having the most expensive restaurants in South Carolina. What on the island might be ranked as moderate would be considered very expensive in other parts of the state.

EXPENSIVE

Marley's Island Grille 🎘🎘 *Kids* SEAFOOD/STEAKS   This is a Caribbean-themed restaurant near Park Plaza, which is noted for its fresh, wood-grilled seafood and steaks. The bartenders make the best margaritas and sangria on island, along with an array of tropical rainbow frozen libations. Marley's has a fun, albeit kitschy, island vibe, and is popular with both islanders and vacationers. It is also a family favorite. Try the lobster tacos with rice and beans or the tortilla-crusted tilapia with jumbo lump crab salsa. Among favorite wood-grilled specialties are jerk grilled chicken or red chili–rubbed flank steak with chimichurri sauce. The grill reaches a temperature of 1,100 degrees Fahrenheit, which creates flavor, moisture, and tenderness. After dinner, you can enjoy dessert next door at Marley's Ice Cream & Trading Company.

35 Office Park Rd. ✆ **843/686-5800.** Reservations recommended. Main courses $16–$35. AE, DISC, MC, V. Sun–Thurs 5–10pm; Fri–Sat 5–11pm.

Michael Anthony's ✸✸✸ ITALIAN Nearly every food critic on the island has declared Michael Anthony's the best place to eat in Hilton Head. Chef Michael Cirafesi has created an exquisite menu blending traditional Italian flavors with Low Country ingredients. It's family owned and operated, and the Fazzinis and Cirafesis bring hands-on attention and care to every detail of the restaurant. Michael Anthony's also has a wine bar where you can enjoy your favorite beverage or dessert or choose to have dinner—no reservations required. We started with the *antipasto della casa al Italiano,* an assortment of Italian meats, cheeses, and marinated vegetables. Our dining companion chose the local favorite *gnocchi di patate ai porcini,* homemade potato gnocchi with a sauce of porcini mushrooms with demi-glace and cream. The flavorful *involtini di vitello con spinachi, formaggio e salsiccia* (medallions of veal with spinach, cheese, and Italian sausage, sautéed with white wine) is a delectable specialty. Don't miss the chocolate soufflé cake, with a melted hot center of chocolate served with vanilla gelato.

37 New Orleans Rd. ✆ **843/785-6272.** www.michael-anthonys.com. Reservations required. Main courses $17–$38. AE, DC, DISC, MC, V. Mon–Sat 5:30–10pm.

Ocean Grille ✸ AMERICAN/STEAKS/SEAFOOD One of the premier restaurants of Hilton Head is a waterfront eatery overlooking a marina. The skilled chefs specialize in fresh seafood and premium choice steaks expertly prepared. Menus, including the soups and salads, are seasonally adjusted. First-rate appetizers include stone crab claws or coconut fried calamari. When available, the fresh catch of the day is served, and it can be grilled, broiled, blackened, or fried. The fish platter is served with rice pilaf and seasonable vegetables. The sauces are sublime, including lobster butter, tangerine coulis, or garlic saffron aioli. New York strip is grilled and served with buttermilk mashed potatoes, or else you might prefer mahimahi or tilapia.

1 Shelter Cove Lane. ✆ **843/785-3030.** Reservations recommended. Main courses $21–$36. AE, DC, MC, V. Mar–Oct daily 5–10pm; Nov–Feb daily 5–9:30pm.

Old Fort Pub ✸ INTERNATIONAL Remote and isolated from the bulk of other Hilton Head eateries, and nestled within the upscale residential community of the Hilton Head Plantation, on the island's northwest coast, this is one of the most consistently reliable and upscale restaurants in the Low Country. It lies only a few paces from the ruin of what was commissioned by the Union army in 1862 as a fort (Fort Mitchell), and as such, some diners make it a point to traipse around the signposted footpaths in the daylight hours preceding an evening meal at this restaurant. You'll dine within a building dating from 1973 that evokes an interconnected series of clapboard-sided houses, amid candlelight and crisp napery, with views over salt marshes and estuaries. Chef Keith Josefiak prepares dishes that include Vidalia onion shoots and goat cheese tarts; spring asparagus *en croûte* with prosciutto and roasted tomato vinaigrette; a succulent version of local bouillabaisse that just happens to include collards and tasso ham; crab cakes; and pork loin with chanterelles, Vidalia onions, and pistachio nuts.

65 Skull Creek Dr. ② **843/681-2386.** Reservations recommended. Main courses $24–$37. AE, DC, DISC, MC, V. Mon–Sat 5–10pm; Sun 11am–2pm (brunch).

Redfish Grill ✿ INTERNATIONAL   One of the more talked-about restaurants on Hilton Head Island occupies a rambling villa that diners quickly discover contains shopping as well as dining options. A popular pastime involves dropping into the on-site wine shop before a meal here, selecting a bottle of wine, and—for a $10 corkage fee, drinking it with your meal. As for exactly where within the building you'd like to dine, we suggest that you wander a bit, since there are three distinct areas. They include two postmodern, vaguely Asian-inspired dining rooms, each with massive, sculptural-looking bouquets of flowers. There are also some tables within the wine shop for a cozy but somewhat offbeat additional option.

The menu changes with the seasons, but might at any time include Asian-style marinated tenderloin of beef with Thai cucumbers in a lettuce leaf wrap; a variety of "naked fish," that's simply grilled and served over salad; grilled sea bass with a wasabi cream sauce and soy glaze on a bed of Udon noodles; seared jumbo scallops served with asparagus and lobster-studded macaroni and cheese; and two of what are probably the most upscale and expensive burgers in the Carolina Low Country: One is made entirely with Kobe beef and accented with foie gras, pepper jack cheese, truffles, and port demi-glace; the other is crafted from chunks of Maine lobster mixed with shrimp. The restaurant lies in an isolated residential neighborhood inland from the sea, close to the Cross-Island Bridge.

8 Archer Rd. ② **843/686-3388.** www.redfishofhiltonhead.com. Reservations recommended. Lunch sandwiches, salads, and platters $8–$12; dinner main courses $21–$32. AE, MC, V. Mon–Sat 11:30am–2pm and 5–10pm; Sun 5–10pm.

MODERATE

All of these so-called moderately priced restaurants have expensive shellfish dishes. However, if you order from the lower end of the price scale, enjoying mainly meat and poultry dishes, you'll find platters that cost $20 or less. Helpings, for the most part, are generous, so you'll rarely need to order appetizers, which will keep your overall cost in the more affordable price range.

Alexander's ✿ SEAFOOD/INTERNATIONAL   One of the most visible independent restaurants (in other words, not associated with a hotel) on Hilton Head lies in a gray-stained, wood-sided building just inside the main entrance to Palmetto Dunes. The decor includes Oriental carpets, big-windowed views over salt marshes, wicker furniture, and an incongruous—some say startling—collection of vintage Harley-Davidson motorcycles, none with more than 1,000 miles on them, dating from 1946, 1948, 1966, and 1993. Each is artfully displayed as a work of sculpture and as a catalyst to dialogues. Powerful flavors and a forthright approach to food are the rules of the kitchen. The chefs don't allow a lot of innovation on their menu—you've had all these dishes before—but fine ingredients are used, and each dish is prepared with discretion and restraint. Try the oysters Savannah or the bacon-wrapped shrimp, and most definitely have a bowl of Low Country seafood chowder. Guaranteed to set you salivating are the scallops encrusted with sun-dried tomatoes, or the bluefin crab cakes. Steak, duck, rack of lamb, and pork—all in familiar versions—round out the menu.

76 Queen's Folly, Palmetto Dunes. ✆ 843/785-4999. Reservations recommended. Main courses $20–$30. AE, DC, DISC, MC, V. Daily 5–10pm.

Antonio's ✿ ITALIAN   Located at the Village at Wexford, this island favorite with its elegant decor and fine Italian cuisine continues its bold quest to duplicate the flavors of sunny Italy, and for the most part succeeds admirably. Chef Mottram is a whiz at using recipes from all the provinces of Italy, although classic preparations of Italian seafood are clearly his favorite. Piano music adds to the ambience, as does a visit to the Wine Room, where you can see Hilton Head's most comprehensive assemblage of Italian wine.

The antipasti selection is one of the island's best, including many classics such as mussels with chorizo sausage, wild mushrooms, grilled ciabatta, Peroni, and lobster consommé; or crispy calamari with a honey chipotle aioli. The chef and his team prepare succulent pastas, including one based on such fruits of the sea as sautéed shrimp, scallops, and mussels flavored with a tomato and saffron broth. Veal saltimbocca appears delectably with crispy prosciutto and creamy roasted pancetta sage potatoes.

1000 William Hilton Pkwy. ⓒ **843/842-5505**. www.antonios.net. Reservations recommended. Main courses $16–$38. AE, DC, DISC, MC, V. Daily 5:30–10pm. Closed Christmas Eve.

Black Marlin Bayside Grill ⓕ SEAFOOD   Partly because of its location beside a marshy inland channel, a few steps from the most battered-looking boatyard and marina on Hilton Head Island, this is the most raffish of the "grand cuisine" restaurants of Hilton Head. With lots of salty cosmopolitan charm, fun, and an insouciance that might remind you of Key West, the restaurant seems a world removed from the manicured, upscale conservatism of the island's secluded residential zones. Thomas Corey is the chef here, a refugee from the cold Northeast, and an expert at crafting flavor from the fresh seafood that arrives directly from fishermen every morning at dawn. Lunch fare includes meal-size salads, at least a dozen hungry-man's sandwiches, pastas, and fried seafood. Dinners are more ambitious, focusing on tuna carpaccio, tempura lobster, fish or shrimp tacos, crab-stuffed flounder, big slabs of steak, and between 7 and 10 dishes that appear only on a blackboard, based on the seafood haul brought in that day.

86 Helmsman Way, at the Palmetto Bay Marina. ⓒ **843/785-4950**. www.hemingways baysidegrill.com. Reservations not accepted. Lunch sandwiches, salads, and platters $8–$15; dinner main courses $20–$33. AE, DC, MC, V. Mon–Fri 11:30am–10pm; Sat–Sun 10am–2pm and 4–10pm.

Boathouse II ⓚⓘⓓⓢ SEAFOOD   The nautical lodge decor and the view over salt marshes and Skull Creek form an appropriate venue for the serving of some fine seafood at affordable prices. From some tables you can see the Pinckney Island Wildlife Preserve and the adjacent marina. Walk under a canopy of giant oaks to enjoy a drink at the Market 13 outdoor bar. Live entertainment is offered, and it's a family-friendly place with a children's menu. Plenty of fresh seafood is prepared with that old Charleston flavor, including shrimp and stone-ground grits, Southern catfish with Carolina fixin's, and the chef's own Boathouse bouillabaisse. Excellent crab cakes are another specialty. For meat fanciers, slow-roasted baby back ribs in a sour mash sauce, served with buttermilk "smashed" potatoes and collards, or filet mignon or prime rib seduce the palate.

397 Squire Pope Rd. ⓒ **843/681-3663**. www.boathouserestaurant.net. Reservations not required. Brunch $9.50–$15; main courses $7–$14 lunch, $17–$28 dinner. AE, DC, DISC, MC, V. Daily 11:30am–3pm and 5–9pm. Closed Christmas.

Charlie's L'Etoile Verte ⓕⓕ INTERNATIONAL   Outfitted like a tongue-in-cheek version of a Parisian bistro, our favorite restaurant on Hilton Head Island was also a favorite of former president Clinton during one of his island conferences. The atmosphere is unpretentious but elegant. The service is attentive, polite, and infused with an appealingly hip mixture of old- and new-world courtesy. Begin with roast portobello mushrooms and crab, and move on to tilapia sautéed in a Parmesan crust. End this rare dining experience with biscotti or a "sailor's trifle." The wine list is impressive.

8 New Orleans Rd. ✆ **843/785-9277.** www.charliesofhiltonhead.com. Reservations required. Main courses $9–$16 lunch, $24–$71 dinner. AE, DISC, MC, V. Mon 6– 9:30pm; Tues–Sat 11:30am–2pm and 6–9:30pm.

CQ's ✿✿ AMERICAN/LOW COUNTRY   With a design based on a 19th-century rice barn, this Harbour Town restaurant is a successful conversion of an already existing property. The extensive wine list, some 400 vintages, is one of the best on the island. A tradition on Hilton Head since 1973, the restaurant will allow you to craft your own unique menu at *La Table du Vin,* with the assistance of a creative culinary team.

The well-thought-out menu of Low Country and American classics reflects the rich bounty of South Carolina—fresh seafood, beef, and game—and also shows a French influence. For a sampling of harmonious appetizers, try such delights as brie *en croûte* with a raspberry purée and crisp apples, or a Maine lobster and Boursin cheesecake with a sherry butter cream—the latter is one of our favorites.

Count yourself lucky if you arrive when game is on the menu. Our party recently took delight in the seared medallions of venison with roasted onion, shallots, leeks, and asparagus; a Madeira wine reduction added that extra special flavor.

140-A Lighthouse Rd. ✆ **843/671-2779.** www.cqsrestaurant.com. Reservations recommended. Main courses $23–$36. AE, DC, DISC, MC, V. Mar–May daily 5– 10pm; June–Nov daily 5:30–10pm; Dec–Feb daily 5–9:30pm.

Crane's Tavern & Steakhouse ✿ STEAK/SEAFOOD   The original Crane's Steakhouse was launched in Philadelphia at the dawn of the 20th century and was one of the most popular taverns there until Prohibition. Always a family business, it was established by Hank Crane, who came over from Ireland and passed the business down to generations of Crane sons, and now daughter Beth Anne. Crane's is now a tradition on Hilton Head.

As Hilton Head restaurants rush to claim the best seafood, Crane's bases its simple, classic fare on prime beef. Each of the choicest cuts is prepared to your taste—can any trencherman cope with the 20-ounce cut? A 12-ounce prime rib was the best we could manage, and it was tender, well flavored, and quite succulent. Steaks get the focus, but the other offerings are good as well, including jumbo lump crab cakes or stuffed chicken. The sweet potato ravioli in a molasses cream was a delightful surprise.

26 New Orleans Rd. © **843/341-2333.** www.cranestavern.com. Reservations recommended. Main courses $17–$46. AE, DC, DISC, MC, V. Daily 5–10pm. Closed Thanksgiving and Christmas.

The Crazy Crab North *(Kids* SEAFOOD   Usually crowded, especially in summer, this is the restaurant that's most likely to be patronized by locals, partly because an entire family can be fed here at relatively modest prices. In a modern, low-slung building near the bridge that connects the island with the South Carolina mainland, it serves baked, broiled, or fried versions of stuffed flounder; seafood kabobs; oysters; the catch of the day; and any combination thereof. She-crab soup and New England–style clam chowder are prepared fresh daily, children's menus are available, and desserts are a high point for chocoholics. There's a second branch of this restaurant with the same hours and virtually the same prices, at Harbour Town in the Sea Pines Resort (© **843/681-5021**).

U.S. 278 at Jarvis Creek. © **843/681-5021.** Reservations not accepted. Lunch sandwiches, salads, and platters $10–$15; dinner main courses $17–$33. AE, DISC, MC, V. Daily 11:30am–10pm.

Harbour Town Grill *(Finds* AMERICAN   For years, this woodsy-looking refuge of golfers was open only to members of the nearby golf club and their guests. Several years ago, however, it opened to the public at large, a fact that's still not widely publicized in Hilton Head and that sometimes seems to catch some local residents by surprise. Decorated with a simple, unpretentious style that's vaguely Scottish and punctuated with occasional pieces of golfing memorabilia, this small-scale affair has views over the 9th hole and room for only about 50 diners at a time. Inside, it's sporty looking and relatively informal during the day, when most of the menu is devoted to thickly stuffed deli-style sandwiches and salads named in honor of golf stars. Dinners are more formal and more elaborate, with good-tasting dishes such as local shrimp sautéed with ginger, Vidalia onions, and collard greens; roasted rack of American lamb with white beans, spinach, and rosemary; and an array of thick-cut slabs of meat that include beef, lamb, veal, and chicken.

In the Harbour Town Golf Links Clubhouse, Sea Pines. © **843/363-8380.** www. seapines.com. Reservations recommended for dinner. Lunch sandwiches and platters $9–$13; dinner main courses $24–$38. AE, DC, DISC, MC, V. Daily 7–3pm and 5–10pm.

Hudson's on the Docks ✦ SEAFOOD   Built as a seafood-processing factory in 1912, and an excellent choice if you're looking for an escape from the island's crowded southern tier, this restaurant still processes fish, clams, and oysters for local distribution, so you know that everything is fresh. If you're seated in the north dining room, you'll be eating in the original oyster factory. We strongly recommend the crab cakes, the steamed shrimp, and the especially appealing blackened catch of the day. Local oysters (seasonal) are also a specialty, breaded and deep-fried. Before and after dinner, stroll on the docks past shrimp boats, and enjoy the view of the mainland and nearby Parris Island. Sunsets here are panoramic. Lunch is served in the Oyster Bar.

1 Hudson Rd. (go to Skull Creek just off Square Pope Rd. signposted from U.S. 278). ℂ 843/681-2772. www.hudsonsonthedocks.com. Reservations not accepted. Main courses $8–$15 lunch, $13–$23 dinner. AE, DC, MC, V. Daily 11am–2:30pm and 5–10pm.

Juleps ✦✦ AMERICAN/SOUTHERN   This is the Hilton Head restaurant where we'd take Jefferson Davis, former president of the Confederacy, should he miraculously appear and want dinner. With its beveled glass, French doors, glass-framed windows, and cream and taupe colors, it has that certain nostalgic atmosphere—like a walk into a time capsule. This is the friendly oasis maintained by Sam and Melissa Cochran—he a longtime islander and she a first-rate chef. Served in three dining areas, with a lively bar, are their original concoctions. Excellent ingredients go into such starters as barbecued duck breast over a corn pancake or Cajun-blackened oysters that are most savory. Here's your chance to try that Southern favorite, fried green tomatoes over creamy grits in a red pepper sauce seasoned with fresh scallions. Nothing is more typical of the Carolinas than a dish of quail with andouille sausage. Desserts are worth making room for, especially the berry shortcake full of strawberries, blackberries, and blueberries.

14 Greenwood Dr. ℂ 843/842-5857. Reservations recommended. Main courses $19–$34. AE, DC, DISC, MC, V. Mon–Sat 11:30am–2pm and 5:30–10pm. Closed July 4 and Christmas.

Jump & Phil's Bar & Grill AMERICAN   Cozy and convivial, with dining tables positioned on three sides of a large rectangular bar that does a thriving business with 40- and 50-something owners of nearby homes and condos, this is the brainchild of entrepreneurs Jump and Phil, who spent 20 years working in other restaurants before branching out on their own. Outfitted with early-20th-century Americana,

some battered antiques, and dark paneling, the place identifies itself
as the headquarters for Hilton Head's Green Bay Packers fan club.
Food is generously portioned, reasonably priced, and utterly unpretentious. Menu items include two-fisted versions of BLTs, Cuban
sandwiches, chili dogs, tuna melts, BBQ'd pork, and burgers. More
substantial fare includes grits with shrimp, fried oyster platters,
chicken potpie, and grilled rib-eye steaks.

In the Hilton Head Plaza, Greenwood Dr. off Sea Pines Circle. © **843/785-9070.**
www.jumpandphils.com. Reservations not necessary. Sandwiches $8–$12; main
courses $13–$22. AE, DISC, MC, V. Daily 11:30am–2am.

Kingfisher Seafood & Steakhouse 🔆 SEAFOOD/STEAK
"Fresh fish—never frozen" is the motto of this popular restaurant at
Shelter Cove, with a panoramic view of the harbor through large picture windows. All three of its dining rooms feature a water view, and
there is live music nightly. You can request the fish catch of the day
to be prepared several ways, including the standards such as grilled
or blackened, but also herb encrusted or else Greek style with tomatoes, onions, mushrooms, spinach, artichokes, and feta cheese.
Served crisp and cold, oysters come on the half shell. Each day different varieties are served. For pasta lovers, the chef makes a creative
lasagna every day. Seafood selections range from a very respectable
Scottish fish and chips to a more typical Charleston-style shrimp 'n'
grits in white gravy. Our recently sampled ahi tuna came seared
medium rare with a *ponzu* sauce, wasabi mashed potatoes, and Asian
slaw. The filet mignons offered here are tender and full of flavor and
served with a creamy béarnaise sauce.

8 Harbour Lane. © **843/785-4442.** www.kingfisherseafood.com. Reservations recommended. Main courses $9–$40. AE, DISC, MC, V. Daily 5–10pm. Closed Christmas
Eve and Christmas.

The Old Oyster Factory 🔆 SEAFOOD/STEAK   Built on the
site of one of Hilton Head's original oyster canneries, this always-
popular landmark offers waterfront dining overlooking Broad Creek.
The restaurant's post-and-beam decor has garnered several architectural awards. At sunset, every table enjoys a panoramic view as diners sip their "sundowners."

All the dishes here can be found on seafood menus from Maine to
Hawaii. But that doesn't mean they're not good. The cuisine is truly
palate friendly, beginning with such appetizers as a tangy kettle of
clams steamed in a lemon-butter sauce, or else a delectable crab cake
sautéed and served in a chile-garlic tartar sauce. Will it be oysters
Rockefeller (baked with spinach and a béarnaise sauce) or oysters

Savannah (shrimp, crabmeat, and smoked bacon)? Almond-crusted mahimahi is among the more tantalizing main courses, as are seafood pasta and broiled sea scallops. Nonseafood eaters can go for a chargrilled chicken breast.

101 Marsh Rd. ✆ 843/681-6040. www.oldoysterfactory.com. Reservations not accepted. Main courses $17–$32. AE, DC, DISC, MC, V. Daily 5–10pm (closing time can vary).

Reilley's Grill & Bar *ⓕ Finds* AMERICAN   It rarely advertises, so much of its business derives from locals, who come here after dark for hobnobbing, gossiping, or eating and drinking within the orbit of patriarch Tom Reilley, the island's ultimate F&B insider. If you can manage to pull yourself away from the mahogany and cherry-paneled bar, you'll discover that food items are the most fussed over and most sophisticated of any other eatery within Hilton Head Plaza. Examples include garlic chicken pasta; grilled loin of beef with peppers and onions; pork chops stuffed with spinach and mozzarella with a Gouda cream sauce; upscale salads such as a version with warm brie and spinach; sandwiches made with such ingredients as tilapia, croissants, meatloaf, and cheddar; and Asian-style chicken salad. There's also a roster of grills and a signature version of sirloin topped with an Irish whiskey peppercorn sauce and cheese grits.

In the Hilton Head Plaza, Greenwood Dr. off Sea Pines Circle. ✆ 843/842-4414. Reservations recommended for dinner. Lunch sandwiches and platters $6–$9; dinner main courses $10–$25. AE, MC, V. Daily 11am–2am.

Santa Fe Cafe *ⓕ* MEXICAN   The best, most-stylish Mexican restaurant on Hilton Head, the Santa Fe Cafe has rustic, Southwestern-inspired decor and cuisine that infuses traditional recipes with nouvelle flair. Live music adds to the allure. Menu items are often presented in colors as bright as the Painted Desert. Dishes might include tequila shrimp, herb-roasted chicken with jalapeño cornbread stuffing and mashed potatoes laced with red chilies, grilled tenderloin of pork with smoked habanero sauce and sweet-potato fries, and worthy burritos and chimichangas. The quesadilla is one of the most beautifully presented dishes in town.

700 Plantation Center. ✆ 843/785-3838. www.santafecafe.com. Reservations recommended. Main courses $7–$12. AE, DISC, MC, V. Mon–Fri noon–2pm and 5–10pm; Sat–Sun 5–10pm.

211 Park AMERICAN/SOUTHERN/ITALIAN   In the Park Plaza Shopping Center, with a contemporary decor, this combined wine bar and bistro is a popular gathering place at night. Actual islanders posed for the mural used as a backdrop. Bill Cubbage, who long ago tired of hearing his name pronounced like a vegetable, opened this place in 1996, and has enjoyed a loyal following ever since.

Many of his dishes are adaptations of international recipes—for example, Bill's takeoff on traditional paella. Here it includes some of the same ingredients as in Spain, but it's served over grits. Shellfish is served in a black Thai sauce, and you might also watch for the specials announced nightly. Pizza comes with smoked salmon, feta cheese, dill, capers, and onions, or you might opt for one of the pasta dishes, the most ordered being a Jamaican-inspired "rasta pasta" with chicken, shrimp, andouille sausage, peppers, and a jerk cream sauce. The chef won our esteem with his cedar-planked salmon topped with whole-grain mustard and broiled to give the fish a slightly smoky flavor. The dish emerged with a sweet-potato waffle and collards (how Southern can you get?).

211 Park Plaza. ✆ **843/686-5212**. www.211park.com. Reservations recommended. Main courses $18–$46; pizzas $10–$14. AE, DC, DISC, MC, V. Mon–Sat 5:30–10pm. Closed New Year's Day, Thanksgiving, and Christmas.

INEXPENSIVE

The British Open Pub BRITISH/AMERICAN   Except for the fact that the hardworking staff speaks with a Carolina accent, you might believe you've stumbled into a remote, woodsy-looking, and unpretentious corner of Britain. And if you opt for a meal here, you'll be in good company, since the town's mayor and a few of his cohorts have to some degree adopted the place as a regular hangout. Since it rarely advertises, prices remain low. Its name derives from the obsession of its owners with the minutiae of the U.K.'s most famous golf tournament. There's British ale on tap, plus ever-popular versions of fish and chips, lobster potpies, shepherd's pie, and meal-size salads. As for Carolina-inspired food, we recommend Chef Jason's twin crab cake platter, or perhaps the baby back barbecued ribs. This is one of the least touristy watering holes on Hilton Head Island, and the drinks are stiff enough to ensure that locals continue to patronize it in droves.

In the Village at Wexford Shopping Center. ✆ **843/686-6736**. www.britishopen pub.net. Reservations not accepted. Sandwiches and platters $8–$24. AE, DC, MC, V. Mon–Sat 11am–10pm; Sun 9am–10pm (bar closes at 2pm).

One Hot Mama's American Grill 𝕗 (Kids) GRILLS/BARBECUE It's fun, it's whimsical, and its reasonably priced platters are served in a setting that evokes a mixture of a rock-'n'-roll cafe and a 1950s-era luncheonette. It's the least expensive of the eateries within "The Triangle" of Hilton Head Plaza, and the most child and family friendly. Food focuses on savory, grease-spattered ribs and barbecue dishes. The baby back barbecued ribs here are scrumptious, and the pit-to-plate hand-pulled pork virtually addictive. Chargrilled steaks and chicken filets will make you call for more, and if you like fried chicken wings, this place serves them in almost 20 different variations, including a version with strawberry-jalapeño sauce. In case you're wondering who the Hot Mama is, she's Orchid, a hardworking entrepreneur who migrated from nearby Bluffton in 2007.

In the Hilton Head Plaza, Greenwood Dr. off Sea Pines Circle. ℂ **843/682-6262.** Reservations not accepted. Lunch platters $7.50–$12; main courses $7.50–$23. AE, DC, MC, V. Daily 11:30am–midnight.

San Miguel's *Kids* MEXICAN This eatery opens onto the same marina as Ocean Grille (p. 145). You can have a fun evening here, enjoying live entertainment on the outside deck overlooking the water. The food is nothing to rave about, but it's good, substantial, and freshly prepared, with south-of-the-border selections and a kids' menu. Every night since 1977 has been fiesta night here. Most guests start with a selection of nachos or quesadillas, or else you might select the freshly made guacamole dip. After that, diners proceed to one of the Mexican platters such as chile relleno or enchiladas. Sizzling fajitas round out the menu. For anyone in your party who doesn't like Mexican food, the chefs also serve a shrimp Alfredo or a New York strip steak from the grill.

Shelter Cove Marina. ℂ **843/842-4555.** Reservations not necessary. Main courses $8–$17. MC, V. Mon–Sat 11:30am–3pm and 5–11pm; Sun 5–11pm.

The Sea Shack *Finds Value* SEAFOOD Completely unpretentious, this seafood shack serves the freshest catch of the day in town; you can order it grilled, fried, or blackened. Stand at the counter and make your selection by reading the specialties on a board. Find a seat at one of the old tables, and your freshly ordered platter of seafood will be brought to you. We always like to begin with the fish soup as an appetizer. At lunch the fried oyster sandwich is a local favorite. At night we prefer the grilled grouper dinner. One of the chef's signature dishes is Caribbean jerk grouper, which you don't encounter too often. It's even been featured on the Food Network. Prices are affordable and the portions are most generous.

6 Pope Ave. ℂ **843/785-2464.** Reservations not necessary. Main courses $5–$14 lunch, $10–$15 dinner. AE, MC, V. Mon–Sat 11am–3pm and 5–9pm.

Signe's Heaven Bound Bakery & Cafe SANDWICHES/PAS-
TRIES Sometime in the early '70s, when Hilton Head was calmer,
quieter, and just beginning to flex its muscles as a world-class resort,
Signe Gardo, a refugee from the snows of Connecticut, opted to
open a bakery. Since then, almost 3,000 wedding cakes and countless danishes later, it's the oldest eatery under single ownership on
Hilton Head, with a roster of clients who'd never give a dinner party
without ending it with a cake, or at least some specialty brownies,
from Signe's. It lies in a relatively underpopulated neighborhood that
you'll quickly surmise is way, way off the island's beaten touristic
track. Many come for breakfast, oohing and aaahing over Signe's signature deep dish French toast, her breakfast polenta, or perhaps her
waffles. (If breakfast is your thing, you'll share something with that
perky *überdiva* from the Food Network, Rachel Ray, who came here
to film a feature story in 2007. Be sure to ask the staff for anecdotes.)
Lunches focus on a half-dozen salads, a spinach and feta *spanikopita*
pie that might have been inspired by Zorba (that handsome Greek)
himself, tomato or crab-cake tarts, or perhaps a steaming ration of
shrimp 'n' grits. Simple tables on an outdoor deck (no view of the
sea, alas) provide a setting for your meal, unless you opt to haul it
away for consumption elsewhere. Few clients can resist carting off
any of the dozen-or-so breads that emerge regularly from the ovens.
Examples you might not have automatically thought of include
Swiss pear bread, French oat and apricot bread, and Hilton Head
sourdough. Cakes include a Forever Valentine and a version flavored
with piña coladas, coconut, and pineapple cream.

93 Arrow Rd. © 843/785-9118. www.signesbakery.com. Reservations not accepted.
Breakfast platters $6–$9; lunch sandwiches, salads, and platters $6–$9. AE, MC, V.
Mon–Fri 8am–4pm; Sat–Sun 9am–2pm. Closed Sun Nov–Feb.

Smokehouse Bar & House of BBQ *Kids* BARBECUE This is
Hilton Head's only authentic barbecue restaurant, serving fine, hick-
ory-smoked meats in a casual Western atmosphere with a large outdoor deck attached to the restaurant. Takeout is also available. It's an
ideal family place with affordable prices. Both native islanders and
visitors come here nightly, raving about the pulled pork, the sliced or
pulled brisket, and the barbecued chicken. The joint has won awards
for its barbecue and its chili, and the portions are man-size. The
menu is corny—salads are called "rabbit food," appetizers
"orderves." But once you get beyond that, the food is rather tasty.
The specialties are smokehouse ribs, either half or full rack. Other
down-home favorites include a pork barbecue plate, barbecued

chicken breast, and fried catfish. Beachgoers are welcome: Management only asks that you wear shoes.

102 Pope Ave. ✆ **843/842-4227.** www.smokehousehhi.com. Reservations recommended. Main courses $6–$21. AE, MC, V. Daily 11:30am–10pm.

Steamer Seafood ✿ SEAFOOD/LOW COUNTRY   In Coligny Plaza, next to the Piggly Wiggly grocery store, lies this fun, affordably priced joint suitable for the whole family. It's a casual, convivial tavern with Low Country specialties on the menu such as Charleston she-crab soup or shrimp gumbo to get you going. The fare is very familiar, and the portions are generous. Many old-time Southern coastal classics are offered, including Frogmore stew (large shrimp, smoked sausage, yellow onion, and red potatoes). You can ask the server to name the catch of the day, which is served grilled or blackened. The "rebel yell" rib-eye is a juicy, well-trimmed 14-ounce slab of beef blackened or chargrilled, as you desire it. The biggest seafood platters on the island are dished up here. After all that, dare you try the rich, creamy chocolate peanut butter pie or the fruit cobbler of the day?

29 Coligny Plaza. ✆ **843/785-2070.** www.steamersseafood.com. Reservations not required. Main courses $8–$36 lunch, $9–$37 dinner. AE, MC, V. Daily 11:30am–10pm.

Truffles Café ✿ *Finds* INTERNATIONAL   It's no longer on the cutting edge of gastronomic newcomers to Hilton Head, but this cafe has been around so long, and garnered so many fans, that it's one of our personal favorites on the island. Set within the shopping center known as Sea Pines Center, within a dark, mostly black decor, it has a large copper-top bar, black banquettes, and a menu that somehow manages to please virtually everybody. Start with a spinach-and-artichoke dip or coconut fried shrimp, followed by baby back ribs or grouper that's grilled and topped with a basil-Parmesan glaze, or perhaps Havana chicken with jack cheese and fresh tomato salsa, or even meatloaf that's grilled with a honey-flavored barbecue sauce and Vidalia onions. Don't confuse this place with the newer and somehow glossier Truffles Grill on Pope Avenue, between Coligny Circle and Sea Island Circle: The Grill is newer and trendier, but many restaurant insiders swear by the original. If you opt for a meal here, you'll have to pay a $5 charge to enter the Sea Island Resort itself. Most islanders accept that fact simply as the cost of doing business and living on Hilton Head Island.

Sea Pines Center, in the Sea Pines Resort. ✆ **843/671-6136.** Reservations recommended for dinner. Lunch sandwiches and platters $9–$26; dinner main courses $17–$28. AE, DISC, MC, V. Daily 11am–10pm.

HILTON HEAD AFTER DARK

Hilton Head doesn't have Myrtle Beach's nightlife, but enough is here, centered mainly in hotels and resorts. Casual dress (but not swimming attire) is acceptable in most clubs.

Cultural interest focuses on the **Arts Center of Coastal Carolina,** in the Self Family Arts Center, 14 Shelter Cove Lane (© **843/842-2787;** www.artshhi.com), which enjoys one of the best theatrical reputations in the Southeast. The **Elizabeth Wallace Theater,** a 350-seat, state-of-the-art theater, was added to the multiplex in 1996. The older **Dunnagan's Alley Theater** is located in a renovated warehouse. A wide range of musicals, contemporary comedies, and classic dramas is presented. Showtimes are 8pm Tuesday to Saturday, with a Sunday matinee at 2pm. Adult ticket prices range from $45 for a musical to $55 for a play. Prices for children 16 and under are $18 to $27. The box office is open 10am to 5pm Monday to Friday, 10am to curtain time on performance days.

The island abounds in sports bars, far too many to document here. We recommend **Callahan Sports Bar & Grill,** 38 New Orleans Rd. (© **843/686-7665**), and **Casey's Sports Bar & Grill,** 37 New Orleans Rd. (© **843/785-2255;** www.caseyshhi.com).

Jazz Corner   Tucked away into an obscure corner of the shopping center known as the Village at Wexford, this is the closest thing to a shadowy, romantic, and permissive jazz bar on Hilton Head. No other nightclub here attracts as diverse and noteworthy collection of jazz artists. Check the website for names and dates of upcoming gigs. Doors open nightly at 6pm, performances begin at 8pm, and intermissions are scheduled at 9:30pm. There's an on-site restaurant and a copious drink menu where many of the martinis are ultraoversize and designed for two drinkers. In the Village at Wexford, Unit C1. © **843/842-8620.** www.thejazzcorner.com. Cover $5–$25.

The Metropolitan Lounge   Consider a martini or two within this very adult, sophisticated nightclub whose decor might be tactfully described as "bordello chic." Here, a sometimes outrageously good-looking female staff in stylish evening décolletage will serve you from a huge martini list. Laura Moretti is the hardworking director of this urban and glossy-looking cocktail lounge, where live music provides highly drinkable music, and where an environment exists that actually celebrates adulthood. Martinis cost from $7 to $13. The lounge is open Tuesday to Saturday from 8pm to at least 2am. In the Park Plaza. © **843/785-8466.**

Quarterdeck   Our favorite waterfront lounge is the best place on the island to watch sunsets, but you can visit at any time during the afternoon and in the evening until 2am. Try to go early and grab one of the outdoor rocking chairs to prepare for nature's light show. There's dancing every night to beach music and Top 40 hits. Quarterdeck is open daily 11am to 2am. Harbour Town, Sea Pines Plantation. ✆ 843/671-2222. www.quarterdeckrestaurant.com.

3 Daufuskie Island ✪

1 nautical mile W of Hilton Head

Rich in legend, lore, and history, Daufuskie Island is relatively cut off from the world. Its heyday came in the mid–19th century when Southern plantations here produced the famous Sea Island cotton, until the boll weevil put an end to that industry. Lying between Hilton Head and Savannah and accessible only by boat, the island is also known to readers as the setting for Pat Conroy's book *The Water Is Wide*. The movie *Conrack* was filmed on Daufuskie.

Half the island has remained an undeveloped wilderness of forest, marshland, and wildlife. In 1980, the other half was purchased for the development of golf courses and elegant "plantations" where people live in condos.

The 5,200-acre island is home to about 300 permanent residents, mostly Gullahs, descendants of slaves freed after the Civil War. The island was originally inhabited by the Cusabo and later the Yamacraw Indians. Indian pottery, some of the oldest in America, has been found on Daufuskie, going back 9,000 years.

The English eventually took over the island and converted it into a plantation culture, focusing on indigo as its main export. Indigo eventually yielded to cotton plantations. After the boll weevil, an oyster-canning industry took over until it was forced out of business by the pollution of the Savannah River.

The island is a nature retreat, with thick, ancient live oaks and angel oaks along with ospreys, egrets, and other waterfowl living among the reeds and rushes.

Because of the recent bankruptcy and the subsequent reorganization of the famous **Daufuskie Island Resort,** most of the conventional hotel facilities there are currently closed, at least until midway through 2009, and possibly later. At press time for this edition, a timetable for a full reopening hadn't been established. Some of the island's privately owned condos and three-bedroom cottages, however, are available for rentals through Hilton Head Rentals & Golf (© **800/445-8664** or www.hiltonheadvacation.com).

GETTING THERE

There is only one way to Daufuskie Island, and that's by boat. See "Cruises and Tours," below.

CRUISES & TOURS

Several tempting tours are offered to Daufuskie, which has beaches, "whispering" marshes (when the wind blows through the marshes, encountering vegetation, locals think the sounds evoke whispering), ancient forests of moss-draped oaks, and two of the best golf courses in America. What it doesn't have are stoplights, crowds, and shopping centers.

The **Calibogue Cruises** ferry (© **843/342-8687**) leaves from Broad Creek Marina off Marshland Road on Hilton Head. The ferry ride is $23 per person, and the tour is $30 per person (the guided tours are only on Tues and Thurs). The tour visits the Mount Carmel and First Union African Baptist churches, the Lighthouse, the Old Winery, and cemeteries dating back hundreds of years. You'll sample delicious Daufuskie Island deviled crab. You also have the option of renting a golf cart for $50 to explore the island on your own. Tours depart once a day Monday to Saturday (call ahead for times).

Outside Hilton Head, **Daufuskie Island Tour** offers two tours to Daufuskie, departing from South Beach Marina at the Sea Pines Resort (© **800/686-6996** or 843/686-6996). The 4½-hour tour is $85 per person (includes boat shuttle, golf cart, and guide). Once on the island, you will board golf carts and tour historic sites. You will be transported to Page Island, where you will kayak to Daufuskie Island. By golf cart, you tour Indian sites, the old Baptist church, Pat Conroy's school, and other locations. Lunch at a "funky" island restaurant is included in the price.

GOLF COURSES

Melrose and Bloody Point golf courses are both at the Daufuskie Island Resort (© **888/909-4653** or 843/341-4810 for both courses; www.daufuskieislandresort.com). **Melrose Golf Course** is an 18-hole, Jack Nicklaus–designed, 7,081-yard, par-72 course that sweeps along the Atlantic Ocean. Greens fees range from $113 to $139 (depending on the season) for resort guests, and $113 to $150 for visitors (includes ferry, greens fees, and cart). Hours are daily 7:30am to 6pm (earlier closing time in winter). **Bloody Point Golf Course** is an 18-hole, Tom Weiskopf and Jay Morrish–designed, 6,900-yard,

72-par course on the Mungen River; it winds through coastal marshes and dark-water lagoons. Greens fees range from $97 to $119 (depending on the season) for resort guests, and $110 to $130 for visitors (includes ferry, greens fees, and cart). Hours are daily 7:30am to 6pm (earlier closing time in winter).

4 Beaufort ★★

46 miles NE of Savannah

The town of Beaufort was the inspiration for the setting of Pat Conroy's novel *The Prince of Tides* (among other bestsellers). The town is full of old-fashioned inns, rustic pubs, and tiny stores along a tailored waterfront park.

Beaufort (Low Country pronunciation: *Bew*-fort) is an old seaport with narrow streets shaded by huge live oaks and lined with 18th-century homes. The oldest house (at Port Republic and New sts.) was built in 1717. This was the second area in North America discovered by the Spanish (1520), the site of the first fort on the continent (1525), and the first attempted settlement (1562). Several forts have been excavated, dating from 1566 and 1577.

Beaufort has been used as a setting for several films, including *The Big Chill*. Scenes from the Paramount blockbuster *Forrest Gump,* starring Tom Hanks, and from *The Prince of Tides* were also shot here.

GETTING THERE

If you're traveling from the north, take I-95 to exit 33; then follow the signs to the center of Beaufort. If you're leaving from Charleston, take U.S. 17 South; then head left on U.S. 21, and follow signs to Beaufort. From Hilton Head, go on U.S. 278 West; after it turns into 278 Alt, you will exit onto S.C. 170. Follow S.C. 170 into Beaufort.

VISITOR INFORMATION

Beaufort Chamber of Commerce, 1106 Carteret St. (PO Box 910), Beaufort, SC 29901 (© 843/525-8531; www.beaufortsc.org), has information and self-guided tours of this historic town. It's open daily 9am to 5:30pm.

ORGANIZED TOURS

If your plans are for early to mid-October, contact the **Historic Beaufort Foundation,** PO Box 11, Beaufort, SC 29901 (© 843/379-3331; www.historic-beaufort.org), for dates and details regarding its 3 days of antebellum house and garden tours.

A tour called the **Spirit of Old Beaufort,** 103 West St. Ext.
(© 843/525-0459; www.thespiritofoldbeaufort.com), takes you on
a journey through the old town, exploring local history, architecture,
horticulture, and Low Country life. You'll see houses that are not
accessible on other tours. Your host, clad in period costume, will
guide you for 1¾ hours Monday to Saturday at 10:30am, 2:30pm,
and 7pm. The cost is $13 for adults and $7.50 for children 6 to 12.
Tours depart from just behind the John Mark Verdier House
Museum.

The most romantic way to see Beaufort is to take a carriage ride
conducted by **Sea Island Carriage Co.** (© 843/476-7789). These
rides leave from the downtown marina at Waterfront Park, lasting 1
hour and costing $18 for adults and $7 for children 5 to 12. Sometimes you'll get an old-timer, a Beaufort native, who speaks Gullah,
which makes for a very informative ride.

SEEING THE SIGHTS

John Mark Verdier House Museum, 801 Bay St. (© 843/379-
6335), is a restored 1802 house partially furnished to depict the life
of a merchant planter from 1800 to 1825. It's one of the best examples of the Federal period and was once known as the Lafayette
Building, because the Marquis de Lafayette is said to have spoken
here in 1825. It's open Monday to Saturday 10am to 4pm. Admission is $6 for adults and $4 for children; children 5 and under are
admitted free.

St. Helena's Episcopal Church, 507 New Castle St. (© 843/
522-1712), traces its origin back to 1712. Visitors, admitted free
Monday to Saturday from 10am to 4pm, can see its classic interior
and visit the graveyard, where tombstones served as operating tables
during the Civil War.

Beaufort is the home of the **U.S. Marine Corps Recruit Depot**
(© 843/228-7100; www.mccssc.com). The visitor center (go to
Building 283) is open daily from 6am to 6pm. You can take a driving tour or a bus tour (free) around the grounds, where you'll see an
Iwo Jima monument; a monument to the Spanish settlement of
Santa Elena (1521); and a memorial to Jean Ribaut, the Huguenot
who founded Beaufort in 1562. Vehicle operators must possess a
valid driver's license, vehicle registration, and proof of automobile
insurance. You can expect tightened security.

The last excursion from Beaufort is the 15-mile drive to the state
park at **Hunting Island** 𝒦𝒦, a lush beach island where the Vietnam
battle scenes from *Forrest Gump* were filmed. This island is not just

a beach but a nature and wildlife refuge. With one of the most beautiful beaches in South Carolina, this 5,000-acre park contains 3 miles of natural sandy beaches. Long a layover for sailors and pirates, including Blackbeard, the island was once a base for hunting deer. There are showers and dressing rooms on the beach, a 200-site campground, plus cabins, a boardwalk, and nature trails, as well as a fishing pier and boat landing.

In the center of the park stands a historic lighthouse, which opens onto a panoramic view. The lighthouse was rebuilt in 1875 after it was destroyed in the Civil War. The park collects a $2 fee to climb its 167 steps. It is open daily April to October 6am to 9pm and November to March 6am to 6pm.

WHERE TO STAY IN BEAUFORT
EXPENSIVE

The Beaufort Inn 𝓕𝓕 Built in 1897, this is the most appealing hotel in Beaufort and the place where whatever movie star happens to be shooting a film in town is likely to stay. The woodwork and moldings inside are among the finest in Beaufort, and the circular, four-story staircase has been the subject of numerous photographs and architectural awards. The guest rooms, each decorated in brightly colored individual style, are conversation pieces.

809 Port Republic St., Beaufort, SC 29902. 𝓒 **843/521-9000.** Fax 843/521-9500. www.beaufortinn.com. 21 units. $159–$179 double; $220–$259 suite. Rates include full gourmet breakfast. AE, DISC, MC, V. No children 7 and under. **Amenities:** Room service; nonsmoking rooms. *In room:* A/C, TV, coffeemaker, hair dryer, iron.

Hilton Garden Inn 𝓕 Of course, any Hilton Garden Inn is not as charming as one of the historic inns of town, but this is a find for those seeking modern, well-maintained, and affordable options for accommodations. It lies a mile from the Historic District and is convenient for those visiting the nearby military bases such as Parris Island, which lies only 3 miles away. The guest rooms are designed in a rather standard motel style, but they are well equipped with all the latest gadgets, including a large work desk and phones with voice mail and dataports. Complimentary newspapers such as *USA Today* are distributed. A freshly prepared breakfast is offered daily in the Great American Grill and drinks are served in the cozy Pavilion Lounge. An on-site pantry sells ready-to-cook meals that can be prepared in the in-room microwave oven.

1500 Queen St., Beaufort, SC 29902. 𝓒 **843/379-9800.** Fax 843/379-9801. http:// hiltongardeninn.hilton.com. 115 rooms. $119–$229 double. AE, DC, DISC, MC, V. **Amenities:** Restaurant; bar; outdoor pool; fitness room; business center; room service; coin laundry; nonsmoking rooms. *In room:* A/C, TV, dataport, Wi-Fi, safe.

The Rhett House Inn ★★★   This inn is certainly very popular, at least with Hollywood film crews. Because it was a site for *Forrest Gump*, *The Prince of Tides*, and *The Big Chill*, chances are that you've seen it before. It's a Mobil and AAA four-star inn in a restored 1820 Greek Revival plantation-type home. Guest rooms are furnished with English and American antiques, and ornamented with Oriental rugs. Eight rooms contain whirlpools. The veranda makes an ideal place to sit and view the gardens.

1009 Craven St., Beaufort, SC 29902. © **888/480-9530** or 843/524-9030. Fax 843/524-1310. www.rhetthouseinn.com. 17 units. $175–$350 double. Rates include full breakfast, afternoon tea, and evening hors d'oeuvres. AE, DISC, MC, V. Free parking. No children 4 and under. **Amenities:** Breakfast room; lounge; nonsmoking rooms. *In room:* A/C, TV, Wi-Fi, minibar (in some), hair dryer, iron, whirlpool (in some).

MODERATE
Country Inn & Suites   Expect clean and friendly accommodations at this four-story chain hotel located 5 miles from Parris Island and 2 miles from the downtown Historic District. This hotel has perks that some chains don't provide, such as a business center, exercise room, indoor pool, and laundry facilities for guests. It's a step above value chains, but still a good deal for families visiting Marine recruits at Parris Island.

2450 Boundary St. (U.S. 21), Beaufort, SC 29906. © **888/201-1746** or 843/379-4000. Fax 843/379-4020. www.countryinns.com. 77 units. $89–$155 double. Rates include continental breakfast. AE, DC, DISC, MC, V. **Amenities:** Breakfast room; indoor pool; fitness center; business center; laundry service. *In room:* A/C, TV, Wi-Fi, microwave, fridge, coffeemaker, iron.

The Cuthbert House Inn ★★   One of the grand old B&Bs of South Carolina, this showcase Southern home was built in 1790 in classic style. The inn was remodeled shortly after the Civil War to take on a more Victorian aura, but its present owner, Sharon Groves, has worked to modernize it without sacrificing its grace or antiquity. Graffiti carved by Union soldiers can still be seen on the fireplace mantel in the Eastlake Room. Guest rooms are elegantly furnished in Southern plantation style, and some have four-poster beds. The inn is filled with large parlors and sitting rooms and has spacious hallways and 12-foot ceilings characteristic of Greek Revival homes. At breakfast in the conservatory, you can order such delights as Georgia ice cream (cheese grits) and freshly made breads.

1203 Bay St., Beaufort, SC 29902. © **800/327-9275** or 843/521-1315. Fax 843/521-1314. www.cuthberthouseinn.com. 7 units. $150–$259 double; $199–$269 suite. Rates include full breakfast and afternoon tea or refreshments. AE, DISC, MC,

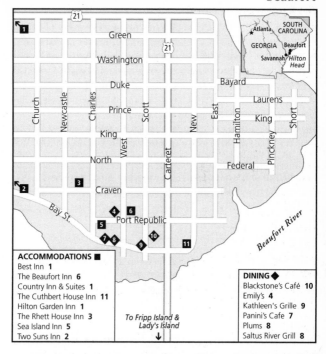

Green

Washington

Duke

Bayard

Laurens

Prince

King

King

North

Federal

Craven

Bay St.

Port Republic

Beaufort River

SOUTH CAROLINA

Atlanta

GEORGIA Beaufort

Savannah Hilton Head

To Fripp Island & Lady's Island

ACCOMMODATIONS ■
Best Inn **1**
The Beaufort Inn **6**
Country Inn & Suites **1**
The Cuthbert House Inn **11**
Hilton Garden Inn **1**
The Rhett House Inn **3**
Sea Island Inn **5**
Two Suns Inn **2**

DINING ◆
Blackstone's Café **10**
Emily's **4**
Kathleen's Grille **9**
Panini's Cafe **7**
Plums **8**
Saltus River Grill **8**

V. Free parking. **Amenities:** Breakfast room; lounge; bikes; nonsmoking rooms. *In room:* A/C, TV, Wi-Fi, fridge, hair dryer, iron.

Two Suns Inn   When this place was built in 1917, it was one of the grandest homes in its prosperous neighborhood, offering views of the coastal road and the tidal flatlands beyond. Every imaginable modern (at the time) convenience was added, including a baseboard vacuum-cleaning system, an electric call box, and steam heat. Later, when it became housing for unmarried teachers in the public schools, the place ran down. Now it's a cozy B&B. Part of the inn's appeal stems from its lack of pretension, as a glance at the homey bedrooms with simple furnishings and neatly kept bathrooms will show.

1705 Bay St., Beaufort, SC 29902. ✆ **800/532-4244** or 843/522-1122. Fax 843/ 522-1122. www.twosunsinn.com. 5 units. $159–$188 double. Rates include full breakfast and afternoon cordials. AE, DISC, MC, V. Free parking. No children 11 and under. **Amenities:** Breakfast room; lounge; nonsmoking rooms; rooms for those w/limited mobility. *In room:* A/C, TV, Wi-Fi, hair dryer.

INEXPENSIVE

Best Inn *Value*   You'll be happiest at this simple member of a local hotel chain if you know what it doesn't have: There's no restaurant, no bar, and no pool. What you do get is a cost-effective hotel room outfitted in a bland contemporary style, with solid, well-maintained furnishings. Set 2 miles north of Beaufort's commercial core, it's a worthy choice for families with children or for business travelers who simply need a no-frills place to spend the night.

2448 Boundary St., Beaufort, SC 29903. ⓒ **843/524-3322.** Fax 843/524-7264. 62 units. $65–$85 double. Rates include continental breakfast. AE, DC, DISC, MC, V. *In room:* A/C, TV, iron.

Sea Island Inn   This is a basic two-story motel with reasonable rates for what you get. Few of the rooms have sea views, but all contain well-kept bathrooms. Although the rooms are nothing special, they're comfortable and well maintained.

1015 Bay St., Beaufort, SC 29902. ⓒ **800/528-7234** or 843/522-2090. Fax 843/521-4858. www.bestwestern.com. 43 units. $112–$160 double. Rates include continental breakfast. AE, DC, DISC, MC, V. **Amenities:** Breakfast room; lounge; pool; fitness center. *In room:* A/C, TV, Wi-Fi, hair dryer, iron.

WHERE TO DINE IN BEAUFORT
EXPENSIVE

Emily's INTERNATIONAL   This is our favorite restaurant in Beaufort, a spot whose ambience and attitude put us in mind of Scandinavia. That's hardly surprising, because the bearded owner is an émigré from Sweden who feels comfortable in the South Carolina lowlands after years of life at sea. Some folks just go to the bar to sample tapas: miniature portions of tempura shrimp, fried scallops, stuffed peppers, and at least 50 other items. Menu items might include rich cream of mussel and shrimp soup, filet "black and white" (filets of beef and pork served with béarnaise sauce), duck with orange sauce, and a meltingly tender Wiener schnitzel. Everything is served in stomach-stretching portions.

906 Port Republic St. ⓒ **843/522-1866.** Reservations recommended. Main courses $18–$30; tapas $8–$12. AE, DISC, MC, V. Mon–Sat 4–10pm, main courses served starting at 6pm.

MODERATE

Kathleen's Grille *Finds* SEAFOOD/SOUTHERN   This local eatery has plenty of Low Country atmosphere and is known for its fresh fish dinners. We'd go here for its Southern starters alone, including fried green tomatoes topped with a shrimp salsa, or the "classy" crab chowder. For lunch, try an offering from the "sandwich showcase," including soft-shell crab or fresh grouper. Salads, including a seafood pasta version, are made fresh daily. At night the restaurant serves some of the best fish platters in the area, including grilled shrimp and boiled oysters. For the meat lover, there is the inevitable rib-eye or pork chop, the latter coming with a sweet-and-spicy berry glaze. One section of the menu is reserved for "Kathleen's kids," but the offerings are so meager (fresh boxed cereals, a hot dog), your little ones may end up nutritionally deprived.

822 Bay St. ⓒ 843/524-2500. Reservations recommended. Main courses $7–$11 lunch, $14–$20 dinner. AE, DISC, MC, V. Mon–Sat 11am–8pm; Sun 11am–6pm. Bar Mon–Sat 11am–1am, Sun 11am–11pm, depending on crowd.

Panini's Café AMERICAN/PIZZA   Known for its pizzas, this restaurant lies on Bay Street with a waterfront view from its terrace. Its stone-baked pizzas are considered the best and most savory in this part of South Carolina. In addition to regular pizzas, you can also order a "Capri," the house specialty with spinach, sun-dried tomatoes, onions, feta cheese, extra-virgin olive oil, and mustard aioli. The building was once a bank and later a movie theater; an award-winning renovation has returned the place to its former grandeur. In this setting, experience lunch specialties like Mediterranean shrimp 'n' grits with pancetta polenta and an olive tomato sauté, or the equally unique crab lasagna with mascarpone, spinach, artichoke, and tomato couli. Dinner main courses include a grilled lobster and shrimp carbonara with applewood-smoked bacon, peas, asparagus, and a light Parmesan cream over capellini; or Spanish paella with shrimp, mussels, clams, red snapper, monkfish, chorizo saffron rice, tomatoes, onions, and garlic.

926 Bay St. ⓒ 843/379-0300. www.paniniscafe.net. Reservations recommended. Main courses $9–$11 lunch, $18–$23 dinner; pizza $15–$17. AE, DC, DISC, MC, V. Daily 11am–10pm. Closed Thanksgiving and Christmas.

Saltus River Grill ⭐⭐⭐ SEAFOOD   Saltus River Grill is the sister restaurant to the more casual Plums in Beaufort, but that's where the similarities end. Elegant and sophisticated, Saltus River Grill looks out over the Intracoastal Waterway and provides spectacular scenery to match its equally spectacular menu. The building was constructed in 1787, and the restaurant was named after shipbuilder John Saltus. Chef Jim Spratling prepares his menu with the freshest ingredients available and produces tantalizing meat selections from the grill. You can also order from the oyster bar or the full-menu sushi bar. Start with the steamed pork dumplings as an appetizer and follow with a main dish of cornmeal-seared jumbo sea scallops with sweet potato–bacon hash, warm pickled onions, and balsamic-fig molasses. If you crave fine beef, order the grilled barrel-cut filet of beef with chèvre scalloped potatoes, shiitake mushrooms, onion confit, and a natural demi-glace.

802 Bay St. ② 843/379-3474. www.saltusrivergrill.com. Reservations required. Main courses $22–$32. AE, DISC, MC, V. Mon–Sat 4–10pm; Sun 10:30am–3pm (brunch) and 4–10pm.

INEXPENSIVE

Blackstone's Café AMERICAN   This is where seemingly everybody gathers for breakfast. Since 1991 locals have met here to eat and gossip. You can order such classics for breakfast as shrimp omelets or, even more authentic, shrimp 'n' grits. You can also drop in for an informal lunch, enjoying the bustling atmosphere and the best selection of sandwiches in town. If kiddies are in tow, you can even get a peanut butter and jelly. House specials include everything from a smoked salmon plate to a bacon cheeseburger platter. Some of the fresh salads are good, especially the almond chicken salad plate or the all-white albacore tuna salad plate with feta cheese and black olives.

205 Scott St. ② 843/524-4330. Reservations not necessary. Breakfast $6–$8; sandwiches $4–$7.75; house specials $7.25–$8.50. AE, DC, MC, V. Mon–Sat 7:30am–2:30pm; Sun 7:30am–2pm.

Plums AMERICAN/SOUTHERN   Centrally located on Bay Street on the waterfront, Plums is one of Beaufort's favorite dining choices. Voted "Best Beaufort Restaurant" in 2006 by the *Island Packet* newspaper, this casual restaurant specializes in sandwiches, soups, and ice cream. While filming *The Prince of Tides* in Beaufort, even Barbra Streisand claimed that Plums was her favorite place to come for a cool, refreshing dish of ice cream after a long day of filming. The chicken salad sandwich, with celery, toasted almonds, and tomato, is as delicious as Plums's Factory Creek Shrimp Roll, with shrimp, celery, lettuce, and spices, all piled high on a French roll. Quesadillas are another choice, as are heartier sandwiches like the blackened catfish sandwich.

904½ Bay St. ② 843/525-1946. www.plumsrestaurant.com. Reservations not necessary. Main courses $6.25–$9 lunch, $15–$30 dinner. AE, DC, MC, V. Daily 11am–5pm (soups, salads, sandwiches) and 5–10pm (pasta, seafood, sandwiches).

5 Sea Island ★★

11 miles E of Brunswick

Since 1928 Sea Island has been the domain of the Cloister hotel (see below). Today, in addition to the hotel, it's home to some of the most elegant villas and mansions in the Southeast. Most of Sea Island's homes—many in the Spanish-Mediterranean style—are second homes to CEOs and other rich folk. Some can be rented if you can afford it. Call **Sea Island Cottage Rentals** (© **800/732-4752;** www.seaislandcottages.com) and be prepared for some higher mathematics.

The island was acquired by Ohio-based Howard Earle Coffin, an automobile executive, in 1925. Still owned by Coffin's descendants, the Cloister combines 10,000 acres of forest, lawn, and marshland, plus 5 miles of beachfront. The island has impressed everybody from Margaret Thatcher to Queen Juliana of the Netherlands, plus four U.S. presidents, including George H. W. Bush, who honeymooned here with his wife Barbara in the 1940s. Many day visitors who can't afford the high prices of the Cloister come over for a scenic drive along Sea Island Drive, called "Millionaire's Row"—there's no tollgate.

ESSENTIALS

GETTING THERE   From Brunswick, take the F.J. Torras Causeway to St. Simons Island and follow Sea Island Road to Sea Island.

VISITOR INFORMATION   There is no welcome center. Information is provided by the Cloister, but the staff prefers to cater to registered guests.

WHERE TO STAY & DINE ON SEA ISLAND

The Cloister ★★★   The Cloister reopened in 2006 as the centerpiece of a $350-million Sea Island Resort redevelopment plan. Georgia's poshest hotel retreat, set amid the most elaborate landscaping on the coast, is a vast compound between the Atlantic Ocean and the Black Banks River. It takes in about 50 carefully maintained buildings, some of them massive and others on neighboring St. Simons Island. The original main building closed in December 2003 after a 75th-anniversary observance and was torn down to make way for construction of a new structure, which is reminiscent of the 1928 Iberian–Moorish Revival style of the resort's original architect, Addison Mizner, and even contains some refurbished remnants of the vintage hotel.

Everyone from honeymooners to golfers checks in here. The hotel offers gorgeous suites and deluxe guest rooms, all with 24-hour butler service. Other perks include 500-thread-count Italian sheets, Bulgari toiletries, Turkish stone bathrooms with deep soaking tubs, and high-speed wireless Internet service.

Sea Island, GA 31561. © **800/732-4752** or 912/638-3611. Fax 912/638-5159. www.cloister.com. $525–$750 double; $1,350–$1,700 suite; $5,000 ultimate suite. Golf, tennis, and honeymoon packages available. AE, DC, DISC, MC, V. **Amenities:** 4 restaurants; 2 bars; 3 outdoor pools; 3 18-hole golf courses; 10 tennis courts; fitness center; spa; boutiques; salon; room service; massage; babysitting; laundry service; dry cleaning; beach club; nonsmoking rooms; rooms for those w/limited mobility. *In room:* A/C, HDTV, Wi-Fi, minibar, hair dryer.

Appendix: Fast Facts, Toll-Free Numbers & Websites

1 Fast Facts: Savannah

AMERICAN EXPRESS The American Express office has closed, but cardholders can obtain assistance by calling ✆ **800/221-7282.**

AREA CODES The area code for Savannah is 912.

AUTOMOBILE ORGANIZATIONS Motor clubs will supply maps, suggested routes, guidebooks, accident and bail-bond insurance, and emergency road service. The **American Automobile Association (AAA)** is the major auto club in the United States. If you belong to a motor club in your home country, inquire about AAA reciprocity before you leave. You may be able to join AAA even if you're not a member of a reciprocal club; to inquire, call AAA (✆ **800/222-4357**; www.aaa.com). AAA is actually an organization of regional motor clubs, so look under "AAA Automobile Club" in the White Pages of the telephone directory. AAA has a nationwide emergency road service telephone number (✆ **800/AAA-HELP** [4357]).

BUSINESS HOURS The following are general open hours; specific establishments may vary. **Banks:** Monday to Friday 9am to 3pm (some are also open Sat 9am–noon). Most banks and other outlets offer 24-hour access to automated teller machines (ATMs). **Offices:** Monday to Friday 9am to 5pm. **Stores:** Monday to Saturday 10am to 6pm, and some also on Sunday from noon to 5pm. Malls usually stay open until 9pm Monday to Saturday, and department stores are usually open until 9pm at least 1 day a week.

CAR RENTALS To rent a car in Georgia, you need a major credit or charge card and a valid driver's license. Sometimes a passport or an international driver's license is also required if your driver's license is in a language other than English. You often need to be at least 25 years of age, although some companies rent to younger people (they may add a daily surcharge). Be sure to return your car with the same amount of gasoline that you started out with; rental companies charge excessive prices for gas. Keep in mind that a separate motorcycle driver's license is required in most states.

DENTISTS   Call **Abercorn South Side Dental,** 11139 Abercorn St. (© **912/925-9190**), for complete dental care and emergencies Monday to Friday 8:30am to 3pm.

DRINKING LAWS   The legal age for purchase and consumption of alcoholic beverages is 21; proof of age is required and often requested at bars, nightclubs, and restaurants, so it's always a good idea to bring ID when you go out. Although local laws can vary, in general, no alcohol is served at bars, restaurants, or nightclubs between 4am and 12:30pm on Sunday. In addition, alcoholic beverages are not sold on Sunday in liquor stores, convenience stores, or grocery stores. Do not carry open containers of alcohol in your car or any public area that isn't zoned for alcohol consumption. The police can fine you on the spot. And nothing will ruin your trip faster than getting a citation for DUI (driving under the influence), so don't even think about driving while intoxicated.

DRIVING RULES   Speed limits are posted on Georgia highways. In addition, the law requires the driver and front-seat passengers to wear seat belts while the car is in motion. Children 4 and under must be buckled into safety seats in the rear; those 5 to 12 must sit in the rear seat if the car is equipped with air bags.

DRUGSTORES   Drugstores are scattered throughout Savannah. A good choice is **CVS,** 12012 Abercorn St. (© **912/925-5568**), open Monday to Friday 8am to 10pm, Saturday 8am to 6pm, and Sunday 10am to 6pm.

ELECTRICITY   Like Canada, the United States uses 110–120 volts AC (60 cycles), compared to 220–240 volts AC (50 cycles) in most of Europe, Australia, and New Zealand. Downward converters that change 220–240 volts to 110–120 volts are difficult to find in the United States, so bring one with you.

EMERGENCIES   Dial © **911** to report a fire, call the police, or get an ambulance. This is a nationwide toll-free call (no coins are required at a public telephone).

HOSPITALS   There are 24-hour emergency-room services at **Candler General Hospital,** 5353 Reynolds St. (© **912/819-6000**), and at the **Memorial Medical Center,** 4700 Waters Ave. (© **912/350-8000**).

NEWSPAPERS   The *Savannah Morning News* is a daily filled with information about local cultural and entertainment events. The *Savannah Tribune* and the *Herald of Savannah* are geared to the African-American community.

POLICE   In an emergency, call ☏ **911.**

POST OFFICE   Post offices and sub–post offices are centrally located and open Monday to Friday 8am to 4:30pm. The main office is at 3601 Montgomery St. (☏ **912/234-8935**).

SAFETY   Although it's reasonably safe to explore the Historic and Victorian districts during the day, the situation changes at night. The clubs along the riverfront, both bars and restaurants, report very little crime. However, muggings and drug dealing are common in the poorer neighborhoods of Savannah.

TAXES   Savannah has a 6% sales tax. It tacks a 6% accommodations tax (room or occupancy tax) on your hotel bill.

TRANSIT INFORMATION   Call **Chatham Area Transit** at ☏ **912/233-5767.**

WEATHER   Call ☏ **912/964-1700.**

2 Toll-Free Numbers & Websites

MAJOR U.S. AIRLINES
(*flies internationally as well)

American Airlines*
☏ 800/433-7300 (in the U.S. and Canada)
☏ 020/7365-0777 (in the U.K.)
www.aa.com

Delta Air Lines*
☏ 800/221-1212 (in the U.S. and Canada)
☏ 084/5600-0950 (in the U.K.)
www.delta.com

US Airways*
☏ 800/428-4322 (in the U.S. and Canada)
☏ 084/5600-3300 (in the U.K.)
www.usairways.com

CAR-RENTAL AGENCIES
Advantage
☏ 800/777-5500 (in the U.S. and Canada)
☏ 021/0344-4712 (in the U.K.)
www.advantage.com

Alamo
☏ 800/462-5266 (in the U.S. and Canada)
www.alamo.com

Avis
- ✆ 800/331-1212 (in the U.S. and Canada)
- ✆ 084/4581-8181 (in the U.K.)
www.avis.com

Budget
- ✆ 800/527-0700 (in the U.S.)
- ✆ 800/268-8900 (in Canada)
- ✆ 087/0156-5656 (in the U.K.)
www.budget.com

Dollar
- ✆ 800/800-4000 (in the U.S.)
- ✆ 800/848-8268 (in Canada)
- ✆ 080/8234-7524 (in the U.K.)
www.dollar.com

Hertz
- ✆ 800/645-3131
- ✆ 800/654-3001 (for international reservations)
www.hertz.com

National
- ✆ 800/227-7368 (in the U.S. and Canada)
www.nationalcar.com

Thrifty
- ✆ 800/367-2277 (in the U.S. and Canada)
- ✆ 918/669-2168 (international)
www.thrifty.com

MAJOR HOTEL & MOTEL CHAINS

Best Western International
- ✆ 800/780-7234 (in the U.S. and Canada)
- ✆ 0800/393-130 (in the U.K.)
www.bestwestern.com

Comfort Inns
- ✆ 800/228-5150 (in the U.S. and Canada)
- ✆ 0800/444-444 (in the U.K.)
www.comfortinn.com

Courtyard by Marriott
- ✆ 888/236-2427 (in the U.S.)
- ✆ 800/228-9290 (in Canada)
- ✆ 0800/221-222 (in the U.K.)
www.marriott.com/courtyard

Crowne Plaza Hotels
- ✆ 888/303-1746 (in the U.S. and Canada)
www.ichotelsgroup.com/crowneplaza

Days Inn
- ✆ 800/329-7466 (in the U.S. and Canada)
- ✆ 0800/280-400 (in the U.K.)
www.daysinn.com

Econo Lodge
- ✆ 800/424-6423 (in the U.S. and Canada)
www.econolodge.com

Fairfield Inn by Marriott
- ✆ 800/228-2800 (in the U.S. and Canada)
- ✆ 0800/221-222 (in the U.K.)
www.marriott.com/fairfieldinn

Four Seasons
- ✆ 800/819-5053 (in the U.S. and Canada)
- ✆ 0800/6488-6488 (in the U.K.)
www.fourseasons.com

Hampton Inn
☎ 800/426-7866 (in the U.S. and Canada)
www.hamptoninn.com

Hilton Hotels
☎ 800/445-8667 (in the U.S. and Canada)
☎ 087/0590-9090 (in the U.K.)
www.hilton.com

Holiday Inn
☎ 800/315-2621 (in the U.S. and Canada)
☎ 0800/405-060 (in the U.K.)
www.holidayinn.com

Howard Johnson
☎ 800/446-4656 (in the U.S. and Canada)
www.hojo.com

Hyatt
☎ 888/591-1234 (in the U.S. and Canada)
☎ 084/5888-1234 (in the U.K.)
www.hyatt.com

Marriott
☎ 877/236-2427 (in the U.S. and Canada)
☎ 0800/221-222 (in the U.K.)
www.marriott.com

Motel 6
☎ 800/466-8356 (in the U.S. and Canada)
www.motel6.com

Quality
☎ 877/424-6423 (in the U.S. and Canada)
☎ 0800/444-444 (in the U.K.)
www.qualityinn.com

Red Carpet Inns
☎ 800/251-1962 (in the U.S. and Canada)
www.bookroomsnow.com

Travelodge
☎ 800/578-7878 (in the U.S. and Canada)
www.travelodge.com

Index

See also Accommodations and Restaurant indexes, below.

RESTAURANTS

Frommer's® Portable Guides

Acapulco, Ixtapa & Zihuatanejo
Amsterdam
Aruba, Bonaire & Curacao
Australia's Great Barrier Reef
Bahamas
Big Island of Hawaii
Boston
California Wine Country
Cancún
Cayman Islands
Charleston
Chicago
Dominican Republic

Florence
Las Vegas
Las Vegas for Non-Gamblers
London
Maui
Nantucket & Martha's Vineyard
New Orleans
New York City
Paris
Portland
Puerto Rico
Puerto Vallarta, Manzanillo & Guadalajara

Rio de Janeiro
San Diego
San Francisco
Savannah
St. Martin, Sint Maarten, Anguila & St. Bart's
Turks & Caicos
Vancouver
Venice
Virgin Islands
Washington, D.C.
Whistler

Frommer's® Cruise Guides

Alaska Cruises & Ports of Call

Cruises & Ports of Call

European Cruises & Ports of Call

Frommer's® National Park Guides

Algonquin Provincial Park
Banff & Jasper
Grand Canyon

National Parks of the American West
Rocky Mountain
Yellowstone & Grand Teton

Yosemite and Sequoia & Kings Canyon
Zion & Bryce Canyon

Frommer's® With Kids Guides

Chicago
Hawaii
Las Vegas
London

National Parks
New York City
San Francisco

Toronto
Walt Disney World® & Orlando
Washington, D.C.

Frommer's® PhraseFinder Dictionary Guides

Chinese
French

German
Italian

Japanese
Spanish

Suzy Gershman's Born to Shop Guides

France
Hong Kong, Shanghai & Beijing
Italy

London
New York
Paris

San Francisco
Where to Buy the Best of Everything.

Frommer's® Best-Loved Driving Tours

Britain
California
France
Germany

Ireland
Italy
New England
Northern Italy

Scotland
Spain
Tuscany & Umbria

The Unofficial Guides®

Adventure Travel in Alaska
Beyond Disney
California with Kids
Central Italy
Chicago
Cruises
Disneyland®
England
Hawaii

Ireland
Las Vegas
London
Maui
Mexico's Best Beach Resorts
Mini Mickey
New Orleans
New York City
Paris

San Francisco
South Florida including Miami & the Keys
Walt Disney World®
Walt Disney World® for Grown-ups
Walt Disney World® with Kids
Washington, D.C.

Special-Interest Titles

Athens Past & Present
Best Places to Raise Your Family
Cities Ranked & Rated
500 Places to Take Your Kids Before They Grow Up
Frommer's Best Day Trips from London
Frommer's Best RV & Tent Campgrounds in the U.S.A.

Frommer's Exploring America by RV
Frommer's NYC Free & Dirt Cheap
Frommer's Road Atlas Europe
Frommer's Road Atlas Ireland
Retirement Places Rated